Public Library Legislation in the New Millennium

Public Library Legislation in the New Millennium

M. Ram

RANDOM

RANDOM PUBLICATIONS

NEW DELHI (INDIA)

Public Library Legislation in the New Millennium

ISBN 978-93-5111-855-8

Published in 2016 in India by

RANDOM PUBLICATIONS

4376-A/4B, Gali Murari Lal, Ansari Road
New Delhi-110 002
Phone : +9111-43580356, 011-23289044, 011-43142548
e-mail: sales@randompublications.com,
info@randompublications.com, randomexports@gmail.com

Reprinted 2026

Type Setting by : Friends Media, Delhi-110089

Preface

Legislation is law which has been promulgated by a legislature or other governing body or the process of making it. Before an item of legislation becomes law it may be known as a bill, and may be broadly referred to as "legislation", while it remains under consideration to distinguish it from other business. Legislation can have many purposes: to regulate, to authorize, to proscribe, to provide to sanction, to grant, to declare or to restrict. It may be contrasted with a non-legislative act which is adopted by an executive or administrative body under the authority of a legislative act or for implementing a legislative act. Under the Westminster system, an item of primary legislation is known as an Act of Parliament after enactment. Legislation is usually proposed by a member of the legislature or by the executive, whereupon it is debated by members of the legislature and is often amended before passage. Most large legislatures enact only a small fraction of the bills proposed in a given session. Whether a given bill will be proposed and is generally a matter of the legislative priorities of government. Legislation is regarded as one of the three main functions of government, which are often distinguished under the doctrine of the separation of powers. Those who have the formal power to create legislation are known as legislators; a judicial branch of government will have the formal power to interpret legislation; the executive branch of government can act only within the powers and limits set by the law.

Legislation is the only way for a systematic and planned development of library service. The work of library legislation in India during the last 50 years has been slow. Even after independence, only thirteen states enacted library legislation. It is happy to note that in almost all remaining states, the work on library legislation is in progress. In the coming few years, there is a grater possibility for library law being enactment in more states.

– Author

Contents

1

Public Library in the New Millennium

INTRODUCTION

A public library is a library that is accessible by the public and is generally funded from public sources and operated by civil servants. There are five fundamental characteristics shared by public libraries. The first is that they are supported by taxes; they are governed by a board to serve the public interest; they are open to all and every community member can access the collection; they are entirely voluntary in that no one is ever forced to use the services provided; and public libraries provide basic services without charge. Public libraries exist in many countries across the world and are often considered an essential part of having an educated and literate population.

Public libraries are distinct from research libraries, school libraries, and other special libraries in that their mandate is to serve the general public's information needs. Public libraries also provide free services such as preschool story times to encourage early literacy, quiet study and work areas for students and professionals, or book clubs to encourage appreciation of literature in adults. Public libraries typically allow users to take books and other materials off the premises temporarily; they also have non-circulating reference collections and provide computer and Internet access to patrons.

SERVICES OFFERED

In addition to print books and periodicals, most public libraries today have a wide array of other media including audiobooks, e-books, CDs, cassettes, videotapes, DVDs, and video games, as well as facilities to access the Internet and inter-library loans. Readers' advisory is a fundamental public library service that involves suggesting fiction and nonfiction titles. Public libraries may also provide other services, such as community meeting rooms, storytelling sessions for infants, toddlers, preschool children, or after-school programmes, all with an intention of developing early literacy skills and a love of books.

In person and on-line programmes for reader development, language learning, homework help, free lectures and cultural performances, and other community service programmes are common offerings. One of the most popular programmes offered in public libraries are summer reading programmes for children, families, and adults. In rural areas, the local public library may have, in addition to its main branch, a mobile library service, consisting of one or more buses furnished as a small public library, serving the countryside according to a regular schedule. Public libraries also provide materials for children, often housed in a special section. Child-oriented websites with on-line educational games and programmes specifically designed for younger library users are becoming increasingly popular. Services may be provided for other groups, such as large print or Braille materials, Books on tape, young adult literature and other materials for teenagers, or materials in other than the national language.

California and Nevada now offer a new service called Link+. This new programme links county libraries across the two states, allowing patrons access to books their library may not have in their collection. Librarians at most public libraries provide reference and research help to the general public, usually at a reference desk but can often be done by telephone interview. As online discussion and social networking allow for remote access, reference is becoming available virtually through the use of the Internet and e-mail. Depending on the size of the library, there may be more than one desk; at some smaller libraries all transactions may occur at one desk, while large urban public libraries may employ subject-specialist librarians with the ability to staff multiple reference or information desks to answer queries about particular topics at any time during regular operating hours.

Often the children's section in a public library has its own reference desk. Public libraries are also increasingly making use of web 2.0 services, including the use of online social networks by libraries. Public libraries in some countries pay authors when their books are borrowed from libraries. These are known as Public Lending Right programme.

DIGITAL DIVIDE

As more commercial and governmental services are being provided online, public libraries increasingly provide Internet access for users who otherwise would not be able to connect to these services. Part of the public library mission has become attempting to help bridge the digital divide. A study conducted in 2006 found that "72.5 per cent of library branches report that they are the only provider of free public computer and Internet access in their communities". A 2008 study found that "100 per cent of rural, high poverty outlets provide public Internet access, a significant increase from 85.7 per cent last year".

The American Library Association (ALA), addresses this role of libraries as part of "access to information" and "equity of access"; part of the profession's ethical commitment that "no one should be denied information because he or she cannot afford the cost of a book or periodical, have access to the internet or information in any of its various formats." In addition to access, many public libraries offer training and support to computer users. Once access has been achieved, there still remains a large gap in people's online abilities and skills. For many communities, the public library is the only agency offering free computer classes and information technology learning. As of 2008, 73.4 per cent of public libraries offered information technology training of some form, including information literacy skills and homework assignment help.

A significant service provided by public libraries is assisting people with e-government access and use of federal, state and local government information, forms and services. Internationally, public libraries offer information and communication technology (ICT) services, giving "access to information and knowledge" the "highest priority." While different countries and areas of the world have their own requirements, general services offered include free connection to the Internet, training in using the Internet, and relevant content in appropriate languagcs. In addition to typical public library financing, non-governmental organizations (NGOs) and business fund services that assist public libraries in combating the digital divide.

ORIGINS AS A SOCIAL INSTITUTION

The culmination of centuries of advances in the printing press, moveable type, paper, ink, publishing, and distribution, combined with an ever growing middle class, increased commercial activity and consumption, new radical ideas, massive population growth and higher literacy rates forged the public library into the form that it is today. Public libraries are not a new idea; Romans made scrolls in dry rooms available to patrons of the baths, and tried with some success to establish libraries within the empire. Naturally, only those few that could afford an education would be able to use the library, where those less than rich or without control of money; women, children and slaves could not.

In the middle of the 19th century, the push for truly public libraries, paid for by taxes and run by the state gained force after numerous depressions, droughts, wars and revolutions in Europe, felt mostly by the working class.

Matthew Battles states that:

> "It was in these years of class conflict and economic terror that the public library movement swept through Britain, as the nation's progressive elite recognized that the light of cultural and intellectual energy was lacking in the lives of commoners."

Libraries had often been started with a donation, an endowment or were bequeathed to various, parishes, churches, schools or towns, and these social and institutional libraries formed the base of many academic and public library collections of today. Andrew Carnegie had the biggest influence in financing libraries in the United States of America, from the east to west coast. From just 1900 to 1917, almost 1,700 libraries were constructed by Carnegie's foundation, insisting that local communities first guarantee tax support of each library built.

The establishment of circulating libraries by booksellers and publishers provided a means of gaining profit and creating social centers within the community. The circulating libraries not only provided a place to sell books, but also a place to lend books for a price.

These circulating libraries provided a variety of materials including the increasingly popular novels. Although the circulating libraries filled an important role in society, members of the middle and upper classes often looked down upon these libraries that regularly sold material from their collections and provided materials that were less sophisticated. Circulating libraries also charged a subscription fee, however the fees were set to entice their patrons, providing subscriptions on a yearly, quarterly or monthly basis, without expecting the subscribers to purchase a share in the circulating library. Circulating libraries were not exclusively lending institutions and often provided a place for other forms of commercial activity, which may or may not be related to print.

This was necessary because the circulating libraries did not generate enough funds through subscription fees collected from its borrowers. As a commerce venture, it was important to consider the contributing factors such as other goods or services available to the subscribers. Many claims have been made for the title of "first public library" for various libraries in various countries, with at least some of the confusion arising from differing interpretations of what should be considered a true "public library". Difficulties in establishing what policies were in effect at different times in the history of particular libraries also add to the confusion.

The first libraries open to the public were the collections of Greek and Latin scrolls which were available in the dry sections of the many buildings that made up the huge Roman baths of the Roman empire. However, they were not lending libraries. The "halls of science" run by different Islamic sects in many cities of North Africa and the Middle East in the 9th century were open to the public. Some of them had written lending policies, but they were very restrictive. Most patrons were expected to consult the books on site. The later European university libraries were not open to the general public, but accessible by scholars.

HISTORY

A public library is a library funded by public money, such as taxpayer money. The purpose of a public library is to provide books, Internet access and many other resources to the public for free. Even DVDs and movies are available for free rentals. Public libraries are not new, in fact the first organization that was considered to be a public library was created in the late 1500s.

- The first public library was created in England. At that time, the only people who were able to use libraries were individuals who joined a cathedral or were enrolled in college. This public library was called Francis Trigge Chained Library. This public library actually still exists and is famous for its long standing history of giving the people free access to all library resources. Although this library was the first, it stood nearly alone in its existence until the mid 1800s. That was the time period in which public libraries began to become popular.
- In England, Parliament decided to make a committee dedicated to considering the creation of multiple public libraries. The committee was supposed to decide if a public library was something that would benefit the public. The committee reported back that public libraries would be beneficial, since so many people were poor. The recommendation was to opcn multiplc public libraries throughout the country. This decision led to the Public Libraries Act of 1850. The act allowed all cities to collect taxes for public library support, providing that the population of the city had at least 10,000 people.
- This was quickly followed by the Public School Law, created in 1870. The point of this law was to raise the literacy rate of the public, since it was very low at the time. The only people who really knew how to read were rich people and scholars. Obviously, this literacy need increased the need for public libraries. By the 1870s, over 50 cities had created public libraries of their own. Only 30 years later, the number of public libraries hit 300. This was the time when public libraries began opening everywhere, and the United States began funding them as well. A public library was funded by public money, but it was also common for the people to help out these public libraries grow and flourish. Womens' clubs and the wealthy donated books to these public libraries to improve their selections.

Today, there are hundreds of thousands of public libraries in the world. The larger the city, the more public libraries will be found there. Unfortunately, despite the great need and desire for public libraries, funding for them are cut consistently by the state legislature. Large amounts of money to fund public libraries are made by private donors who have the wealth and desire to see a public library being used.

17th Century

In the early years of the 17th century, many famous collegiate and town libraries were founded throughout the country. Francis Trigge Chained Library of St. Wulfram's Church, Grantham, Lincolnshire was founded in 1598 by the rector of nearby Welbourne. Norwich City Library was established in 1608, and Chetham's Library in Manchester, which claims to be the oldest public library in the English-speaking world, opened in 1653.

Other early town libraries of the UK include those of:

- Ipswich (1612),
- Bristol (founded in 1613 and opened in 1615), and
- Leicester (1632).

Shrewsbury School also opened its library to townsfolk. In Bristol, an early library that allowed access to the public was that of the Kalendars or Kalendaries, a brotherhood of clergy and laity who were attached to the Church of All-Hallowen or All Saints. Records show that in 1464, provision was made for a library to be erected in the house of the Kalendars, and reference is made to a deed of that date by which it was "appointed that all who wish to enter for the sake of instruction shall have 'free access and recess' at certain times".

Early 18th Century

At the turn of the 18th century, libraries were becoming increasingly public and were more frequently lending libraries. The 18th century saw the switch from closed parochial libraries to lending libraries. Before this time, public libraries were parochial in nature and libraries frequently chained their books to desks. Libraries also were not uniformly open to the public. In 1790, The Public Library Act would not be passed for another sixty-seven years. Even though the British Museum existed at this time and contained over 50,000 books, the national library was not open to the public, or even to a majority of the population.

Access to the Museum depended on passes, of which there was sometimes a waiting period of three to four weeks. Moreover, the library was not open to browsing. Once a pass to the library had been issued, the reader was taken on a tour of the library. Many readers complained that the tour was much too short. At the turn of the century, there were virtually no public libraries in the sense in which we now understand the term *i.e.* libraries provided from public funds and freely accessible to all. Only one important library in Great Britain, namely Chetham's Library in Manchester, was fully and freely accessible to the public.

However, there had come into being a whole network of library provision on a private or institutional basis. Subscription libraries, both private and commercial, provided the middle and middle to upper class with a variety of books for moderate fees. The increase in secular literature at this time encouraged the spread of lending libraries, especially the commercial subscription libraries. Commercial subscription libraries began when booksellers began renting out extra copies of books in the mid-18th century. Steven Fischer estimates that in 1790, there were 'about six hundred rental and lending libraries, with a clientele of some fifty thousand. The mid to late 18th century saw a virtual epidemic of feminine reading as novels became more and more popular. Novels, while frowned upon in society, were extremely popular.

In England there were many who lamented at the 'villanous profane and obscene books' and the opposition to the circulating library, on moral grounds, persisted well into the 19th century. Still, many establishments must have circulated many times the number of novels as of any other genre. In 1797, Thomas Wilson wrote in The Use of Circulating Libraries: "Consider, that for a successful circulating library, the collection must contain 70% fiction". However, the overall percentage of novels mainly depended on the proprietor of the circulating library. While some circulating libraries were almost completely novels, others had less than 10% of their overall collection in the form of novels.

The national average at the turn of the century hovered around novels comprising about 20% of the total collection. Novels varied from other types of books in many ways. They were read primarily for enjoyment instead of for study. They did not provide academic knowledge or spiritual guidance; thus they were read quickly and far fewer times than other books. These were the perfect books for commercial subscription libraries to lend. Since books were read for pure enjoyment rather than for scholarly work, books needed to become both cheaper and smaller. Small duodecimo editions of books were preferred to the large folio editions. Folio editions were read at a desk, while the small duodecimo editions could be easily read like the paperbacks of today. Much like paperbacks of today, many of the novels in circulating libraries were unbound.

At this period of time, many people chose to bind their books in leather. Many circulating libraries skipped this process. Circulating libraries were not in the business of preserving books; their owners wanted to lend books as many times as they possibly could. Circulating libraries had ushered in a completely new way of reading. Reading was no longer simply an academic pursuit or an attempt to gain spiritual guidance. Reading became a social activity. Many circulating libraries were attached to the shops of milliners or drapers. They served as much for social gossip and the meeting of friends as coffee shops do today. Another factor in the growth of subscription libraries was the increasing cost of books.

In the last two decades of the century, especially, prices were practically doubled, so that a quarto work cost a guinea, an octavo 10 shillings or 12 shillings, and a duodecimo cost 4 shillings per volume. Price apart, moreover, books were difficult to procure outside London, since local booksellers could not afford to carry large stocks. Commercial libraries, since they were usually associated with booksellers, and also since they had a greater number of patrons, were able to accumulate greater numbers of books. The United Public Library was said to have a collection of some 52,000 volumes--twice as many as any private subscription library in the country at that period. These libraries, since they functioned as a business, also lent books to non-subscribers on a per-book system.

Private Subscription Libraries

Private subscription libraries functioned in much the same manner as commercial subscription libraries, though they varied in many important ways. One of the most popular versions of the private subscription library was a gentleman's only library.

The gentlemen's subscription libraries, sometimes known as proprietary libraries, were nearly all organized on a common pattern. Membership was restricted to the proprietors or shareholders, and ranged from a dozen or two to between four and five hundred.

The entrance fee, *i.e.* the purchase price of a share, was in early days usually a guinea, but rose sharply as the century advanced, often reaching four or five guineas during the French wars; the annual subscription, during the same period, rose from about six shillings to ten shillings or more. The book-stock was, by modern standards, small and was accommodated, at the outset, in makeshift premises--very often over a bookshop, with the bookseller acting as librarian and receiving an honourarium for his pains. The Liverpool Subscription library was a gentlemen only library. In 1798, it was renamed the Athenaeum when it was rebuilt with a newsroom and coffeehouse.

It had an entrance fee of one guinea and annual subscription of five shillings. While no records survive of the commercial library lendings, we have the Bristol Library's continuous record of borrowings from 1773 to 1857. An analysis of the registers for the first twelve years provides some fascinating glimpses of middle-class reading habits in a mercantile community at this period. The largest and most popular sections of the library were History, Antiquities, and Geography, with 283 titles and 6,121 borrowings, and Belles Lettres, with 238 titles and 3,313 borrowings. Far below came Theology and Ecclesiastical History, Natural History and Chemistry, Philosophy, Jurisprudence, Miscellanies, Mathematics, etc., and Medicine and Anatomy, all with fewer than 100 titles.

The most popular single work was John Hawkesworth's Account of Voyages in the Southern Hemisphere which was borrowed on 201 occasions. The records also show that in 1796, membership had risen by 1/3 to 198 subscribers and the titles increased five-fold to 4987. This mirrors the increase in reading interests. A patron list from the Bath Municipal Library shows that from 1793 to 1799, the library held a stable 30% of their patrons as female. It was also uncommon for these libraries to have buildings designated solely as the library building during the 1790s, though in the 19th century, many libraries would begin building elaborate permanent residences. Bristol, Birmingham, and Liverpool were the few libraries with their own building.

The accommodations varied from the shelf for a few dozen volumes in the country stationer's or draper's shop, to the expansion to a back room, to the spacious elegant areas of Hookham's or those at the resorts like Scarborough, and four in a row at Margate. Private subscription libraries held a greater amount of control over both membership and the types of books in the library. There was almost a complete elimination of cheap fiction in the private societies. Subscription libraries prided themselves on respectability.

The highest percentage of subscribers were often landed proprietors, gentry, and old professions. Towards the end of the 18th century and in the first decades of the nineteenth the need for books and general education made itself felt among social classes created by the beginnings of the Industrial Revolution. The late 18th century saw a rise in subscription libraries intended for the use of tradesmen. In 1797, there was established at Kendal what was known as the Economical Library, "designed principally for the use and instruction of the working classes".

There was also the Artizans' library established at Birmingham in 1799. The entrance fee was 3 shillings. The subscription was 1 shilling 6 pence per quarter. This was a library of general literature. Novels, at first excluded, were afterwards admitted on condition that they did not account for more than one-tenth of the annual income.

Rate-supported Libraries

Although by the mid-19th century, England could claim 274 subscription libraries and Scotland, 266, the foundation of the modern public library system in the U.K. is the Public Libraries Act 1850. Prior to this, the municipalities of Warrington and Salford established libraries in their museums, under the terms of the Museums Act of 1845. Warrington Municipal Library opened in 1848. Salford Museum and Art Gallery first opened in November 1850 as "The Royal Museum and Public Library", as the first unconditionally free public library in England. The library in Campfield, Manchester was the first library to operate a free lending library without subscription in 1852.

Norwich lays claims to being the first municipality to adopt the Public Libraries Act 1850 but theirs was the eleventh library to open, in 1857, being the eleventh in the country after:

- Winchester,
- Manchester,
- Liverpool,
- Bolton,
- Kidderminster,

- Cambridge,
- Birkenhead and
- Sheffield.

The Scottish-American philanthropist and businessman, Andrew Carnegie, helped to increase the number of public libraries from the late 19th century. County libraries are a later development which were made possible by the establishment of County Councils in 1888. They normally have a large central library in a major town with smaller branch libraries in other towns and a mobile library service covering rural areas.

NORTH AMERICA

Canada

In 1779 Frederick Haldimand, the Governor of Québec City, founded the first subscription library in Canada. Until then, Canada's libraries were mostly religious institutions, and the general public was not admitted. However, even though "Haldimand's library, like other subscription libraries, appealed primarily to an urban elite", it was the nation's first step towards the public library as it is known today. Haldimand's library later merged with the Literary and Historical Society of Quebec, which displays the original Québec Library collection within its library. This and similar association/social libraries were examples of early prototypes of public libraries.

They were public in that membership was allowed regardless of class or religion, and many in Canada eventually evolved into free public libraries. Subsequently legislative collections were established in 1791 in Upper and in 1792 in Lower Canada; and in 1796 the first public library was founded in Montreal. In 1800, libraries were established in King's College, Nova Scotia, and at Niagara, where the first public library in Upper Canada operated for twenty years, in spite of losses during the War of 1812. In Saint John, New Brunswick in 1883, following the efforts of Colonel James Domville in procuring a collection of materials to replace the many private collections lost in the Great Fire of Saint John, New Brunswick the first free, tax-supported public library was established. Guelph, Ontario and Toronto, Ontario opened public libraries that same year as well. Due to Canada's size and diversity, the development of the modern Canadian public library was more of a slow evolution than a quick transition as each of the provinces' specific conditions had first to be addressed.

The public library therefore took on many forms in Canada's earlier years; the three most prevalent of these forms were school-district libraries, Mechanics Institutes, and association/social libraries. In 1850, school-district libraries were initiated in Canada. Public servant Joseph Howe started one in Nova Scotia, and politician Egerton Ryerson started one in Ontario. New Brunswick and Prince Edward Island followed suit in 1858 and 1877, respectively. The hope was that both children and adults could benefit from the local school authorities, where financial assistance was provided from colonial legislatures, but the departments of education proved to be too centralizing for locals and this practiced was phased out. Mechanics Institutes also contained libraries that the working class could access inexpensively. The first Canadian library of its kind was established in 1828 in Montréal, Québec. Other communities took up this idea as well – notably those in Halifax, Nova Scotia, Hamilton, Ontario, Toronto, Ontario and Victoria, British Columbia. Like the school-district libraries, these institutes eventually ceased or were replaced by public libraries.

The public library that opened in Toronto, Ontario, was mostly due to a campaign by city alderman John Hallam. James Bain became the first chief librarian, and built a comprehensive collection of Canadian literature and history. The Toronto Public Library was one of the first libraries to choose free status, and it was the largest of them all. Its development flourished after 1900 when Carnegie grants began to aid in building construction and the expansion of collections and services. During this time, open access and children's departments were introduced, and standard cataloguing and classification systems were adopted. Many of the original branches, funded by a Carnegie grant, still stand and continue to be operated by the Toronto Public Library. Other provinces were affected by Carnegie as well and followed Ontario's lead in legislating tax support for library services. British Columbia acted in 1891, Manitoba in 1899, Saskatchewan in 1906, and in Alberta, the first legislation officially passed by the legislative assembly was the Library Act.

The act was passed March 15, 1907. The next provinces to follow were New Brunswick in 1929, Newfoundland in 1935, Prince Edward Island in 1936, Nova Scotia in 1937, Québec in1959, and then the Northwest Territories in 1966. As they stand today, public libraries in Canada are "governed by provincial statues and are primarily financed by municipal tax revenues and other local income, with provincial grants supplementing local funding. [They are also] the responsibility of a local or regional library board with authority to appoint or dismiss employees, control library property, establish policies, and budget for library operations."

Though the services offered vary from local branch to local branch, public libraries in Canada are not only places to read and borrow books; they are also hubs of community services, such as early reading programmes, computer access, and tutoring and literacy help for children and adults. Throughout the years, Canadian libraries have been subject to the political and economic influence of the nation. During World War II, public libraries experienced development setbacks, but expansion resumed in 1945. Then, in the 1960s, Canadian public libraries felt the benefits of the era's emphasis on education – service expanded, buildings were remodeled or constructed from scratch, and

Centennial Grants were provided in order to improve the system. This period of growth ended in due to the inflationary period in the 1970s and the two recessions during the 1980s. However, in the late 1990s this trend reversed and the National Core Library Statistics Programme reported in 1999 that public libraries served 28.5 million municipal residents – a total of 93% of the Canadian population. Nevertheless, in 2011 the tides turned for public libraries in Canada once again, specifically in Toronto. The city is now undergoing a heated debate regarding Mayor Rob Ford's proposed budget cuts for the Toronto Public Library, which is currently one of the most efficient public library systems in all of North America.

Mexico

In 1646, Don Juan de Palafox y Mendoza, bishop of Puebla and Viceroy of New Spain, expelled the Jesuits from New Spain, and with the confiscated books founded the Biblioteca Palafoxiana—the first public library in New Spain. It was in Puebla and open to all readers. The Biblioteca Palafoxiana exists today and is listed on the UNESCO Memory of the World Programme.

United States

As the United States developed from the 18th century to today, growing more populous and wealthier, factors such as a push for education and desire to share knowledge led to broad public support for free libraries. In addition, money donations by private philanthropists provided the seed capital to get many libraries started. In some instances, collectors donated vast book collections. William James Sidis in *The Tribes and the States* claimed the public library, as such, was an American invention. But exactly what constitutes a "free public library" is subject to dispute, and the term "invention" doesn't seem applicable to the many facets of an institution such as a library.

Throughout history, knowledge in different forms has been shared in different ways. Writing was recorded on papyrus and stored in scrolls and kept in vast libraries such as the Library of Alexandria in Egypt. In ancient Greece, knowledge was passed by one person reading aloud to a group of scribes from a text; this resulted in sometimes different and error-prone versions of the same text. Monks in the Middle Ages copied manuscripts by hand. After the invention of the printing press by Johann Gutenberg, books became prevalent, and different institutions such as universities and governments and churches found ways to keep and share them. There are disputes about which was the first public library in the nation. Early American cities such as Boston and Philadelphia and New York had the first organized collections of books, but which library was truly "public" is subject to dispute. Sidis claims the first public library was Boston's in 1636, although the official Boston Public Library was organized later in 1852.

In 1698, Charleston's St. Philip's Church Parsonage had a parish library. In 1731, Benjamin Franklin and his friends, sometimes called "the Junto", operated the Library Company of Philadelphia partly as a means to settle arguments and partly as a means to advance themselves through sharing information. Franklin's subscription library allowed members to buy "shares" and combined funds were used to buy more books; in return, members could borrow books and use the library. Today, the Library Company continues to exist as a nonprofit, independent research library.

A town in Massachusetts wanted to name itself Franklin in honour of the famous Pennsylvanian, and in return, Benjamin Franklin donated books for use by local residents; while Franklin had been asked to donate a church bell instead, he declined on the basis that "sense" was preferable to "sound". One source considers the Franklin library in Massachusetts to be the first public library in the United States. Another source claims the library in Darby, Pennsylvania which opened in 1743 is the "oldest continuously operating free public library" in the United States. But other libraries claim to be the first public library, including the Scoville library in Salisbury, Connecticut, which was established in 1803. The library in the New Hampshire town of Peterborough claims to be the first publicly-funded library; it opened in 1833. And a library in Massachusetts in the town of Arlington claims to have had the first free children's library; it opened in 1835.

Finances

In the trend from private to public libraries, big city libraries had the largest book collections and the most funding. The forerunner of the New York Public Library in Manhattan was a library established by the Earl of Ballamont around 1700. A newspaper described the call for the "first public librarian" demanding that "he must not be too young, for this would render him liable to be despised by the youth" and "he must be of an even temper" with "great diligence" and "sufficient learning" and "have a genius peculiarly adapted to the calling." In 1849, the library was officially established, and consolidated in 1901.

Today, it is considered to be one of the most important public libraries in the nation. New York governor and book lover Samuel J. Tilden bequeathed millions to build the New York Public Library. He believed Americans should have access to books and a free education if desired. In 2005, the library offered the "NYPL Digital Gallery" which made a collection of 275,000 images viewable over the web; while most of the contents are in the public domain, some images are still subject to copyright rules.

In 1902, one account suggested "the village library is growing more and more an indispensable adjunct to American village life." Around the turn from the 19th to the 20th century, Scottish-American businessman Andrew Carnegie donated over $60 million, which was a vast fortune in 20th century dollars, to build over 2,811 free public library buildings in the United States. They were often known as Carnegie libraries. Carnegie envisioned that libraries would "bring books and information to all people." Libraries have been started with wills from other benefactors; for example, the Bacon Free Library in South Natick, Massachusetts was founded in 1881 after a benefactor left $15,000 in a will; it has operated as a public library since then. Once the idea of the public library as an agency worthy of taxation was broadly established during the nineteenth and early twentieth centuries, librarians through actions of the American Library Association and its division devoted to public libraries, the Public Library Association, sought ways to identify standards and guidelines to ensure quality service.

In 2009, with the economic downturn, many public libraries have budget shortfalls. The library in Darby, Pennsylvania found expenses were greater than revenues from local property taxes, state funds, and investment income; it was on the risk of closing, according to a newspaper report. Many public libraries face budgetary problems; the report noted that "tax dollars that support them are dwindling as property tax revenue declines along with home values and sales taxes fall as consumers spend less. As local funding drops, libraries are turning to their endowments and draining the investments." Many libraries have foundations behind them to support them financially, and rely on the help of well-heeled donors as well as local corporations for funds.

Services

Most public libraries today are supported by tax monies from local and state governments, and some have foundations to support them with additional capital. Libraries lend books and materials freely, but charge fines if materials are returned late or damaged. Libraries often keep many historical documents relevant to their particular town, and serve as a resource for historians in some instances; for example, the Queens Public Library kept letters written by unrecognized Tiffany lamp designer Clara Driscoll, and the letters remained in the library until a curator discovered them. In 2009, big city libraries have multiple branches and offer numerous services. For example, the Boston Public Library has 26 neighbourhood branches and offers free Internet service; it has two restaurants and an online store which features reproductions of photographs and artwork; and it promotes itself with a website. It answers more than one million reference questions annually.

The library uses wireless technology software networks to offer more services and keep costs under control. The Boston library offers digitized content, video, a wider range of formats and, as a result, "research documents now have broader accessibility within the community and around the world," and help communities by offering public access computers, mobile Wi-fi access, and free job search tools. Libraries promote cultural awareness; in Newark,

New Jersey, the public library celebrated black history with exhibits and programmes. Libraries also partner with schools and community organizations to promote literacy and learning. One account suggested libraries were essential to "economic compet-itiveness" as well as "neighbourhood vitality" and help some people find jobs. Some library buildings are notable for their particular architectural styles; in the town of Beaver Dam, Wisconsin, architects designed the Williams Free Library in the style of Richardsonian Romanesque.

EUROPE

France

The National Library of France is one of the oldest libraries in the world still in service today as it traces its origin to the royal library founded at the Louvre by King Charles V in 1368, but at the time it was conceived as the private library of the French kings and it opened to the public only in 1692, during the reign of Louis XIV. Claude Sallier, the philologist and churchman, had an idea that was advanced for its era—to make culture accessible to all. From 1737 to 1750 he made books available to the town of Saulieu, forming France's first public library. The pioneer of modern public libraries in France was Eugène Morel, a writer and one of the librarians at the Bibliothèque nationale. He put forward his ideas in the 1910 book La Librairie publique.

Italy

The Malatestiana Library also known as the Malatesta Novello Library, is a public library dating from 1452 in Cesena, Emilia-Romagna. It was the first European civic library, *i.e.* belonging to the Commune and open to everybody. It was commissioned by the Lord of Cesena, Malatesta Novello. The works were directed by Matteo Nuti of Fano and lasted from 1447 to 1452.

Poland

The Zaluski Library was built in Warsaw 1747– 1795 by Józef Andrzej Zaluski and his brother, Andrzej Stanis³aw Zaluski, both Roman Catholic bishops. The library was open to the public and indeed was the first Polish public library, the biggest in Poland and one of the earliest public libraries in Europe. In 1794, the library was looted on orders from Catherine II of Russia. Much of the material was returned in the period of 1842-1920, but once again the library was decimated during World War II during the period following the Warsaw Uprising. The Zaluski Library was succeeded by the creation of the National Library of Poland in 1928.

Australia

Library services in Australia developed along different paths in the different States. In 1809 the Reverend Samuel Marsden advertised in England for donations to help found a 'Lending Library for the general benefit of the inhabitants of New South Wales'.

The library would cover 'Divinity and Morals, History, Voyages and Travels, Agriculture in all its branches, Mineralogy and Practical Mechanics'. No Public Library came to fruition from this although some of the books brought to the colony after this call survive in the library of Moore Theological College.

The place of Public Libraries was filled by Mechanics' Institutes, schools of arts, athenaeums and literary institutes. Some of these provided free library services to visitors. However lending rights were available only to members who were required to pay a subscription. In 1856, the Victorian colonial government opened the Melbourne Public Library. This was however purely a reference library. In September 1869, the New South Wales (NSW) government opened as the Free Public Library, Sydney by purchasing a bankrupt subscription library. In 1896, the Brisbane Public Library was established. The Library's collection, purchased by the Queensland Government from the private collection of Mr. Justice Harding. In 1932, the Carnegie Corporation of New York, funded a survey into Australian libraries. It found 'wretched little institutes' which were 'cemeteries of old and forgotten books'.

There was also criticism of the limited public access, poor staff training, unsatisfactory collections, lack of non-fiction, absence of catalogues and poor levels of service for children. Lending libraries in Sydney and Prahran were praised as examples of services which were doing well, but these were seen as exceptions. In NSW, The Free Library Movement was established in response to the Munn-Pitt Report. This collection of concerned citizens, progress associations, returned servicemen and trade unions advocated a system of public libraries to serve the needs of all people. The birth of the movement took place at a public meeting in the Chatswood-Willoughby School of Arts, Sydney, in 1935. George Brain, President of the Middle Harbour Progress Association, ran the meeting.

George Brain initiated the resolution which brought the Free Library Movement into existence in NSW as well as the election of provisional office bearers, including himself as Honourary Secretary. This movement was stalled by the onset of World War II in 1939. In 1943, the Queensland Parliament passed the Libraries Act, establishing the Library Board of Queensland to manage the operations of the Public Library of Queensland, and coordinate and improve library facilities throughout the State of Queensland. In November 1943, at the official opening of the new Public Library of New South Wales building, William McKell, the New South Wales Premier, announced that the Library Act would be fully proclaimed from 1 January 1944. After the war, and with George Brain now in NSW parliament as a principle advocate for the Free Library Movement, the passing of Library Acts in NSW and the other states at the end of the war marked the beginning of modern public libraries in Australia.

Even after the war, the development of free lending libraries in Australia had been agonizingly slow: it was not until the 1960s that local governments began to establish public libraries in suburban areas. Currently there are 1402 Australian public libraries plus 78 mobile libraries. Australians generate more than 110 million library visits per year. There are more than 9.9 million library members more than 41.5 million items to use and borrow, plus more than 11,600 computers for public use. It costs $882.3 million to run Australian public libraries. They return at least $2.6 billion-worth of community benefits. All this costs Australians $830 million - just over 10c a day each with a benchmark for best practice funding being 20c per day.

The 2007 Americans for Libraries Council (ALC) report on library valuation stated, 'A benefit-to-cost ratio of 3:1 or better is common among the library valuation studies ALC reviewed. Because this type of economic analysis is commonly used across industries and businesses, it puts libraries into an evaluative framework that permits comparisons with other types of organizations. When this occurs, public libraries consistently outpace other sectors, such as transportation, health, and education, on the efficient use of tax dollars'.

FUNDING PROBLEMS

Most public libraries rely heavily on local government funding. Some proactive librarians have devised alliances with patron and civic groups to supplement their financial situations. Library "friends" groups, activist boards, and well organized book sales supplement government funding. With the cost of running local government increasing at a rate far above inflation, libraries are compelled to look beyond the tax base of the communities they serve. In the United States, among other countries, libraries in financially strapped communities compete financially with other public institutions, such as police, firefighters, and schools.

Many communities are closing down or reducing the capability of their library systems, at the same time balancing their budgets. Jackson County, Oregon, closed its entire 15-branch public library system for six months in 2007, reopening with a private-public 'partnership' and a reduced schedule. This example of a funding problem followed the failure to pass of a bond measure and cessation of federal funding for counties with dwindling timber revenue, in a state with no sales tax. In December 2004, Salinas, California almost became the first city in the United States to completely close down its entire library system. A tax increase passed by the voters in November 2005 allowed the libraries to open, but hours remain limited.

The American Library Association says media reports it has compiled in 2004 showed some $162 million in funding cuts to libraries nationwide. Survey data suggests the public values free public libraries. A Public Agenda survey in

2006 reported 84 per cent of the public said maintaining free library services should be a top priority for their local library. Public libraries received higher ratings for effectiveness than other local services such as parks and police. But the survey also found the public was mostly unaware of financial difficulties facing their libraries. Recently, many US cities, including Philadelphia, New York, Trenton and San Diego, have been facing the issue of making job cuts and service reductions in order to save money.

Most of these cities have decided to cut library funding by closing down several branches and cutting hours and staff members in the branches that will remain open. Philadelphia, however, has decided to keep their 54 branches open. In order to save money during this financial crisis, Mayor Michael Nutter has proposed to cut funding for recreational parks and decrease the budget for police and fire services. Nutter has announced that the Philadelphia public library branches will not be affected by the budget cuts at this time. In various cost-benefit studies libraries continue to provide an exceptional return on the dollar. A 2008 survey discusses comprehensively the prospects for increased funding in the United States, saying in conclusion "There is sufficient, but latent, support for increased library funding among the voting population." Public libraries, long supported by various government entities, have seen a decline in monetary support for several decades, due to various influences.

The American Library Association states that 41% of states saw a decline in state budgets for public library funding in 2009 Cases in point are the libraries in Salinas, California, Rochester, New York, and Buffalo, New York, but there are many other long-standing public libraries now having to find new sources of income to keep them operating.

- In California, the passage of Proposition 13 in 1978 removed the property tax as a source of funding for libraries, school programmes, and other public services. This action provided tax relief for homeowners on one hand, but forced severe budget cuts to the services they enjoyed.
- The cost of creating, maintaining, and upgrading electronic hardware, networks, and resources has put a strain on many library budgets.
- The cost of printed matter such as books and magazines has risen over time, while funding has remained static or declined.

DEVELOPMENT OF PUBLIC LIBRARIES IN INDIA

Public libraries arose worldwide along with growth in education, literacy, and publications. Every country has its own public library history with influential leaders. Monarchs, wealthy people, and philanthropists have all made a contribution to society in the form of public library development. India is no exception. Libraries were established in ancient India mainly by the patronage extended by emperors, major capitalists, and scholars. Indian emperors and kings were supported scholars and scholarship. There is evidence of well-developed libraries even in the sixth century A.D. The famous Nalanda University in Bihar had its own magnificent library with a massive collection of manuscripts covering the universe of knowledge. Admission to library was restricted to scholars.

Other ancient universities, such as Taxila and Vikramashila, also had valuable libraries. Muslim influence in India during the 13th century A.D. marked the dawn of another era of learning and scholarship. The Mughal period gave a further stimulus to the growth of libraries. Mughal rulers attached considerable importance to libraries and appointed scholars as librarians. The Mughal emperors were patrons of art and literature. In the period of Emperor Babur, Humayun, and Akbar many new libraries were established and existing ones further developed. Mughal libraries featured magnificent buildings, rare manuscripts, and scholar librarians.

The names of Maharaja Sawai Man Singh of Jaipur and Maharaja Ranjit Singh of Punjab will be remembered with appreciation in the history of library services in India. The Maharaja of Tanjuar started the famous Saraswati Mahal Library in 17th century A.D. It remains a unique institution in its nature of collection and services Libraries established by the kings and capitalists functioned like private institutions and the admission was limited. Service to the general public had to wait for the British. Unfortunately, the arrival of the British and resulting political disorder also brought chaos to the Indian way of life.

This was a severe blow to the cultural heritage of India, which had arisen from the Indus valley civilization. When libraries began developing in India during the early nineteenth century, they were a western product. In 1808, the Government of Bombay proposed to register libraries, which were to be given copies of books published from the "funds for the encouragement of literature". The "Sinha Committee", this was the beginning of the first phase of public library development in India. During the first half of the 19th century, the three presidency towns of Bombay, Calcutta, and Madras had public libraries. These libraries were mostly financed by Europeans residing in these towns. Of these, the establishment of the public library at Calcutta in 1835 was the most significant. This was the library which later developed into the National Library of India. Almost simultaneous, subscription libraries were started in many Indian cities.

These were, of course, not public libraries in the true sense of the term, and did not provide free books for all. Founded in imitation of their western counterparts, the use of these libraries was confined to small, affluent portion of society. The first three decades of the 20th century can be looked on as the golden age of the Indian library system. On January 31, 1902, the Imperial Library Act was passed and Lord Curzon transformed the Calcutta Public Library into the Imperial Library in 1906. Developments in Baroda were also notable. The development of public libraries in Baroda was unique. Baroda developed a network of public libraries to serve the entire Princely State. Maharaja Sayaji Rao Gaekwad III of Baroda who traveled all over the world was deeply impressed by the role played by public libraries in the promotion of education in the United States and thought of extending such benefits to his own subjects. In 1910 he invited an American expert, William Alson Borden to organize the public library system for his state. The public library movement that flourished in Baroda was a glorious one. But that was not a general trend of that period because in no other part of India, a parallel development occurred.

Yet another development during the period was the organisation of a host of conferences such as:

- The first conference of library workers and persons interested in the library movement was held at Beswada, Andhra in 1914.
- The first All India Library Conference of Librarians was held in 1918 at Lahore.
- The first All India Library Conference was held at Calcutta in 1933.
- The first All India Public Library Conference was held at Madras in 1934.

With the existence of democratic governments in several provinces beginning in 1937, another phase of the library movement began. Between 1937 and 1942, a number of village libraries and travelling libraries sprang up in Assam, Bihar, Punjab, and Travancore. It was estimated that there were about 13,000 village libraries in India in 1942. Another remarkable development was the appointment of the 'Library Development Committee' by the Government of Bombay, with A.A.A. Fyzee as its chairman. The Committee ambitiously recommended a comprehensive library system to be implemented in three successive stages. Because of financial constraints, the government could only implement part of the recommendations.

After Independence

After independence, the growth of libraries in general has been remarkable, although not as remarkable as that of academic and special libraries. At the time of independence, India was facing a host of challenges. Those in the rural population, 88 per cent of the total, were nearly all illiterate. Transportation was poor and mass media merely nominal. Nevertheless, the public library scene in India improved considerably during the post independence period, though it is still lacking on several fronts.

Verma and Agrawal argue that to compare our public libraries with those of the developed nations on equal footing, we have to go a long way. The 1951 census, the first conducted after independence, found 2,843 local governments in the urban and rural areas in India, of which 320 were rural district boards. Only about one third of local governments maintained public libraries, about 950. In addition, there were about 1,500 subscription libraries. So-called public libraries were primarily reading rooms with a few hundred books for reading on the premises. The Delhi public library deserves special mention. It was founded in 1951 as the first UNESCO Public Library Pilot Project under the joint auspices of UNESCO and Government of India.

The purpose of the library was to adapt "modern techniques to Indian conditions" and to serve as a model public library for Asia. The establishment of Delhi Public Library, the involvement of union government in the public library movement, and the enactment of public library legislation in some states are the main factors which contributed to the improvement of public libraries after independence. Although the government of India allotted funds for public library development in its five-year plans, this funding was not connected to effective planning.

Advisory Committee for Libraries

The Government of India appointed a committee in 1957 to report on the status of public library development in the country. It is also called the Sinha Committee, after its chair, the late Dr. A.P. Sinha, who was at that time Director of Public Instruction in Bihar.

The Sinha Committee's charge included:

- Determining present reading needs, how they are met, and what part existing library systems play in meeting the needs;
- Determining reading tastes, what agencies provide suitable literature, and how reading taste can be improved;
- Recommending future library structure in India;
- Recommending areas of cooperation between libraries and education systems;
- Considering the training of librarians and the conditions of their service;
- Recommending the administrative and financial measures necessary to support public libraries in India.

The committee submitted its report to Dr. K.L. Shrimali, who was Minister for Education, on the 12th of November, 1958. The Committee described the situation as dismal and called libraries in most cases, "a stagnant pool of books," because new books were not added regularly. The committee at the same time observed that wherever large collections did exist, they were not fully used because of rigid rules. Library users were not trusted and were required to deposit large sums of money as a kind of insurance, which lower income people could not afford.

As of March 1954 there were 32,000 libraries in India, with a little more than 7,100,000 books and a total circulation of about 37,700,000. The report observed that genuine public library service was rarity, and that public library service throughout the country was unsatisfactory. The committee recommended creating state library networks based on uniform library legislation.

The chief recommendations of the report were:

- Library service should be made free to every citizen of India;
- The hierarchy of public library service in the country should begin with National Library, and proceed to State Central Library, District Library, Block Library, and Panchayat Library;
- An independent Director of Social Education and Libraries should be set up in every state, with a fulltime senior class-1 officer of the rank of Deputy Director of Education to plan, organize, and administer library services;
- An All India Library Advisory Council should be constituted as a central agency to review and assess the work done at the state level;
- Library Associations should actively assist the development of libraries in the country;
- University libraries should cooperate with public library systems by allowing selected public readers to use their collection;
- State governments should accept responsibility for public library services in their states;
- Librarians and social education workers should cooperate to promote literacy;
- A library cess of six paisa for each rupee of property tax should be levied with the permission of local bodies.
- The Government of India should match the amount collected in the states. State governments should also give matching grants to local bodies over the succeeding 25 years, their contribution should be raised to three times the cess collected.
- State and national governments should enact comprehensive state library laws incorporating the right of every citizen to have free access to libraries. The Government of India should provide necessary financial assistance to the state governments for this purpose.

RAJA RAM MOHAN ROY LIBRARY FOUNDATION

Another positive step taken by the Central Government was the establishment of the Raja Ram Mohan Roy Library Foundation (RRRLF) at Calcutta on May 22, 1972, as a part of the bicentenary celebrations of the birth of Raja Ram Mohan Roy, a social reformer of the early 19th century.

Its objectives are library development in general and rural library development in particular. It provides financial assistance to public libraries in the form of matching grants. It assists State Central Libraries and District Central Libraries, which has helped many states and Union Territories develop rural public library services.

Main Objectives of RRRLF

The main objectives of RRRLF are:

- Promotion of the library movement in India;
- The adoption of a national library policy by the central and state governments;
- Development of a National Library System by integrating the services of National Libraries, State Central Libraries, District Libraries, and other types of libraries through an interlibrary lending system;
- Propagation and adoption of library legislation in the country;
- Provision of financial and technical assistance to libraries;
- Provision of financial assistance to voluntary organizations and library associations for the promotion of library development;
- Periodic publication of reports on library development;
- To act as a clearing house for ideas and information on library development in India and abroad;
- To advise the Government of India library development;
- Promotion of research in problems of library development

The primary objective of RRRLF is the promotion of the library movement. The rest are subsidiary objectives. RRRLF is the first government-sponsored body specifically created for this purpose.

The foundation also has a programme of assistance to libraries for workshops, conferences, and exhibits. The foundation has taken the major initiative for the formulation of a national policy on library and information systems by the Government of India.

The current programmes of assistance are:

- Collection building;
- Rural libraries and mobile library service for rural areas;
- Seminars, workshops, conferences, training courses, and exhibits;
- Facilities and equipment for storage and display of materials;
- Public library buildings;
- Television and VCR equipment for educational purposes;
- Assistance to voluntary organisations providing public library services;
- Assistance to children's libraries or children's sections of general public libraries

During the last three decades, the foundation has assisted more than 500 libraries, including many in rural areas

NATIONAL POLICY ON LIBRARY AND INFORMATION SYSTEM (NAPLIS)

In 1985, a committee was set up under the chairmanship of Prof. D.P. Chattopadhyay to formulate a National Policy on Library and Information System (NAPLIS). The Committee submitted its report in May 1986. Following that, another committee looked at implications of the report and created an action plan for its implementation. The Empowerment Committee submitted its report in April 1988 and an Implementation Cell was formed to implement its recommendations within a period of six months. Yet another Working Group, under the Joint Secretary to the Government of India in the Department of Culture, was constituted to examine its recommendations for implementation. The Working Group submitted its report in July 1993 and suggested implementing only 29 of 60 recommendations made by the NAPLIS.

The following are some of the recommendations of NAPLIS related to public libraries:

- Proposals for maintenance and development of public libraries should preferably come from State Legislative Enactment. The Central Government may revise the Model Public Library Bill. Funds for library development should come from each state, either from general revenue or from local taxation. Central Government agencies may provide funds under Plan Expenditure.
- Efforts should emphasize rural public libraries. A village or a cluster of villages with an adequate population should have a community library/rural community centre, which will also serve as an information centre. Resources from various agencies engaged in the public health, adult education, State and central government, etc., should be used to build up and maintain this centre.
- The central government increase its assistance to state governments in the development of public libraries. The RRRLF, as the national agency for coordinating and assisting the development of public libraries, should be suitably strengthened in order to do this.
- Standards and guidelines for library service should be created.
- There should be a system of national libraries consisting of National Library, Calcutta as the National Library of India, National Depository libraries in Delhi, Bombay, Madras, National Subject Libraries, and others. These national libraries should form part of one integrated system.
- A National Commission on Libraries and Information System or National Commission on Informatics and Documentation may be constituted by an Act of Parliament to serve under the Ministry of Human Resource Development. The Commission will have representation from appropriate central and state agencies and could

provide guidance and coordinate library development programmes in all sectors. This body will have the primary responsibility for the implementation of NAPLIS programmes.

- National Depository libraries; Connemara Public library, Chennai; Central Library, Bombay; and Delhi Public Library, Delhi should concentrate on development of collections and preservation of Indian culture produced in the languages of their regions, supplementing and complementing the efforts of the Indian National Library.
- The Indian National Bibliography should have a comprehensive coverage of the national output of documents and should be updated regularly. This responsibility should be vested in the National Library.
- Government should create a national awareness of the need to preserve the nation's cultural heritage. National libraries should be responsible, with preservation facilities created there. Links between libraries, archives, and museums should be established for the purpose of national preservation.
- The Ministry of Rural Development has a plan for one community centre in every Panchayat Centre. The Department of Culture and the Ministry of Rural Development have agreed to provide library services at each of these Rural Community Centres.
- An important link should be established between community centre library and primary schools. If the schools do not have libraries of their own, the community centre library should provide children with adequate services.
- A community centre library should have an important role in adult education programmes.
- A district library should provide facilities and recreation for the disabled and low-income people, *e.g.*, literature in Braille.
- Libraries should be built in areas of tribal concentration and in minority communities to help in developing and sustaining their distinctive cultures.
- Libraries should be equipped with relevant resources, such as publications covering Open University and vocational educational courses, for their role in support of distance education.
- All public libraries within a state should form a part of a network extending from village library through community centre library, district library, and state network, and should be linked to the national information grid.

1951-1956

- The first five-year plan for educational development included a proposal for "Improvement of Library Service." This proposal envisioned a network of libraries throughout the country, coordinated by National Central Library at New Delhi

- During the first five-year plan, nine state governments, *i.e.* Assam, Madhya Pradesh, West Bengal, Punjab, PEPSU, Rajasthan, Savarashtra, Bhopal, and Vindhya Pradesh, decided to set up State Central Libraries.

1956-1961

- At this time, the government allocated funds to set up a national network of libraries in its 320 districts. As a result, most states established State Central Libraries and District Libraries as the main distributing centres

1961-1966

- During this period, the system of central government assistance to the states was changed, and funding for libraries was kept to a minimum. It was up to the individual states to take initiative and develop their public libraries. The programme to assist state governments in establishing state central libraries, district central libraries, and block development libraries was abandoned.
- The decision was a major setback to the development of public libraries. During this period four national libraries were established at Delhi, Calcutta, Bombay, and Madras. A Working Group on libraries was appointed by the Planning Commission in 1964 to take a stock of library development.

The working group submitted its report on 7th September 1965 with following recommendations:

- The central and state governments should share responsibility for providing adequate public library service. New government agencies in the central government under the Minister of Education, a directorate of libraries and a state library advisory council in each state should be set up to execute the programmes effectively.
- State central libraries should be established in four states: Madhya Pradesh, Mysore, Nagaland, and Orissa.
- States which do not possess adequate functional buildings for their state central libraries should be provided with library buildings.
- The state central library must have a children's section.
- There should be 335 District Libraries for the 327 districts in the country, *i.e.*, in large and populous districts, two district libraries may be provided.

- New buildings should be constructed for the existing 100 district libraries.
- Block libraries are the chief feeding centre for the rural reading public, and therefore, 2,500 new block libraries, covering 75% of blocks in the country should be constructed.
- A sum of 10 million rupees shall be provided for distribution of grant in aid to such libraries of urban and rural areas which depend on subscription and donations.
- Three public libraries on model of Delhi Public Library should be set up
- The Institute of Library Science established by the Ministry of Education at Delhi University in 1958-59, and then closed in 1962, should be reopened. Such institutes should be established at the state levels also to train graduate and undergraduate librarians to meet future requirements.
- A sum of Rs.10,000 shall be allocated as financial assistance to all national level and state level library associations to create library consciousness in the country by organizing seminars, conducting surveys, and producing library literature.
- A programme of book production should be undertaken.
- A draft of the Library Act should be produced

1969-1974

This plan proposed a substantial sum for the social education programme. A much lower sum was allocated. Of this, only a very small amount was available for the development of libraries in the country.

1974-1979

This plan included measures to strengthen the buildings, collections, and staff of the central and state libraries, as well as strengthening the district, block, and village libraries. During this period, attempts were made to develop a district-level library system, so that district library could act as a leader for the smaller libraries in the district. The adult education programme was the hallmark of this plan. The programme was to be supported by a network of libraries at the village and block levels and various community centres. Thus steps were taken to strengthen not only the village and block libraries, but also the central, state libraries and the district libraries

1980-85

This plan emphasized establishing a network of rural public libraries to sustain literacy and disseminate information to rural areas. It discussed the necessity of integrating school and college libraries with the system of public libraries. During this period, 26 states or union territories out of 31 had established state central libraries and 291 district libraries.

1985-90

During this period, the Commission's objective was to address the needs of 90 million people in the Adult Education Programme. The network of libraries was to play a role in the development of literature for neo-literates. Library systems were to be strengthened, with specific attention given to improvement of facilities at national level institutions. An important development was the 1986 adoption of National Literacy Mission, which emphasised the education of women and the establishment of rural libraries. In addition, the RRRLF set up an Integrated Research Cell-cum-Computer Unit for promoting research in librarianship and database of public libraries in the country There were two annual plans for the years 1990-91 and 1991-92.

1992-97

During this period it was proposed to reorganize the Central Reference Library into the National Bibliographical and Documentation Centre, which would also have a computer centre. The Delhi Public Library set up two new libraries in its service area. RRRLF created programmes to help state central libraries purchase reprographic equipment, to help libraries process rare books, and to give special assistance to networks of public libraries that were at least 100 years old.

1997-2002

During the 9th five year plan, the National Library, Kolkatta, undertook several major initiatives to upgrade and modernize its collection building programme, reader services, and conservation of library material. The major activities completed during the period were automation of the circulation system in the lending section, setting up of a local area network, improved reader services, and more efficient collection management. The conservation activities in the library got a major advance with the purchase of modern equipment to preserve rare books and other materials. The Central Reference Library, Kolkatta computerised various functions during the Ninth Plan.

As a result, the publication of the Indian National Bibliography is now up to date, with records available online. Funds were provided to the Delhi Public Library and Central Secretariat Library, Delhi, for acquisition of new material in different languages and media as well as for modernizing their infrastructure. The benefits of these efforts can be seen in improved reader services, networking, and resource sharing.

The Central Secretariat Library organized a number of computer training programmes for resource sharing, standardization of cataloguing formats, and co-operative acquisition. Funds for modernizing and computerization were also provided from central grants to the Connemara Library, Chennai, Thanjavur Maharaja Serovji Sarasvati Mahal Library, Thanjavur and the State Central Library, Mumbai. Besides these, the RRRLF provided assistance to public libraries across the country for collections and storage, construction, and seminars and workshops.

Tenth Five-year Plan (Action Plan)

The Planning Commission proposed further modernization of central and public libraries during the Tenth Plan. A national bibliographic database would be developed to encourage resource sharing, networking, and to improve reader services. The Commission resolved to strengthen public library infrastructure through the RRRLF. The Tenth Plan focused on upgrading existing libraries, including private collections, and widening the programme for bibliographic control and documentation. To make readers services more comprehensive and effective, the National Library is expected to act as the ultimate referral centre for various subjects. To keep pace with the latest developments in information technology in public libraries, the upgrading and networking of central and state libraries was also planned.

STATE LIBRARY AGENCIES

Continuing education for professional and support staff in all the professions has been receiving increasing emphasis in recent years. The need to update current practice through new knowledge and insight of societal conditions and client needs has had its impact in the library and information science fields.

The advances in automation and technology, the proliferation of knowledge, and the growing recognition of the need to provide access to the rapid delivery of information in many formats have given priority emphasis to continuing library education as a means of responding to the changes taking place in our society. State library agencies have a continuing responsibility for a planned approach to the development of library and information services in each state. This planned approach includes the need for the continuing education of library personnel to meet changing service demands.

This object reviews the background for the continuing education role of the state library agency, the development of continuing education for libraries, the implications of these developments, current programmes in progress, and trends which may indicate future change. Historically, state library agencies have had the responsibility for statewide library development, particularly public library development. The provision of advice, assistance and consultant services has been one of the primary means employed. Included in the advisory activities were the conducting of workshops and other educational and staff development programmes. State library agencies having responsibility for school library development as units of state departments of education carried on similar programmes and activities to improve school libraries.

Following the enactment of the federal Library Services Act (LSA), state library agencies moved into a new era of growth and influence. The requirement to develop state plans and the attendant emphasis on establishing libraries, creating library systems and extending library services created the need for staff development and continuing education activities as a major component in the achievement of desired objectives.

A U.S. Office of Education study of state library extension resources and services compares the data from 1955-56 prior to LSA with the re- sources and services of state library agencies in 1960-61. For the purposes of this chapter, the report of consultant activity and training programmes during this period is of interest. Forty-eight States reported 16,466 field visits compared to 6544 in 1955-56; 44 states held or sponsored some 1600 training programmes for over 56,000 persons from 1956 to 1961. These pro- grams served professional (36 %) and nonprofessional (22 %) personnel and public library trustees (26 %).

The responsibility of state library agencies for the planning and administration of federal funds under the Library Services Act of 1956 and the Library Services and Construction Act (LSCA) of 1964 gave added impetus to national documents and conferences concerned with improving the capabilities of state library agencies. These reports emphasize a stronger focus on goals, purposes and long-range plans with the attendant need for highly skilled consultants and related staff development activities in the field in order to implement the statewide programme.

All state library agencies view continuing education and consultant services as a major responsibility of the agency. In a recent survey, about one-half of the state library agencies considered the continuing education responsibility to be a shared responsibility and not solely the responsibility or of the state library agency.

In recent years national activities of major importance have contributed to an increased awareness of continuing education responsibility and to an increase in planned activities of state library agencies.

In the regional hearing conducted in 1972 by the National Commission on Libraries and Information Science (NCLIS), one of the identified priorities was the availability of continuing education for the development and maintenance of competencies which are needed to deliver the library and information services required by the nation. Subsequently, NCLIS funded a study in 1973 to recommend a nationwide programme of continuing education which culminated in Continuing Library and Information Science Education. This report made recommendations which eventually led to the formation of the Continuing Library Education Network Exchange (CLENE). The NCLIS report outlines the develop-ment of library continuing education and comments on the necessity for continuing life- long learning.'

Based on responses from the field, an operational definition of continuing education was developed which includes the following:

- The implication that lifelong learning is necessary to keep the individual up to date,
- Assurance that the individual carries the basic responsibility for his/her own development,
- Diversification to new areas of interest, and
- Involvement in educational activities beyond those considered necessary for entrance into the field.

In comparison with other professions, the librarians felt that continuing education should be pro- vided for all levels of personnel, not solely professional, and that it not be limited to improved competence for the job held now or aspired to in the future. In its plan for continuing education, the report suggests roles and responsibilities of the individual agencies and organizations in order to coordinate efforts, including those of the individual employee, the employing library, the state library agency, the library schools, and state, regional and national associations.

Major responsibilities outlined for the state library agencies include coordination of continuing education programmes on a statewide basis, identification of continuing education needs of the state, provision of a link between librarians in the state and national and regional plans, and the appointment of a continuing education coordinator on the state library agency staff. The other major responsibility is three- fold: the planning, implementation and evaluation of statewide continuing education programmes based on identified needs.

These initial efforts to provide a suggested outline of responsibilities continued to receive attention through CLENE as a newly formed national organization. State library agencies which joined CLENE as sustaining members, as well as the state library agency directors and continuing education staff members, influenced some of the priorities of CLENE. In 1976 CLENE received a USOE, Title II-B grant to provide an "Extended Institute to Train State Library Agency.Personnel to Implement and/or Strengthen Statewide Systems of Continuing Education for Library/Information/Media Personnel." The workshop phase of the institute was held November 7-13, 1976, at the Illinois State Library. Continuing education personnel from twenty-five state library agencies met to develop planning and implementation skills in continuing education. For participating states the institute spurred development of statewide coordinated planning among providers of continuing education in the state.

During this period several regional consortia of states were formed with a primary concern for continuing education. CELS grew out of a survey of members of six state library associations where the need for Continuing education was strongly expressed. State library agencies are major financial contributors to this programme. The Western Interstate Commission on Higher Education (WICHE) had a major continuing education component funded in large part by five state library agencies. The Western Council of State Libraries has succeeded WICHE in this regional effort.

State library agencies were asked to report on activities in needs assessment, programmes in continuing education, the extent of cooperation of other agencies in planning and implementing continuing education programmes, recent changes and improvements in state library agency continuing education programmes, and trends and new developments in continuing education. Forty responses to the questionnaire were received. State library replies indicate that all state library agencies have a responsibility for continuing education. Several have stated that the agency statutes define this responsibility but most suggest that agency planning documents cover these functions.

Cooperation with other continuing education agencies is extensive; 63 per cent of the respondents work closely with state library associations, and 34 per cent with library schools. State universities, higher education commissions, state departments of education, and other agencies were also listed. State staff are active participants on the continuing education committees of other agencies, and either library associations or the state library agency has formed a continuing education committee for coordinated planning and programmes. The formation of continuing education planning committees representing all types of libraries is a recent development in many states.

These committees are in various stages of the development of guidelines, policy statements or state plans for coordinated continuing education programmes. Examples of plans underway can be found in Illinois, Michigan, Ohio and Louisiana. Oklahoma reported the formation of a state committee in 1978, Maryland in 1977. Pennsylvania is planning a special project in 1978 with a director and task force to develop continuing education coordination. States participating in the Western Council of State Libraries and CELS are the primary planners for the continuing education programme of the regional consortia. Coordinated planning appears to be one of the more significant activities now underway.

Continuing education needs were identified by the majority through surveys and questionnaires at state, regional or local levels;consultations with local staffs and "perceived changes in the library climate," evaluation of current programmes and of new national library trends and programmes were also cited. The responses did not indicate the types of libraries involved in the needs assessment process. The influence of continuing education committees and recently formed task forces has not yet been felt to any great degree in the development of continuing education programmes as reported.

The continuing education programmes sponsored by state library agencies are directed primarily to public library staffs, although programme offerings to reach a broader group were listed. All respondents listed public library directors and public library professional staff as participants; twenty-six listed nonprofessional public library staffs. However, twenty- one listed academic librarians;twelve, school librarians;twelve, multi-type participants; and two listed institutional and special library staffs.

Principal topics in continuing education programmes covered a wide range including copyright, networking, automation, planning, management, public relations and audiovisual materials. However, over one-third of the respondents offered basic or refresher courses to public library staffs in such areas as reference, children's services, storytelling, and young adult services. A few states mentioned law materials, oral history, censorship, and government documents. Workshops on community needs and development of special services to disadvantaged, senior citizens and other groups reflect the outreach programme priorities of some states.

Wisconsin reported a continuing education programme for public library and staff through the University of Wisconsin using the Education Telephone Network (ETN). Once a month for about two hours, several topics are discussed by a group or panel. Local libraries may purchase sets of materials related to the programme.

Topics covered in the last two years include:

- Networks,
- Censorship,
- School-public library cooperation,
- The independent adult learner,
- Deaf awareness, and
- Service to special groups.

Alaska and Hawaii reported the use of video cassettes to bring continuing education programmes to remote areas, and West Virginia reported that the capability now exists there to provide this form of continuing education programming.

Frequently, continuing education programmes sponsored by the state library agency are executed by contract with a university or other educational organization. Some states do this extensively; others use this method for institutes in such areas as management.

Recent changes and improvements in the continuing education activities of state library agencies reflected the increased emphasis and direction given a planned and coordinated programme. The establishment of a new position of continuing education coordinator was listed by five states; assignment of this responsibility to an established position was listed by many states.

Several states were engaged in "train the trainer" programmes with the shift to local library systems of responsibility for staff development and training in their own institutions, particularly for nonprofessional staff. State programmes will provide for more advanced and intensive training and attempt to ensure continuity in programme offerings. At least two states - North Carolina and Maryland -provide reimbursement to public library staffs for attending out-of-state institutes.

The responsibility of the continuing education coordinator for developing and disseminating information on continuing education offerings in-state and nationally; for maintaining a master calendar; for providing continuing liaison with library schools, library associations and other educational agencies; and for assuring a programme of needs identification and developing plans to meet needs were mentioned.

These activities reflect to a marked degree the influence of the CLENE report and subsequent programmes and activities of CLENE. It should be noted that state library agency personnel active in CLENE are frequently those most active in continuing education development in their respective states.

Several states commented that NCLIS and CLENE had provided the impetus for renewed continuing education activity at the state level; one saw CLENE as the key to noteworthy, effective state library agency work in continuing education.

The continuing education programmes of CLENE itself provide state library agency personnel the opportunity to gain knowledge, exchange information, and encourage the further coordinated development of continuing education activities of state library agencies.

Changes and trends seen as important and needed for further development of continuing education include the development of more non- traditional methods for the delivery of continuing education programmes, as well as education techniques more suitable to adult learners. States ex- pressed the need for improved needs assessment and evaluation skills and techniques.

At least one-half the states were interested in a recognition system for continuing education. This seemed to be the national trend of greatest interest. Some states are currently using the continuing education unit (CEU) in institutions of higher education for library programmes. CEUs are directly related to certification in several states. South Dakota State Library provides voluntary certification for public libraries based on CEUs. Michigan and North Carolina have proposals for recertification of public librarians through approved programmes in continuing education and the CEU. The "college without walls" programme in New Hampshire and Vermont has prompted library staff to indicate that continuing education programmes should provide some academic credit.

A nationally recognized CEU programme for librarians was specifically cited by several respondents. The study recently completed by CLENE, Model Continuing Education Recognition System in Library and Information Science, was first discussed in January at a CLENE meeting and is to be further examined and discussed at a national convention sponsored by NCLIS in June 1978. State library agencies will need to give the proposal and comments from the field serious study, since it has implications for an increased state library agency role.

This object has attempted to provide a summary of the development of continuing education responsibilities in state library agencies as viewed in the literature and reported from the agencies themselves. A few other points and issues need to be raised. State library agencies have a continuing responsibility for the improvement of the quality of library services in the state. In that respect they are in a unique position to assess the impact of continuing education programmes on library services in the state, and have a responsibility to do so. There is no documentation to determine whether this is being done, but the need to develop the evaluation and performance criteria for this purpose is evident. In the author's opinion this would lead to fewer programmes of longer duration, involving participants in more appropriate learning situations and plans for implementation in their libraries.

Another issue is the responsibility of the individual for his own continuing education and for the pursuit of programmes that satisfy individual needs and interests. State library agency programmes are geared primarily to the perceived needs of the institution and to the priorities of the state library plans and objectives. To the extent that these coincide with individual needs and interests and that participation is voluntary and encouraged, the interests of both can be served.

By publicizing continuing education programmes at state, regional or national levels, state library agencies are helping individuals to become aware of other opportunities. Each state library agency needs to define its own role in continuing library education in relation to those of library schools, library associations and other providers of continuing education programmes.

State library agencies should continue efforts to make possible situations in which innovators and practitioners can reach each other, invent ways to be mutually instructive and supportive, define steps by which to strengthen the drive towards improved continuing education programmes, and undertake cooperative endeavours that ultimately may matter greatly in the capacity of library personnel to deliver the library and information services needed in today's society.

EMERGING ROLE OF PUBLIC LIBRARIANS AS E-GOVERNMENT PROVIDERS

In an effort to become more efficient, governments are moving more information and services to the Internet. As part of this transition, some agencies have begun to use technology and EGovernment to justify the elimination of staff, many of whom provide face-to-face programme support. The result is fewer agency staff able to assist government programme applicants and beneficiaries. This increase in E-Government at the expense of agency staffing raises a number of issues regarding government service delivery and support. In particular, as fewer government agency staff are able to assist existing and potential beneficiaries, citizens seek a range of assistance elsewhere.

One such institution is the public library. As local agency offices close, more citizens use the public library to: use free access to computers and the Internet; receive computer and Internet skills training; search for government servicerelated information and forms; seek government programme assistance; and receive assistance in accessing government websites, navigating programme requirements, and completing online forms. In short, the need for government agency programme and service support has not diminished, but rather, it is possible that some agencies shifted the burden of support to other entities. Although E-Government offers the potential to increase the efficiency and effectiveness of government services, E-Government as a means to reduce staff and service support may limit this potential. This is particularly the case if local agencies such as public libraries – where staff members are neither programme experts nor case workers – are expected to compensate for the reduction in government agency staff and services.

This chapter presents findings from an exploratory study that assesses the impact of E-Government on public libraries, the E-Government support roles of public libraries, and citizen expectations from public libraries regarding E-Government services. For the purposes of this chapter, the term "citizen" will be used to represent all residents of the state of Florida, regardless of nationality or country of citizenship.

Role of Public Libraries in E-Government

The E-Government Act of 2002 states the goal of E-Government as enhancing "governmental functions and service," achieving "more efficient performance," and increasing "access to Government information, and...citizen participation in Government". Since the passage of the E-Government Act, E-Government has quickly become an increasingly popular element of service delivery at the federal, state and local levels. If E-Government services are planned and executed well, they allow government agencies to increase effectiveness and efficiency, and can increase citizen trust in government. The challenges that libraries encounter in providing E-Government vary geographically, as planning and execution of E-Government service varies between states, municipalities, and counties. Even different agencies within county governments approach E-Government in a number of different ways, and with varying levels of success. In addition to increasing effectiveness and efficiency of services, governments have increased their use of E-Government in an effort to cut operating costs. The Florida Department of Children and Families' (DCF) eliminated almost ten thousand staff positions between 1999 and 2007 with the introduction of its ACCESS Florida E-Government programme, three thousand of which are attributable directly to the ACCESS Florida initiative. The DCF ACESS programme is a "modernized public assistance service delivery system... based on streamlined workflows, policy simplification, technology innovations and partnership with local community organizations".

This programme largely eliminates DCF offices, instead, funneling applicants and programme participants to a network of Community Partners for assistance with applications and administration of accounts. DCF now counts public libraries among its Community Partners – agencies and organizations willing to provide Internet access and service assistance applicants. A close examination of the DCF Community partners list reveals that, in most counties, libraries are the only partners charged with providing free Internet access to any citizen who enters requesting service. Other partners are limited to specific constituencies. Since 1994, the Information Use Management and Policy Institute at Florida State University has conducted a national survey of public library internet connectivity. Between 1994 and 2007, Internet availability in libraries grew from approximately 21% to over 99%. Bertot, Jaeger, Langa and McClure write, "...by meeting user information needs through public access computing and Internet services, public libraries were able to serve a larger community need for access to e–government services and resources".

The 2008 national survey found that approximately 95% of public libraries provide asneeded assistance to patrons with understanding and using E-Government resources, while 69% help with E-Government applications and services. Sixty three per cent of respondents indicated that the public library was the only free public internet access point in the surrounding community. Thus, public libraries provide substantial E-Government service and resource support. One can view Government to Citizen EGovernment as a three-part system comprised of the public, the government agency involved and the networks and points of access that allow citizens to participate in EGovernment with that agency. By seeking EGovernment information at the library and requesting assistance from librarians, citizens have added a fourth component to the system: the local librarian as a surrogate agency service provider.

In this capacity, the librarian facilitates what ideally develops into discourse around the design of the E-Government implementation in question. As library activities write:

"To develop citizen-oriented EGovernment services that achieve cost savings implies that governments...actively seek to discover what citizens want from E-Government"

Some provides a useful framework for understanding the implications of this "fourth party" service provider. The object outlines a four-part chain of interaction in E-Government development that includes developers (agencies), local designers (developers), service providers (libraries) and citizens.

The framework proposed by the library activities it is in the best interest of all parties to collaboratively develop effective ways to collect and channel patron feedback for successful, iterative development of the E-Government system. Citizens in need of government services do not bear sole responsibility for involving librarians in EGovernment service. Some agencies refer citizens to public libraries to access web-based forms or applications that are not available in their offices.

The DCF ACCESS website encourages applicants to "apply for public assistance (food stamps, temporary cash assistance, and Medicaid) using the internet wherever it is available including home, a library, or a school". Because they are, in many cases, the only organizations offering free Internet access in their communities, the public library plays an instrumental role in leveling out differences in citizen access to personal computers and the Internet, moving the E-Government system away from exclusion of segments of the population, and towards "design for all".

In this role, many libraries have begun to evolve into "one-stop shops" that now include assistance with government service programmes, access, and delivery.

This is a substantive departure from a longstanding role of public libraries that serve as access points to government information and forms (*i.e.*, tax forms during tax season). For example, though librarians provided tax forms in the past, they did not serve as tax accountants who assisted patrons complete and file their taxes.

Now, citizens come to the library seeking government programme and services assistance, not simply access to information. This shift seems to occur in direct relation to government agencies cutting back in their provision of programme support services due to the adoption of E-Government technologies.

PURPOSE AND OBJECTIVES

The purpose of this exploratory study was to identify the E-Government related needs of citizens who access government related information at the library, and to identify current library E-Government practices in order to provide practical guidance to public libraries in meeting the needs of local community members they serve.

Specifically, the study addresses the following questions:

- What E-Government services and resources do public libraries typically provide?
- What types of E-Government assistance and/or resources do members of libraries' community members request?
- Why do citizens seek E-Government services and resources at the public library?
- What barriers and issues do librarians face in providing E-Government services and resources?

Answers to these questions can help ascertain EGovernment needs from a user perspective, but also foster understanding the impacts of E-Government on community-based support organizations such as public libraries.

The study was exploratory and used an iterative multi-method approach.

Limited to public libraries in the state of Florida, the study used:

- Interviews with public librarians. The interviews explored and identified the E-Government services public librarians provided, and the issues encountered by public librarians in providing EGovernment services and resources.
- E-Government workshops. The study team conducted five E-Government workshops in key geographic regions to explore E-Government service provision by libraries in the regions.
- Survey of workshop attendees. The survey asked librarians to identify the most frequently provided E-Government services, and to identify issues encountered by patrons seeking E-Government assistance in local libraries.
- Librarian-maintained reference log files. The log files captured specific E-Government service and resource transactions provided to users in libraries.
- User survey. The survey explored the reasons why users came to the public library for E-Government services and resources, library services requested and used to engage in E-Government services, and issues encountered while engaging in E-Government services. The survey was available in English, Spanish, and French Creole. The survey was primarily in print format, though a web-based Survey Monkey version of the survey was available in English.

The interviews and workshops informed the development of the log file and user surveys. User surveys and log files were pre-tested to ensure their usability and ability to capture valid and reliable data.

Key Issues

The study found a number of issues raised due to local, state and federal E-Government implementations.

Access and the Digital Divide

The transfer of some services from face-to-face to Internet-only highlights the gap between those who have and do not have access to the Internet. The digital divide continues to exist, to the detriment of citizens without access. In many communities, public libraries provide the only free access to the Internet, and thus the only link to E-Government. In some cases, E-Government is a matter of convenience. Some patrons seek websites and forms that make application for a service simpler than walking into an agency office or calling a phone number. In other cases, E-Government is the only option. The Florida Department of Children and Families, which deals primarily with a low-income constituency, has moved its services and applications to an Internet-based application system. Since DCF closed many of its offices, applicants have begun seeking help at public libraries. In many locations in South Florida, the only way to make an appointment at the United States Citizenship and Immigration Service office, which processes immigrant visas, permanent residence and citizenship applications, is to use the web-based appointment system.

ECitizenship and E-Participation rely on access to the Internet, making access an issue of democratic participation. But access is only part of the divide, and a basic one. Users require computer and Internet use training, information resource selection, web site navigation, and a range of other types of assistance to engage in successful E-Government efforts. It is not the case that the library simply opens its doors and provides access to a computer and the Internet. Rather, that technology access leads to a number of other types of assistance requests and needs from government service applicants and beneficiaries that agencies are unable or unwilling to provide.

Resolving Life Events: The Evolving Role of the Librarian as Case Worker

The increased emphasis on E-Government in public libraries threatens to alter the role of the librarian from neutrally situated information provider to that of social worker. Instead of being asked to provide information, reference staff report being asked to help patrons resolve problems, advise patrons on which forms they need to use, and at times, assist patrons in completing applications. Patron requests ranged from help with enrolling children in childcare, to finding family members, to setting up businesses, to help going through the trademark process.

Increasingly, librarians are taking on the role of the social worker, referring patrons to one agency or another, and becoming more involved in patrons' personal lives. In addition, the needs of citizens change over the course of the year.

Librarian surveys, conducted in late 2007, suggested that the greatest volume of EGovernment services were provided on behalf of the Department of Children and Families. In contrast, librarian log data collected in early 2008 suggested that most E-Government services were provided on behalf of the IRS. Together, the data demonstrate that E-Government related information needs change fluidly with external life events, such as tax season, and DCF application deadlines.

This evolution of librarian as information provider to case worker has multiple and profound implications. Not only is this a substantial shift in librarian duties, but it also requires librarians to become facile with multiple agency programmes.

And, given that user life events can cut across multiple agencies, programmes, and eligible benefits, the knowledge and skills librarians need are numerous. A number of librarians commented that they had no training in being a social case worker and felt uncomfortable serving in that role.

Skills and Training

Librarians expressed concern and anxiety that they are unprepared to provide the services requested by users. While some agencies have made significant efforts to reach out to libraries and community centers that serve their target populations, many have not made any efforts to provide training to nonagency staff. As a result, libraries that embrace the role of E-Government service provider must pour significant resources into training staff, most often without assistance from local agencies. In short, librarians that engage in the provision of EGovernment services and resources are self-taught and can often lack an essential programmatic perspective.

There is a need for increased communication and cooperation between libraries and the government agencies on state and local levels. Local agency offices are often unaware of the level of service libraries are able to offer, and direct patrons to the library for services they may not provide. They also argued that state agencies often shut down local offices without consideration for the restrictions of the local library's funding, resources, or space. To some degree, librarians do not have a choice whether to assist or not assist someone needing help in using E-Government resources or services. If the person is present and needs assistance then the librarian will likely try to assist them as best they can – regardless of the level of training the librarian has received regarding E-Government. Thus, an area for additional research is the quality of the EGovernment services that librarians can provide – especially in the current Florida context of severe budget cutbacks, reduced library hours of operations and increasing overall library use.

Liability

As library staff members are asked to assist patrons with forms and applications, and to handle more sensitive personal information, librarians and administrators grow more concerned over possible liability issues. This anxiety includes civil and criminal concerns. Fear over possible lawsuits against library staff, administrators, and city/county councils, and criminal consequences associated with entering false information on behalf of library patrons lead some libraries to avoid EGovernment altogether. A few local library administrators restrict librarians from providing assistance with E-Government forms. In some cases, library staff members are instructed to limit EGovernment help to locating forms as requested, and to provide no help in interpreting or completing applications. But overall, there are no clear guidelines as to "how much assistance" in filling out forms requiring a range of personal information and explanation is too much assistance on the part of the librarian.

Forcing Technology Management Changes

Library public access computer and Internet resources are not limitless. Libraries only have a certain number of public access computers available for use. Indeed, 82.5% of libraries report that they have insufficient public access computers some or all of the time and 93.4% have time limits on workstation use. Given this, libraries have had to purchase, install, and maintain public access management software that manages user workstation registration process, enforces time limits, and resets the computers after each session.

Time limits, imposed to alleviate public access computer and Internet access demands on limited library resources, are often in direct conflict with E-Government services requirements, which can often take considerable time and effort.

Librarians either have to try and remove the time limit features, set up E-Government workstations, or risk the loss of E-Government application and other information by users. Thus, EGovernment service provision can impose a substantial management and infrastructure burden on libraries.

An Unfunded Mandate: Resources and Burden Shifting

When state and federal agencies send citizens to county-funded public libraries to access EGovernment forms, schedule appointments and seek information instead of providing that information in the traditional office setting, they add to an overall increase in the number of patrons requesting EGovernment services.

Library services are provided by local tax revenue and libraries' budgets are significantly stressed. The increase in EGovernment users taxes the human and financial resources of already strained local libraries, increasing costs associated with staff time, computer equipment, and Internet bandwidth.

Although Florida's budget reductions represent an extreme case, reduced library funding is a national issue, made worse by downturns in the economy Agencies that choose to exchange face-to-face services for Internet based services are, in many cases, actually shifting personnel and operating costs to locally funded organizations that provide "free" public Internet access and assistance. Local agency offices are often unaware of what level of service libraries are prepared to offer, and direct patrons to the library for services they may not be in a position to provide.

State agencies often shut down local offices without consideration for the restrictions of the local library's funding, resources, or space. While some local libraries are able to absorb the costs associated with a spike in use, others cannot, and risk closure when local agency offices close their doors. This burden shift amounts to an unfunded mandate from state agencies to local, city and county governments that fund local library systems. Libraries are put in the position of providing services that they may not have the staff, expertise, equipment, or funding to deliver, or risk the ire of a patron base that provides the library's funding. Because public libraries are not legally mandated, community support is sometimes the only protection a library has at its disposal to maintain its operations. The extent to which reductions in state staffing at DCF, for example, have resulted in increased costs for public libraries in Florida, reductions in other library services, and staff time to meet E-Government service demands is an area for future investigation.

RULES AND REGULATIONS

DEFINITIONS

- *Board of Governors:* The Board of Governors of the National Academy of Higher Education/ University Grants Commission.
- *Competent Authorty:* Any authority of the University Grants Commission/National Academy of Higher Education having full financial and administrative powers or part thereof.
- *Director General:* The Director General of National Academy of Higher Education.
- *Employees:* The employees of the National Academy of Higher Education, University Grants Commission and University Grants Commission's Regional Offices.
- *Inter-Library Loan:* Giving or taking of books and other reading material on loan to and from other libraries or agencies.
- *Librarian:* The Librarian of the National Academy of Higher Education's library.
- *Library:* The Library of the National Academy of Higher Education.

- *Members:* Registered members of the National Academy of Higher Education Library as laid down in rules 3and4.
- *Officers:* The employees declared by the Government as officer *i.e.* all employees of BP&-16 and above of the National Academy of Higher Education and the University Grants Commission.
- *Officials:* All employees BP&-1 to BP&-15 of the University Grants Commission and the National Academy of Higher Education.
- *Pre-Service/In-Service Training Participatnts:* Participants attending training Programmes in the National Academy of Higher Education.
- *University:* Any University in Pakistan recognized by the Government.
- *University Librarian:* Librarian/ Incharge Librarian/ Acting Librarian/ Chief Librarian of any of the Pakistani Universities.
- *University Departmenta Librarian:* Librarian of a departmental library of any of the Pakistani Universities.

LIBRARY RULES

Working Hours

- The library shall remain open for service during the working hours observed by the National Academy of Higher Education/University Grants Commission.
- The" library hours may be changed from time to time according to the service of the National Academy of Higher Education/University Grants Commission.

Loan Privileges

- The following categories of persons will be allowed to make use of the library resources:
  - Employees of the University Grants Commission/National Academy of Higher Education.
  - In-service and Pre-Service training participants.
  - Teachers/resources persons etc. deputed by UGC/NAHE for teaching.
  - Members of the Board of Governors of UGC/NAHE.
  - Other persons allowed in writing by Director General/Librarian.
  - University/University Department Librarians.
- Persons desirous of using the library must apply for membership on a form obtainable from t he library.
  - A borrower's card will be issued to each member on presentation of which reading material will be issued (except rule 3.6 for which the Librarian will maintain a proper record). The same

procedure will be followed when the books are returned. This card will not be transferable and should be surrendered at the time of obtaining a clearance certificate.

- A borrowers card will be valid up- to the date mentioned on it. A borrower should get the card renewed before it expires, if he so desires.
- Members should not mark or write on their borrower cards in any way Defaulters may be dealt with as per rule 30.

• A Member, who loses his card shall at once inform the Librarian. A duplicate card will be. issued. Any member sub- lending reading material from the library on his card to any other person shall do so at his own responsibility.

Loan Period

• The following categories of members shall observe the loan schedule mentioned against each.

• Books borrowed once may be issued provided these are not required by other members. Books will not be reissued more than twice. Books will have to be presented for re-issue. However, in case of need the Librarian may relax the condition.

• Reading material of the following nature shall not be issued but can be consulted in.the library (except in special cases *e.g.* classroom use of a teacher for a short period/photocopying purposes)

  - Reference material (*i.e.* Encyclopedias, dictionaries, atlases and the material marked 'R')
  - Theses, reports, pamphlets, syllabi, acts etc.
  - Microfilms, slides, cassettes, tape recorders and other allied material.
  - All unprocessed material.
  - Current periodicals.
  - Other material assigned by the Librarian.

Damage and Loss of Books

• Book(s) lost, dam ed, or mutilated in any way by a member shall have to be replaced or paid for. The cost of such book(s) shall be double the prevailing cost plus an additional 25% departmental charges. The price of rare book(s) shall be decided by the Librarian.

• If books and other materials borrowed from the library are not returned notices will be issued. In case the books are r even after the second notice, Rule 9 will be applied.

Relaxation of loan schedule will be at the discretion of the Librarian:

- The amount realised from a member as cost of lost or damaged book(s) or material(s) or for not returning the books after due notices shall be credited to NAHE Library's head 'Books and Journals'.
- Book.,(s) or other material lost or found to be lost on stock-taking shall be reported to the competent authority for write-off.
- If a member leaves his organization without returning books borrowed from this library, the price of the book(s) will be adjusted against his dues with the organization. (In case there is no outstanding balance in his name, the price will be paid by his guarantor).

Weeding

- On receipt of a written request from the Librarian, the Director General shall depute one or two members other than the library staff for weeding out outdated worn-out and/ or seriously damaged or mutilated books and other materials. He/ She/ they shall submit their recommendations in writing to the competent authority for approval.

Write-off Losses

- The Librarian shall report all books/ non- print material damaged, and/or worn-out through fair wear and tear to the competent authority for write off action.
- Losses to the extent of 3% per annum of the available stock in an open access library shall be written off by the competent authority.
- Losses to the extent of 2% per annum of the available collection of a close access or partially open access library shall be written off by the competent authority.
- Losses written off by the competent authority shall be struck off from the stock and the records of the library, including public catalogues, and transferred to the with-drawl register indicating the authority under which the losses were written off.
- The permanent irrecoverable loans of mutilated, damaged and worn-out books found to be beyond repairs during the physical verification of the library shall also be reported to the competent authority for write-off.

Mail Loan

- The library shall offer postal loan service to the Librarian(s) of the out station Universities provided Rule 4.2 is followed. University Librarian/ Department Librarian will be responsible for Safe return.
- In view of the insecurity of mail, inconveniences of the postal-loan service and other discrepancies of non-receipt of materials expected

to arise by this/these facility (ies) loss of book(s) and other materials shall be safeguarded by adopting the Registered Parcel procedure of dispatch to avoid loss in transit.

- In case there is a loss in transit, it shall be recorded by the Librarian and reported to the competent authority for write-off action.

Inter-Library Loans

- With a view to extending and/or utilizing book and non-book resources of other institutions of higher education in the country, the Librarian shall enter into, and maintain any mutually agreed upon interlibrary loan system with Academic, Research, Special, Public and Government Departmental Libraries.

General Rules

- Members shall not mutilate, or damage by writing or marking on pages, any book or publication, nor shall they trace or perform mechanical reproduction of any material belonging to the library without formal permission of the Librarian. Violation of this rule shall require replacement of the damaged volume or payment of its price as specified under rule 9.
- If one volume of a set/series is damaged and it is not available separately, the whole set shall have to be replaced or paid for by the member as specified under rule 9.
- Following Rules 24 and 25 paying the cost the member may, if he/ she so desires, retain the damaged book(s) or volumes for which the price has been recovered from him/her.
- Members are advised to inspect books or other material at the time of issue. They must direct the attention of the staff at the Charging Desk to defects, if any.
- The Library Reading Room shall remain open during stock-taking but the borrowing privileges will remain suspended for the same period. All books on loan 'with the members must irrespective of the date-due, be returned to. the library before the date of stock-taking. Two week advance notice will be given.
- All members must without fail intimate, the librarian of any change of address.
- The Librarian is authorized to withdraw library facilities from any member who is found misusing the library material or facilities.
- Members of the library shall deposit their personal belongings at the counter near the entrance.
- In case any personal reading material has to be taken in-side the

library, permission must be sought from the Librarian. All reading material issued to them shall be shown to the attendant at the exit before leaving.

- Eating, sleeping, smoking and audible conversation within the library premises is prohibited.
- Members shall make their own arrangement for carrying book(s) etc. from and to the library.

2

Public Libraries, Legislation and Information Technology

THE ROLE AND PURPOSE OF THE PUBLIC LIBRARY

DEFINING THE PUBLIC LIBRARY

Public libraries are a world-wide phenomenon. They occur in a variety of societies, in differing cultures and at different stages of development. Although the varied contexts in which they operate inevitably result in differences in the services they provide, and the way those services are delivered, they normally have characteristics in common, which can be defined as follows. A public library is an organisation established, supported and funded by the community, either through local, regional or national government or through some other form of community organisation. It provides access to knowledge, information and works of the imagination through a range of resources and services and is equally available to all members of the community regardless of race, nationality, age, gender, religion, language, disability, economic and employment status and educational attainment.

THE PURPOSES OF THE PUBLIC LIBRARY

The primary purposes of the public library are to provide resources and services in a variety of media to meet the needs of individuals and groups for education, information and personal development including recreation and leisure. They have an important role in the development and maintenance of a democratic society by giving the individual access to a wide and varied range of knowledge, ideas and opinions.

Education

The need for an agency available to all, which provides access to knowledge in printed and other formats to support formal and informal education, has been the reason for the foundation and maintenance of most public libraries and remains a core purpose for the public library. Throughout their lives people require education either at formal institutions, for example, schools, colleges and universities, or in a less formal context related to their employment and daily life.

Learning does not end with the completion of formal education but is, for most people, a lifelong activity. In an increasingly complex society people will need to acquire new skills at various stages of their life. The public library has an important role in assisting this process. The public library should provide material in the appropriate media to support formal and informal learning processes.

It should also help the user to make use of these learning resources effectively as well as providing facilities that enable people to study. The ability to access information and make effective use of it is vital to successful education and, where possible, public libraries should co-operate with other educational organisations in teaching the use of information resources. Where adequate library facilities exist to support formal education the public library should complement them rather than duplicating library provision available elsewhere.

The public library should also actively support literacy campaigns, as literacy is the key to education and knowledge and to the use of libraries and information services. Newly literate people need easy access to appropriate reading materials to maintain and develop their skills. In some countries the need for educational development is seen to be paramount and the focus of public libraries is to support formal education. There are, however, a variety of ways in which public libraries can support both formal and informal education. How this is achieved will depend on the local context and the level of available resources.

Information

It is a basic human right to be able to have access to and an understanding of information, and there is now more information available than ever before in the world's history. As a public service open to all, the public library has a key role in collecting, organising and exploiting information, as well as providing access to a wide range of information sources. The public library has a particular responsibility to collect local information and make it readily available. It also acts as a memory of the past by collecting, conserving and providing access to material relating to the history of the community and of individuals. In providing a wide range of information the public library assists the community in informed debate and decision-making on key issues. In collecting and providing information the public library should, wherever possible, co-operate with other agencies to make the best use of available resources. The rapid growth in the volume of available information and the continuing technological changes, which have radically affected the way information is accessed, have already made a significant effect on public libraries and their services. Information is very important to the development of the individual and of society, and information technology gives considerable power to those able to access and use it.

Despite its rapid growth it is not available to the majority of the world's population, and the gap between the information rich and the information poor continues to widen. A vital role for the public library is to bridge that gap by providing public access to the Internet as well as providing information in traditional formats. Public libraries should recognise and exploit the opportunities provided by the exciting developments in information and communications technology. They have the opportunity to become the electronic gateway to the information world.

Personal Development

The opportunity to develop personal creativity and pursue new interests is important to human development. To achieve this, people need access to knowledge and works of the imagination. The public library can provide access, in a variety of different media, to a rich and varied store of knowledge and creative achievement, which individuals cannot acquire on their own behalf. Providing access to major collections of the world's literature and knowledge, including the community's own literature, has been a unique contribution of the public library and is still a vitally important function.

Access to works of the imagination and knowledge is an important contribution to personal education and meaningful recreational activity. The public library can also make a fundamental contribution to daily survival and social and economic development by being directly involved in providing information to people in developing communities; for example, basic life skills, adult basic education and AIDS awareness programmes. In communities with a high illiteracy rate the public library should provide services for non-literates and interpret and translate information where necessary. It should also provide basic user education.

CHILDREN AND YOUNG PEOPLE

The public library should attempt to meet the needs of all groups in the community regardless of age and physical, economic or social circumstances. However, it has a special responsibility to meet the needs of children and young people. If children can be inspired by the excitement of knowledge and by works of the imagination at an early age, they are likely to benefit from these vital elements of personal development throughout their lives, both enriching them and enhancing their contribution to society. Children can also encourage parents and other adults to make use of the library. It is also important that young people who experience difficulty in learning to read should have access to a library to provide them with appropriate material.

Public Libraries and Cultural Development

An important role of the public library is providing a focus for cultural and artistic development in the community and helping to shape and support the cultural identity of the community. This can be achieved by working in partnership with appropriate local and regional organisations, by providing space for cultural activity, organising cultural programmes and by ensuring that cultural interests are represented in the library's materials. The library's contribution should reflect the variety of cultures represented in the community. It should provide materials in the languages spoken and read in the local community, and support cultural traditions.

The Social Role of the Public Library

The public library has an important role as a public space and meeting place. This is particularly important in communities where there are few places for people to meet. It is sometimes called 'the drawing room of the community'. Use of the library for research and for finding information relating to the user's education and leisure interests, brings people into informal contact with other members of the community. Using the public library can be a positive social experience.

AN AGENCY FOR CHANGE

In carrying out its role in these key areas the public library is acting as an agency for social and personal development and can be a positive agency for change in the community. By providing a wide range of materials to support education and by making information accessible to all, the public library can bring economic and social benefits to individuals and to the community. It contributes to the creation and maintenance of a well–informed and democratic society and helps to empower people in the enrichment and development of their lives and that of the community in which they live. The public library should be aware of the issues that are being discussed within the community and provide information that will inform that debate.

FREEDOM OF INFORMATION

The public library should be able to represent all ranges of human experience and opinion, free from the risk of censorship. In some countries a Freedom of Information Act will help to ensure these rights are maintained. Librarians and governing bodies should uphold these basic human rights and resist pressure from individuals and groups to limit the material available in the public library.

ACCESS FOR ALL

A fundamental principle of the public library is that its services must be available to all and not directed to one group in the community to the exclusion of others. Provision should be made to ensure services are equally available to minority groups who for some reason are not able to use the mainstream services, for example, linguistic minorities, people with physical and sensory disabilities or those living in remote communities who are unable to reach library buildings.

The level of funding, development of services, the design of libraries and their opening hours should all be planned with the concept of universal access as a basic principle.

The development of collections should also be based on the principle of access for all and include access to formats appropriate to specific client groups, for example, Braille and talking books for blind people. Information and communications technology should be used to allow access to the library's collections and those of other information sources, both from within the library or from remote sites.

LOCAL NEEDS

Public libraries are locally based services for the benefit of the local community and should provide community information services. The services and collections they provide should be based on local needs, which should be assessed regularly.

Without this discipline the public library will get out of touch with those it is there to serve and will, as a result, not be used to its full potential. Librarians should, therefore, be aware of the changes in society arising from such factors as social and economic development, demographic change, variations in the age structure, levels of education, patterns of employment and the emergence of other educational and cultural providers.

LOCAL CULTURE

The public library should be a key agency in the local community for the collection, preservation and promotion of local culture in all its diversity. This can be achieved in a variety of ways, for example, the maintenance of local history collections, exhibitions, storytelling, publishing of items of local interest and developing interactive programmes on local themes. Where the oral tradition is an important method of communication the public library should encourage its continuation and development.

THE CULTURAL ROOTS OF THE PUBLIC LIBRARY

It is important to the long-term success of the library that it should be based on the culture, or cultures, of the country or area in which it operates. It is less likely to succeed if the form and structure of the public library are introduced from a country or area with a very different cultural background.

LIBRARIES WITHOUT WALLS

In developing policies to fulfil the role and purpose of the public library the emphasis should be on the services it provides. In meeting the needs of its community the public library will provide a range of services, some of which can be most effectively delivered from a library building. However, there will be many circumstances where it is more effective to provide the service beyond the walls of the library. Examples will vary in different societies but the principle of planning library development from a service rather than a building perspective is important in all public library policy development.

The provision of services using information and communications technology also presents exciting opportunities to take library and information services direct to the home and the workplace. A variety of forms of transport are used to deliver services to sparsely populated areas. The provision of library and information services to people unable to visit a library due to physical or sensory disability or lack of transport, for example, ensures that access to these services is available to all at their home or workplace regardless of their circumstances.

LIBRARY BUILDINGS

Library buildings play an important part in public library provision. They should be designed to reflect the functions of the library service, be accessible to all in the community and be sufficiently flexible to accommodate new and changing services. They should be located close to other community activities, for example, shops and cultural centres. Wherever possible the library should also be available for community use, for example, for meetings and exhibitions and in larger buildings for theatrical, musical, audiovisual and media performances. A well used public library will make a significant contribution to the vitality of an urban area and be an important learning and social centre and meeting place, particularly in scattered rural areas. Librarians should, therefore, ensure that library buildings are used and managed effectively to make the best use of the facilities for the benefit of the whole community.

RESOURCES

To fulfil its roles satisfactorily the public library must have adequate resources, not just when it is established but also on a continuing basis, to enable it to sustain and develop services that meet the needs of the local community.

This means it should provide materials in all formats, up-dated regularly to meet the changing needs of groups and individuals, including newly-published and replacement materials. It should also provide adequate levels of staff with appropriate training and sufficient funds to support whatever methods of service delivery are needed for it to meet its vital role in the community.

THE LEGAL AND FINANCIAL FRAMEWORK

Public libraries are a community agency providing access at local level to a range of knowledge and information for the benefit of the individual and society as a whole. In order to maintain the level of service required to fulfil their functions public libraries should be supported by legislation and sustained funding.

THE PUBLIC LIBRARY AND GOVERNMENT

There are many different models of the relationship between public libraries and government. Equally, the laws that govern their activities and funding arrangements are varied and complex. In different countries, provinces, regions, states or municipalities are, either in whole or in part, responsible for library services. As public libraries are a locally based service local government is often the most appropriate place in the government structure for them. However, in some countries public libraries are provided at regional or state level and the national library sometimes has responsibility for providing the public library service. There are instances of two or more levels of government co-operating in the provision of the service.

Alternative Structures

In some countries, although the local authority has nominal responsibility for the public library, it does not have the required funds and non-governmental organisations or private foundations undertake the practical operation of the public library services. However, to ensure sustained development and its role in the information network, the public library should be closely related to and funded by the appropriate level of government. The eventual aim should be to bring public libraries into the formal government structure operating under national legislation and with appropriate levels of funding.

National Information Policies

In order to make the most effective use of available library and information resources, and take full advantage of the opportunities offered by the development of electronic information sources, many countries are developing national information policies. Public libraries should be a key element in such policies and public librarians should ensure they are fully involved in their development.

PUBLIC LIBRARY LEGISLATION

Public libraries should be based on legislation, which assures their continuance and their place in the government structure. Public library legislation takes various forms. In some countries or regions the legislation is specific to public libraries whereas in others it is part of wider legislation which includes different types of libraries. Public library legislation is also varied in its provisions. It can be simple, allowing the establishment of public libraries but leaving standards of service to the level of government directly responsible for the library, or more complex, with specific detail on what services should be provided and to what standard. Examples of public library legislation are available on the IFLA web site. Because governmental structures vary so much in different countries the form and detail of public library legislation is also likely to vary significantly. However, legislation governing public libraries should state which level of government is responsible for their provision and how they should be funded. It should also place them in the framework of libraries in the country or region as a whole.

Related Legislation

Public libraries are subject to a range of legislation apart from the specific legislation relating to them. This can include legislation on financial management, data protection, health and safety and staff conditions and there will be many other examples. Library managers should be aware of all legislation affecting the operation of the public library. They should also be aware of global trade negotiations, which can result in policies and agreements, which could have a serious impact on public libraries. In such cases librarians should take every opportunity to bring the effect of such policies on public libraries to the notice of the public and politicians.

Copyright

Copyright legislation, especially that relating to electronic publications, is of particular importance to public libraries. It is constantly subject to amendment and review and librarians should keep up-to-date with the legislation in relation to all media. Librarians should promote and support copyright legislation, which achieves an equitable balance between the rights of creators and the needs of users.

Public Lending Right

In some countries, public lending right legislation has been introduced which provides a payment to authors and others involved in the creation of a book, related to its provision in, and loan from, public libraries. It is important that funds for payment of public lending right should not be taken from libraries' funds for the purchase of materials. However, public lending right, if separately funded, does provide support for authors without affecting public libraries' budgets. In some schemes it can also provide useful statistics on the loans of books by specific authors. Librarians should participate in the development of public lending right schemes to ensure they are not financed from library budgets.

FUNDING

Adequate levels of funding are crucial to the success of a public library in fulfilling its roles. Without suitable levels of funding over the long-term it is impossible to develop policies for service provision and make the most effective use of available resources. This can be seen in number of examples: a new library building without adequate funds to maintain it, collections of new books with no money for their replacement and computer systems without funds to maintain and update them. Funding is required not only when a public library is established, but should also be sustained on an assured and regular basis.

Priorities

A public library and the services it provides is a long-term investment on behalf of the community and should be funded appropriately. It is recognised that even in the wealthiest of societies it may not be possible to provide appropriate levels of funding for every service requirement. It is vitally important, therefore, that service development should be conducted on a planned basis with clear priorities. This process is necessary whatever level of funding is available to the library service. To determine strategic planning and the maintenance of agreed priorities, written policy statements should be developed for services. They should be reviewed at regular intervals and revised where necessary.

Partnership

No public library, however large and well funded, can meet all the needs of its users on its own. Participation in partnerships and networks with other libraries and related organisations, and the provision of access to other sources of information, enables the public library to satisfy the information needs of its users by increasing the range of available resources.

Sources of Funding

A number of sources of funding are used to finance public libraries but the proportions of funding from each source will vary depending on local factors in each country.

The primary sources are:

- Taxation at local, regional or central level
- Block grants from central, regional or local level.

Secondary sources of income may include:

- Donations from funding bodies or private individuals
- Revenue from commercial activities, *e.g.*, publishing, book sales, sale of works of art and handicrafts
- Revenue from user fees, *e.g.*, fines

- Revenue from charges to users for individual services, *e.g.*, photocopying and printing facilities
- Sponsorship from external organisations
- Lottery funds for specific initiatives.

Charging the User

The *IFLA/UNESCO Public Library Manifesto* states: 'The public library shall in principle be free of charge'. Charging users for services and membership should not be used as a source of revenue for public libraries, as it makes the ability to pay a criterion in determining who can use a public library. This reduces access and therefore breaches the fundamental principle that the public library should be available to all. It is recognised that in some countries subscriptions to join the library or charges for specific services are levied. Such charges inevitably deny access to those unable to afford them.

They should be seen as an interim situation and not as a permanent feature of public library funding. It is common in some countries to ask users to pay a fee or fine when keeping an item after it is due for return to the library. This is sometimes necessary to ensure that items are kept in circulation and not retained for a long time by one user. The fine should not be set at a level that would deter anyone from using the library. Charges are also sometimes levied for personalised services, for example photocopying or use of a printer. These charges should also not be set at a level which will deter the user.

Funding for Technology

Public libraries must, whenever possible, make use of the new technologies to improve their services and provide new ones. This means a considerable investment in various kinds of electronic equipment, and a reliance on this equipment for the delivery of services. To continue to perform effectively equipment should be upgraded and replaced. This has significant funding consequences and a plan for the replacement and upgrading of technological equipment should be developed.

External Funding

Librarians should be imaginative in seeking external sources of funding for the public library. However, they should not accept funding from any source if, by so doing, the fundamental status of a public library as an agency available to all is compromised. Commercial organisations, for example, may offer funding with conditions which might prejudice the universal nature of the services provided by the public library.

THE GOVERNANCE OF THE PUBLIC LIBRARY

Public libraries should be governed by a properly established body made up largely of representatives of the local community including those elected either to the local council or to the library board. Library committees and boards should have rules of procedure and their proceedings should be open to the general public. They should meet on a regular basis and publish agenda, minutes, annual reports and financial statements. Normally the governing body will be responsible for matters of policy rather than the day-to-day operation of the library. In all cases the chief librarian should have direct access to the meetings of the governing body of the library and work closely with it. Policy documents should be made available to the public and, where possible, steps should be taken to involve local citisens in the development of the public library.

Public librarians must be fully accountable both to their governing bodies and local citizens for their actions by providing reports, holding public meetings and through consultation. They must also maintain the highest professional standards in carrying out their duties and in advising the governing body. Although the final decisions on policy will be taken by the governing body and the librarian, ways should be sought to involve the local citizens who are the actual or potential library users.

The concept of a 'library charter', which identifies and publicises the level of service the public library provides has been developed in some countries. This establishes a 'contract' between the public library and the users. Library charters have more credibility if they are developed in consultation with users.

THE ADMINISTRATION OF THE PUBLIC LIBRARY

Public libraries should be well managed and administered. The administration of a public library should be directed towardss improving the quality of service to the users and not as an end in itself. It should be efficient and accountable. To get best results the administrative and management staff of a large public library service should be multidisciplinary, involving staff with specialist skills, for example, librarians, accountants, public relations officers and system managers. It may also be necessary to draw on the expertise of staff of the parent authority or other related organisation in certain areas, for example, lawyers, payroll and pensions staff.

PUBLICITY AND PROMOTION

Public libraries operate in an increasingly complex society, which makes many calls on people's time and attention. It is important, therefore, that libraries publicise their presence and the range of services they provide. Publicity ranges from simple techniques, like signs on library buildings stating what they are, and leaflets advertising opening hours and services, to more sophisticated methods like marketing programmes and the use of web sites to promote the library's services and activities.

MEETING THE NEEDS OF THE USERS

To be successful in fulfilling its goals the public library service must be fully accessible to all its potential users. Any limitation of access, whether deliberate or accidental, will reduce the ability of the public library to fully achieve its primary role of meeting the library and information needs of the community it serves.

The following are important elements in delivering an effective public library service:

- Identifying potential users
- Analysing users' needs
- Developing services to groups and individuals
- Introducing customer care policies
- Promoting user education
- Co-operating and sharing resources
- Developing electronic networks
- Ensuring access to services
- Providing library buildings.

IDENTIFYING POTENTIAL USERS

The public library has to aim to serve all citizens and groups. An individual is never too young or too old to use a library.

The public library has the following potential target groups.

- People at all ages and at all stages of life:
- Children
- Young adults
- Adults.
- Individuals and groups of people with special needs:
- People from different cultures and ethnic groups including indigenous people
- People with disabilities, *e.g.*, blind and partially sighted, hearing impaired
- Housebound people
- Institutionally confined people, *e.g.*, in hospitals, prisons.
- Institutions within the wider community network:
- Educational, cultural and voluntary organisations and groups in the community
- The business community
- The governing body of the parent organisation, *e.g.*, local authority.

As resources are limited in even the wealthiest society it is not always possible to serve all users to the same level. The library must establish priorities based on an analysis of user needs and related to their access to alternative services.

ANALYSING NEEDS WITHIN THE COMMUNITY

It is important to establish who uses and who does not use the library service. It is also necessary to collect and analyse data that identifies those needs of individuals and groups within the community that can be met by the public library.

SERVICES TO USERS

The public library must provide services based on an analysis of the library and information needs of the local community. In planning services, clear priorities must be established and a strategy be developed for service provision in the medium to long term. Services should be developed for identified target groups and only provided if such groups exist in the local community.

The services of the library should not be subject to any form of ideological, political, religious or commercial pressure. Services must be able to adjust and develop to reflect changes in society, for example, variations in family structures, employment patterns, demographic changes, cultural diversity and methods of communication. They should take account of traditional cultures as well as new technologies, for example, support for oral methods of communication as well as making use of information and communication technology. In some countries the services that the public library must provide are defined in library legislation.

Service Provision

Public libraries provide a range of services, both within the library and in the community, to satisfy their users' needs. The library should facilitate access to its services for all, including those who have difficulty reading print.

The following services, which should be easily accessible to the user in a variety of formats and media, should be provided:

- Loan of books and other media
- Provision of books and other materials for use in the library
- Information services using print and electronic media
- Readers' advisory services including reservation services
- Community information services
- User education including support for literacy programmes
- Programming and events.

This is not an exhaustive list but an indication of some of the key services of the public library. The range and depth of provision will depend on the size of the library and the community it serves. Every library should aim to be an active participant in one or more networks, which will give the user access to a wide range of material, however small the access point. Service provision should not be confined to the library building but also taken direct to the user where access to the library is not possible. In providing services, both within the library and beyond, use should be made of information and communications technology as well as the printed word.

Services to Children

By providing a wide range of materials and activities, public libraries provide an opportunity for children to experience the enjoyment of reading and the excitement of discovering knowledge and works of the imagination. Children and their parents should be taught how to make the best use of a library and how to develop skills in the use of printed and electronic media. Public libraries have a special responsibility to support the process of learning to read, and to promote books and other media for children.

The library must provide special events for children, such as story telling and activities related to the library's services and resources. Children should be encouraged to use the library from an early age as this will make them more likely to remain users in future years. In multilingual countries books and audiovisual materials for children should be available in their mother tongue.

Services for Young Adults

Young people between childhood and adulthood develop as individual members of society with their own culture. Public libraries must understand their needs and provide services to meet them. Materials, including access to electronic information resources, that reflect their interests and culture should be provided.

In some cases this will mean acquiring materials that represent youth culture, in a variety of media that are not traditionally part of a library's resources, for example, popular novels, book and television series, music, video tapes, teenage magazines, posters, computer games, graphic novels.

It is important to enlist the help of young people in selecting this material to ensure that it reflects their interests. In larger libraries this material, with appropriate furniture, can form a special section of the library.

This will help them to feel that the library is for them and help to overcome a feeling of alienation from the library, which is not unusual among this age group. Relevant programmes and talks to young adults should also be provided.

SERVICES FOR ADULTS

Adults will have different requirements of an information and library service related to the variety of situations they will encounter in their studies, employment and personal life. These requirements should be analysed and services be developed on the outcome of that analysis.

They should include support for:

- Lifelong learning
- Leisure time interests
- Information needs
- Community activities
- Cultural activity
- Recreational reading.

Services meeting these needs should also be available to children and young adults.

Lifelong Learning

The public library supports lifelong learning, working with schools and other educational institutions to help students of all ages with their formal education. The challenge of providing educational support provides an opportunity for public libraries to interact and network with teachers and others involved in education.

The public library should also provide a range of materials on a variety of topics which will allow people to follow their interests and support their formal and informal education. It should also provide materials to support literacy and the development of basic life skills. In addition the library must provide study facilities for students who have inadequate or no access to these facilities in their homes.

The development in distance learning is having an impact on the public library. Distant learners, studying at home, are likely to make use of their local library as their primary source for material. Many will require access to the Internet which the public library should provide. Public libraries play an increasingly important role within the educational network and should provide space and access to materials to meet this demand.

Leisure Time Interests

People need information to support their leisure time interests and meeting this need by a range of resources in a variety of formats is another key role of the public library. Public libraries must be aware of the cultural, social and economic changes in the community and develop services that are sufficiently flexible to adjust to these changes. The public library should also help to preserve the culture, history and traditions of the local community and make them readily available. The public library, by organising activities and exploiting its resources, should encourage artistic and cultural development in people of all ages. The library is also an important social centre for individuals and groups to meet both formally and informally. This is of special importance in communities where other meeting places are not available.

Information Services

The rapid development of information technology has brought a vast amount of information within reach of all those with access to electronic media. Information provision has always been a key role of the public library and the ways in which information can be collected, accessed and presented have changed radically in recent years.

The public library has a number of roles in providing information:

- Providing information about the local community and making it readily accessible, often in co-operation with other organisations
- Training people of all ages in the use of information and the associated technology
- Guiding users to the appropriate information sources
- Providing opportunities for disabled people to have independent access to information
- Acting as a gateway to the information world by making it accessible to all, thus helping to bridge the gap between 'the information rich' and 'the information poor'.

The dramatic development of the Internet has been largely unstructured and uncontrolled. The vast amount of information that can be accessed via the Internet is of variable quality and accuracy and a key role of the librarian is to guide users to accurate information sources, which will meet their requirements.

Services to Community Groups

The public library should be at the centre of the community if it is to play a full part in its activities. It should, therefore, work with other groups and organisations in the community. This will include departments of government and local government, the business community and voluntary organisations.

An analysis of the information needs of these bodies should be conducted, and services be provided to meet these needs. This will not only help the organisations involved but will also demonstrate, in a practical way, the value of the public library to people in the community who are likely to have some influence on the future of the library service.

Many public libraries, for example, provide an information service to local government politicians and staff, giving a practical demonstration of the value of the public library.

Services to Special User Groups

Potential users who, for whatever reason, are unable to use the regular services of the library have a right to equal access to library services. The library should, therefore, establish ways of making library material and services accessible to these users.

These will include:

- Special transport, *e.g.*, mobile libraries, book-boats and other forms of transport to serve those living in isolated areas.
- Services taken to the home of those people who are housebound.
- Services taken to factories and industrial premises for employees.
- Services for those confined in institutions, *e.g.*, prisons and hospitals.
- Special equipment and reading materials for those with physical and sensory disabilities, *e.g.*, hearing impaired and visually impaired people.
- Special materials for people with learning difficulties, *e.g.*, easy-to-read materials and cassettes.
- Services for immigrants and new citizens to help them to find their way within a different society and to provide access to media of their native culture.
- Electronic communication, *e.g.*, Internet catalogues.

Services for people with special needs can be enhanced by the use of new technology, for example, speech synthesisers for the visually impaired, online access catalogues for those in isolated areas or unable to leave their home, connections to remote sites for distance learning. Mainstream service provision, for example, public access catalogues (OPACs) can often be adapted to meet the needs of those with physical and sensory disabilities. Those who can benefit the most from technological developments are often the least able to afford the investment needed.

Innovative schemes should, therefore, be developed by the public library to exploit the new technology in order to make services available to as many people as possible. Services for ethnic groups in the community and for indigenous peoples should be developed in consultation with the group concerned.

They are likely to include:

- The employment of staff from the group in the library.
- Collections including the native literature of the group and reflecting the oral tradition and non-written knowledge of the people.
- The application of special conditions, developed in conjunction with local people, to culturally sensitive material.

Reading Promotion and Literacy

Reading, writing and the ability to use numbers are basic prerequisites to being an integrated and active member of society. Reading and writing are also the basic techniques needed for making use of new communication systems.

The public library should support activities that will enable people to make the best use of modern technology. It should support other institutions that are combating illiteracy and promoting media competence.

It can achieve this by:

- Promoting reading.
- Providing appropriate materials for those with poor literacy skills.
- Working with other agencies in the community involved in combating illiteracy.
- Participating in campaigns to combat illiteracy and improve numeracy
- Organising events to promote an interest in reading, literature and media culture.
- Promoting and providing training in the use of computer technology
- Promoting awareness of new developments in the media market.
- Helping people to find the information they need in the appropriate format.
- Co-operating with teachers, parents and other contact persons to help new citizens acquire the necessary educational skills that will help them to manage their lives in the new context.

The public library provides a range of creative literature and can use promotional techniques to bring its variety and range to the attention of its users. It can also organise interactive programmes that enable users to exchange views about books that they have read.

CUSTOMER CARE

The policies and procedures of the library should be based on the needs and convenience of the users and not for the convenience of the organisation and its staff. Quality services can only be delivered if the library is sensitive to the needs of its users and shapes its services to meet those needs. Satisfied users are the best advocates of the library service. The public library should have a positive policy of customer care. This means ensuring that in all policy planning, design of libraries and of systems, preparation of operational procedures and drafting of information and publicity material, a positive effect on the user should be a prime objective.

The following actions should be elements in a customer care policy:

- The image projected by all libraries must be neutral and objective.
- Staff should be courteous, friendly, respectful and helpful at all times
- There should be a regular programme of staff training in customer care.
- All staff should receive basic awareness training on how to deal with people with disabilities or from ethnic minorities.

- Jargon should be avoided in all forms of communication, verbal and written.
- Staff should have a friendly and informative telephone manner.
- Methods of communication with the users must be provided, *e.g.*, billboards, bulletins, web site.
- Library services should be properly planned, adequately prepared and reliable.
- The design of the library should be as convenient and inviting as possible.
- Opening hours should be convenient for the users.
- Open public access catalogues should be available on the Internet so that the user can access services from home and outside opening hours.
- There should be efficient renewal and reservation services.
- Services should be delivered beyond the library building when users' needs require it.
- Users should receive a response in the shortest possible time; letters and other forms of communication should be answered promptly and courteously.
- Equipment should be provided to make library use convenient, *e.g.*, drop-in boxes for returning materials out of hours, self-service issue and return equipment in the library, answering machines for communicating with the library out of hours.
- All printed information about services should be available in appropriate alternative formats, *e.g.*, large print, tape; they should also be available in minority languages.
- When resources allow, good quality electronic equipment should be provided in the library including special equipment for the partially sighted and hearing impaired.

User Participation

Customers should be involved in service development:

- By asking them through surveys what services they use and require.
- By analysing and responding to users' complaints.
- By monitoring users' reactions to services and new initiatives.
- By ensuring the input received from users is considered in the development of policy and procedures.
- By providing feedback to users about the effects of their input on service development.
- By providing suggestion boxes and a complaints and commendations procedure.

USER EDUCATION

The public library should help its users develop skills that will enable them to make the most effective use of the library's resources and services. Library staff must act as information navigators to help users of all ages to make the most effective use of information and communications technology, and programmes of user education should be developed. As the new technologies become more commonly available, the role of the public library both in providing access to these technologies and in helping people learn how to make best use of them is of vital importance.

Guided tours of the library should take place regularly to introduce people to the library building and services and how to use its tools, for example, catalogues and technical equipment. These guided tours have to be carefully planned according to the needs of those taking part. Tours for groups should be organised in co-operation with the institution from which they come.

CO-OPERATION AND RESOURCE SHARING

Overall service to the community is enhanced when libraries develop links for exchanging information, ideas, services and expertise. Such co-operation results in less duplication of service, a combining of resources for maximum effect, and an overall improvement in community services. In addition, individual community members may in some cases be of great assistance in helping the library to carry out special tasks or projects.

Formal Links

The library should establish formal links with other organisations in the local community, for example, schools, cultural institutions such as museums, galleries and archives, literacy programmes, chambers of commerce or boards of trade. The links should be used to co-ordinate the resources and efforts of each partner and thereby jointly improve services to the community.

Relations with Schools

One of the most important institutional relationships for a public library is that with the local schools and the education system in the service area.

Types of linkages and/or forms of co-operation include:

- Sharing resources
- Sharing staff training
- Co-operative collection development
- Co-operative programming
- Co-ordination of electronic services and networks
- Co-operation in the development of learning tools
- Class visits to the public library

- Joint reading and literacy promotion
- Programme of web-awareness for children
- Sharing of telecommunications and network infrastructures
- Jointly arranged authors' visits.

Resource Sharing

Each library collection is in some degree unique. No collection can contain all the materials that the members of its public require. Libraries, therefore, can greatly enhance services to their users by providing them with access to the collections of other libraries. Libraries can participate in resource-sharing schemes at any level, local, regional, national and international, involving libraries of a wide range of organisations with information resources. The library should also make its collection available for loan to other libraries through participation in a network, for example, in a union catalogue or in a local network of information providers, such as schools, colleges and universities.

Bibliographic Records

The library should classify and catalogue its resources according to accepted international or national bibliographic standards. This facilitates their inclusion in wider networks.

Borrowing from Other Libraries

In order to meet the information needs of users the library should borrow materials from other libraries both within the same organisation and beyond.

The library should establish interlending policies, which address such issues as:

- Lending materials to other public libraries
- The type of materials it is prepared to lend or not to lend
- The length of time for which materials will be lent
- When it will request materials from other libraries
- Methods of shipment
- How the costs of the service will be met
- Action to be taken if materials are lost or damaged.

ELECTRONIC NETWORKS

Public libraries are instruments of equal opportunity and must provide a safety- net against alienation and social exclusion from technological advance by becoming the electronic doorway to information in the digital age. They should enable all citizens to have access to the information that will enable them to manage their lives at the local level, to acquire essential information about the democratic process and to participate positively in an increasingly global society.

The library should provide access to the resources of the library and to those of other libraries and information services through the creation and maintenance of and participation in effective electronic networks at all levels from local to international. This can include participation in community networks, programmes to develop technologically advanced communities and electronic networks linking two or more agencies. They should also be part of national information policies.

User Access

The library should provide free public access to the Internet/world wide web to enable all citizens, regardless of economic means, to have access to information available in electronic form. It should have at least one public-access workstation with Internet access and a printer that is not shared with staff.

Remote Access

The library should exploit information and communications technology to enable the public to gain access to as many of its electronic resources and services as possible from their home, school or workplace. If possible they should be made accessible 24 hours a day, seven days a week. Making the library catalogue available on the Internet increases its accessibility to the public, and to other libraries, and improves the quality of the service.

Staff Access

Library staff should have access to the Internet/world wide web to enable them to provide better reference and readers' advisory service to users. Staff should have regular training in using the Internet.

Information Navigator

The public library's role is becoming one of mediator, of being the public's electronic doorway to digital information and of helping citizens cross the 'digital divide' to a better future. The librarian's role is increasingly one of 'information navigator' ensuring that the user gets accurate and reliable information.

ACCESS TO SERVICES

Physical accessibility is one of the major keys to the successful delivery of public library services. Services of high quality are of no value to those who are unable to access them. Access to services should be structured in a way that maximizes convenience to users and potential users.

Location of Service Outlets

Public library service outlets should be located for the maximum convenience of residents of the community. If possible they should be near the centre of transport networks and close to areas of community activity, for example, shops, commercial centres, cultural centres. Where appropriate the public library may share buildings with other services such as arts centres, museums, art galleries, community centres and sports facilities. This can help to attract users and achieve capital and operational economies. The outlet should be highly visible and easily reached by foot, public transport, where available, or by private vehicle. In well-developed urban and suburban areas a public library should be available within a journey by private vehicle of about 15 minutes.

Opening Hours

In order to provide the best possible access to the library service, the library must be open at times of maximum convenience to those who live, work and study in the community.

LIBRARY BUILDINGS

In general when planning a library, the librarian and governing body should consider the following elements:

- The function of the library.
- The size of the library.
- Designated spaces.
- Design features.
- Accessible shelving.
- Sign-posting.
- The ambience of the library.
- Electronic and audiovisual equipment.
- Safety.
- Parking.

The Function of the Library

The library should have adequate space to implement the full range of library services that are consistent with the library's strategic plan and that meet local, area or national standards/guidelines.

The Size of the Library

The amount of floor-space required by a public library depends on such factors as the unique needs of the individual community, the functions of the library, the level of resources available, the size of the collection, the space available and the proximity of other libraries. Because these elements will vary significantly from country to country and between different building projects it is not possible to propose a universal standard on the space required for a public library.

Designated Spaces

The library should include space for services to adults, children and young adults and for family use. It should aim to provide a range of materials to meet the needs of all groups and individuals in the community. The range of functions provided and the space available for each will depend on the size of the library.

In planning a new library the following should be considered for inclusion:

- The library collection including, books, periodicals, special collections, sound recordings and video cassettes and other non-print and digital resources.
- Reader seating space for adults, children and young adults to use for leisure reading, serious study, group work and one–one tutoring; quiet rooms should be provided.
- Outreach services: space should be provided to house special collections and preparation areas for outreach services.
- Staff facilities, including work space rest space for eating and relaxing during breaks and meeting rooms where staff can meet with colleagues and supervisors in private.
- Meeting room space for large and small community groups, which should have separate access to the washrooms and to the exterior to enable meetings to be held while the library is closed
- Technology, including public access workstations, printers, CD-ROM stations, copiers, microfilm/fiche readers, public typewriters and facilities for listening to recorded sound.
- special equipment, including atlas cases, newspaper racks, self-service book circulation, dictionaries, wall-mounted display racks, display stands, filing cabinets, map cases, etc.
- Sufficient space for ease of circulation by both public and staff; this can be 15 per cent–20 per cent of public areas and 20 per cent–25 per cent in staff areas.
- In larger libraries a café area for the public is a desirable facility.
- Space must be allowed for the mechanical services of the library, *e.g.*, elevators, heating, ventilation, maintenance, storage of cleaning materials, etc.

Design Features

The library should guarantee easy access for all users and in particular persons with physical and sensory disabilities.

The following features should be included in the planning of a new library:

- The exterior of the library should be well lit and identified with signs clearly visible from the street.

- The entrance of the library should be clearly visible and located on that part of the building that most users approach.
- The library should focus on eliminating barriers to use.
- There should be no design features that limit the ability of an individual or groups to use any part of the library.
- Care should be taken to avoid steps as much as possible in both interior and exterior design.
- Lighting levels should comply with those stated in international or national standards.
- Libraries that occupy two or more floors should provide elevators that are close to the library entrance and that easily accommodate wheelchairs and child strollers.
- The library should provide facilities for the return of library materials when the library is closed; after-hours deposit boxes should be both theft and waterproof.
- A library should undertake an 'accessibility' audit on a regular basis to confirm that there are no barriers to easy use.
- Local, national or international standards on making public buildings accessible to the disabled should be followed, wherever possible.

Accessible Shelving

Materials should be displayed on open shelves and arranged at a height within easy reach for users. All shelving should be adjustable and preferably on lockable wheels so that it can easily be moved. The furniture in the children's section should be appropriately sized. Shelves should be of accessible height and width for persons using a wheelchair.

Sign-posting

The library's exterior signs not only identify the particular function of the building but are also the library's most basic form of publicity. Signs should therefore be carefully planned to communicate an appropriate image of the library. Internal areas of the library and parts of the collection should be clearly identified by signs of a professional standard so that users can easily find them, for example, the library catalogue, magazines, reference services, the children's area, washrooms, Internet stations, copy machines, etc. Signs should also be posted in Braille where necessary. Where appropriate, signs should be provided in languages used by ethnic groups in the community. A sign displaying the opening hours of the library should be clearly visible from outside the library. Talking kiosks could also be considered to help all users find their way in the library. Directional signs should be erected in nearby streets and town centres to guide the public to the library.

The Ambience of the Library

The library should provide a physical setting for the library service that is inviting to the public and that provides:

- Adequate space to store and display the library collection.
- Adequate, comfortable and attractive space for the public to make proper and convenient use of the library's services.
- Sufficient space for the library staff to carry out their duties in an efficient and comfortable setting.
- Adequate space and flexibility for the future.

The climate of the library should be maintained at a comfortable temperature, using efficient heating and air conditioning. Humidity control helps to protect the stock as well as increasing the comfort of the library. Larger libraries may include a café open either throughout the opening hours of the library or for special occasions. Such facilities are sometimes contracted out to a commercial provider.

Electronic and Audiovisual Equipment

As a major function of the public library is to bridge the gap between the information rich and the information poor, it has also to provide access to the necessary electronic, computer and audiovisual equipment. This will include personal computers with Internet access, public access catalogues, microform readers, tape recorders, slide projectors and equipment for the visually and physically handicapped. Wiring should be up-to-date and easily accessible for alterations at a later date. It should also be inspected regularly.

Safety

Every effort should be made to ensure that the library is safe for the public and the staff. Smoke and fire alarms should be provided and security protection for staff and resources. The location of fire extinguishers and emergency exits should be clearly marked. Staff should be trained in first aid and first aid supplies be made readily available. Evacuation drills should be carried out regularly. The library manager in co-operation with the emergency services should prepare a disaster plan to be put into action in the event of a serious incident, for example fire.

Parking

Where users travel to the library in private vehicles there should be sufficient safe and well lit parking either at or close to the library with appropriately identified spaces for persons with disabilities. If bicycles are a common mode of transport, secure cycle racks should be provided outside the library.

COLLECTION DEVELOPMENT

The public library should provide equality of access to a range of resources that meets the needs of its users for education, information, leisure and personal development. The library should provide access to the heritage of its society and develop diverse cultural resources and experiences. Constant interaction and consultation with the local community will help to ensure this objective is achieved.

COLLECTION MANAGEMENT POLICY

Each public library system requires a written collection management policy, endorsed by the governing body of the library service. The aim of the policy should be to ensure a consistent approach to the maintenance and development of the library collections and access to resources. It is imperative that collections continue to be developed on an ongoing basis to ensure that people have a constant choice of new materials and to meet the demands of new services and of changing levels of use.

In the light of today's technological advances, the policy must reflect not only a library's own collections but also strategies for accessing information available throughout the world. The policy should be based upon library standards developed by professional staff related to the needs and interests of local people, and reflecting the diversity of society. The policy should define the purpose, scope and content of the collection, as well as access to external resources.

Content of the Policy

The policy may proceed from statements of universal applicability that are relevant to all library services, through more general statements that are relevant to particular countries, or regions, to statements that are specific to particular library services and could include the following elements.

Universal

- Article XIX of the Declaration of Human Rights.
- IFLA statement on freedom of access to information.
- Statements on intellectual freedom, free access to library collections.
- Freedom of information.
- Consideration of the International Copyright Convention.
- IFLA/UNESCO Public Library Manifesto.

General

- Purpose of the collection management policy and its relation to the corporate plan of the library service.

- Long and short term objectives.
- Access strategies.
- History of the collection and/or library service.
- Identification of relevant legislation.

Specific

- Analysis of community needs.
- Priorities of the library service.
- Parameters of the collection, including special collections and collections for special needs, such as multicultural material, literacy and resources for people with disabilities.
- Selection and discard principles and methods.
- Budget allocation.
- Responsibility within the organisation for collection development, selection and discard.
- Access to electronic resources including online access to periodicals, databases and other information sources.
- The role of the library as an electronic gateway to information.
- Co-operative relationships with other libraries and organisations.
- Preservation and conservation policies.
- Auditing requirements: accessioning, recording, control, discard, sale or disposal.
- Financial accountability.
- Donations policy.
- Complaints procedure.
- A resource management plan assessing the current and future needs of the collections.
- Review and assessment of the policy.

This is not an exhaustive list but an indication of some of the issues that may be included.

RANGE OF RESOURCES

The public library should provide a wide range of materials in a variety of formats and in sufficient quantity to meet the needs and interests of the community.

The culture of the local community and society must be reflected in the resource collection. Public libraries must keep abreast of new formats and new methods of accessing information. All information should be as readily available as possible, irrespective of format. The development of local information sources and resources is vital.

Collections

The following categories of library materials may be represented in a typical public library, although this list is not exhaustive:

- Fiction and non-fiction for adults, young adults and children.
- Reference works.
- Access to databases.
- Periodicals.
- Local, regional and national newspapers.
- Community information.
- Government information, including information by and about local administrations.
- Business information.
- Local history resources.
- Genealogical resources.
- Resources in the primary language of the community.
- Resources in minority languages in the community.
- Resources in other languages.
- Music scores.
- Computer games.
- Toys.
- Games and puzzles.
- Study materials.

Formats

The following formats may be included in a public library collection although this list is not exhaustive and new formats are continually appearing:

- Books, both hard and soft covers.
- Pamphlets and ephemera.
- Newspapers and periodicals including cuttings files.
- Digital information through the Internet.
- Online databases.
- CD-ROM databases.
- Software programmes.
- Microforms.
- Tapes and compact discs (CDs).
- Digital versatile discs (DVDs).
- Videocassettes.
- Laser discs.

- Large print materials.
- Braille materials.
- Audio books.
- Electronic books.
- Posters.

COLLECTION DEVELOPMENT

Collections complement services and should not be seen as an end in themselves, unless their specified primary purpose is the preservation and conservation of resources for future generations. Large collections are not synonymous with good collections, particularly in the new digital world. The relevance of the collection to the needs of the local community is more important than the size of the collection.

Collection size is determined by many factors, including space, financial resources, catchment population of the library, proximity to other libraries, regional role of the collections, access to electronic resources, assessment of local needs, acquisition and discard rates, and policy of stock exchanges with other libraries.

Criteria for Collections

The main criteria for collections should be:

- A range of resources that cater for all members of the community.
- Resources in formats that enable all members of the community to make use of the library service.
- Inflow of new titles.
- Inflow of new books.
- A wide range of fiction categories and of non-fiction subject coverage
- Provision of non-print resources.
- Access to external resources such as libraries of other institutions, electronic databases, local societies, government departments or the community's knowledge of oral cultures.
- Discard of old, worn and outdated books, non-print resources and information sources.

COLLECTION MAINTENANCE PRINCIPLES

Public libraries of any size will contain materials in a variety of formats. Collection maintenance applies equally to all materials whatever their format. Materials on open access should be in good physical condition and contain current information. A smaller, high quality stock will result in more usage than a large stock with a high proportion of old, worn and outdated books, in which newer titles can be lost among mediocre stock. Using outdated reference material can result in the user being given inaccurate information. Materials in electronic formats complement book collections and will replace them in certain areas. Reference works and periodicals on the Internet and on CDs are viable alternatives to printed formats.

Acquisition and Discards

The library collection is a dynamic resource. It requires a constant inflow of new material and outflow of old material to ensure that it remains relevant to the community and at an acceptable level of accuracy. Acquisition rates are more significant than collection size. The acquisition rate is often determined largely by the size of the resource budget.

However, it can also be affected by other factors, for example:

- The number of books published in local languages.
- The population served.
- The level of use.
- The multicultural and linguistic diversity.
- Age distribution of the population.
- Special needs such as people with disabilities or older persons.
- Access to online information.

The size and quality of the stock should reflect the needs of the community.

Reserve Stocks

It may be necessary to maintain a collection of older and lesser-used books on shelves not directly accessible to the public. This should only contain books that have a current or future use and that cannot be replaced or found in any other format.

This may include special subject collections that are used on a regular, if limited, basis and out-of-print fiction. Books that contain outdated information or are in poor condition and can be replaced, should be discarded and not held in a reserve stock. It is efficient to maintain a cooperative reserve with other libraries. The maintenance of a reserve stock should be a regular and on-going activity. The availability of a wide range of information on the Internet and electronic databases reduces the need for public libraries to keep extensive reserve stocks.

Interlending

No library or library service can be self-sufficient in stock, and an efficient and effective interlibrary loan system should be an essential part of every public library service. Within a library service with several outlets a regular programme of exchange of stock between libraries makes maximum use of the stock and provides users with a greater variety of titles from which to choose.

STANDARDS FOR BOOK COLLECTIONS

The following proposed standards relate to book collections. Local and financial circumstances could lead to variations in these proposed standards. Where resources are severely limited these may be regarded as target figures and medium and long-term strategies should be developed to work towards achieving these standards in the future. In the smallest collections materials for children, adult fiction and adult nonfiction may be provided in equal proportions. In larger collections the percentage of non-fiction titles will tend to increase. These ratios can vary according to the needs of the local community and the role of the public library.

Relevant collections to serve the needs of young adults should be developed. Where the library has a strong educational role this is likely to be reflected in the composition of the stock. Where reliable population figures are not available alternative methods of developing standards are needed. The estimated size of the community served, the size of the library, and the number of current and anticipated users can be used as a basis for developing standards for the size of the collection. Comparisons with a number of existing libraries serving communities of a similar size and make-up can be used to determine a target figure for the size of the collection and the resources needed to maintain it.

STANDARDS FOR ELECTRONIC INFORMATION FACILITIES

The development of standards for the provision of electronic information facilities is at an early stage.

Current standards include the following:

- An assessment is required of the demographics of the community in the catchment areas of proposed new library developments to determine the initial mix of collections. The development of local and regional standards should be undertaken to take account of variations in the catchment population to be served by the new library. The following recommended standards relate to book provision. Additional standards will be required for other media.

Establishment Phase

A basic collection should be established in new libraries to serve the needs of the general population within the catchment area. A sufficient range and depth of resources to meet general needs should be the aim at this stage rather than comprehensive coverage. The interlibrary loan system should be at its peak utilisation during this phase to supplement the developing collections. In some countries materials from a national or provincial centre are used to supplement the local stock. Where this is not achievable a modest growth plan should be implemented to establish this minimum base stock over a period of three years. Access to electronic information sources should also be included in this phase of development.

Consolidation Phase

The objective under this phase is to achieve growth in the stock size, range and depth. Special conditions of the population are taken into account and collections developed to meet the more in-depth needs of the population served. The book discard factor comes into play and the collection growth rate decreases as discards begin to offset acquisitions.

Steady-state Phase

The collections meet the needs of the community in depth, range and quantity. The quality of collections is maintained by acquisition rates matching discard rates. New formats are accommodated within the collections as they become available and access is provided to the widest possible range of resources through the use of technology.

Content Creation

The service should become a content creator and a preserver of local community resources. Content creation includes publication of information booklets and the development of web content by providing access to information about the library or held by the library in printed formats. This positions the library as an electronic gateway by the creation of links to useful web pages.

ACQUISITION AND DISCARD RATES

For general book stock in an established library service the following acquisition rates may be applied:

Population	Books Per Capita Per Annum	Books per 1000 Population Per Annum
Below 25 000	0.25	250
25 000–50 000	0.225	225
50 000+	0.20	200

The following examples suggest the size of book stock for communities of different sizes.

Scenario 1:

- Established library service serving 100 000 population.
- Median book stock of 200 000 volumes.
- Annual acquisition rate of 20 000 volumes.

Scenario 2:

- Established library service serving 50 000 population.
- Median book stock of 100 000 volumes.
- Annual acquisition rate of 11 250 volumes.

Scenario 3:

- Established library service serving 20 000 population.

- Median book stock of 40 000 volumes.
- Annual acquisition rate of 5000 volumes.

Small Libraries and Mobile Libraries

The general acquisition rates would be inadequate to meet the needs of small libraries and mobile libraries where stock numbers are limited. All libraries require a certain minimum stock in order to provide a sufficient range of books from which users may make their selection. The acquisition rate of 250 books per 1000 population may not be relevant in the smallest service points, where physical limitations may reduce stock levels below the minimum recommended level of 2500 volumes.

In these cases the acquisition rates, renewal rates or exchange rates should be based upon the collection size rather than the population served, and be in the order of 100 per cent or more per annum. An efficient interlibrary loan system is essential in these situations.

Special Collections

General acquisition and discard rates may not be relevant to some parts of the collection or to particular special collections or where special circumstances prevail. In these cases the collection policy must reflect the special needs.

Particular examples of these exceptions are:

- *Indigenous Resources* – the public library has a role in maintaining and promoting collections of resources related to the culture of indigenous people and ensuring access to them.
- *local History Resources* – material relating to the history of the locality should be actively collected, preserved and made available.
- Libraries in Communities with a high proportion of particular groups, *e.g.*, children, retired people, young adults, indigenous peoples, ethnic minorities or unemployed people should reflect the needs of these groups in their collections and services.
- Reference Collections – older reference material may need to be retained to provide historical data for research.

HUMAN RESOURCES

Staff are a vitally important resource in the operation of a library. Staff expenses normally represent a high proportion of a library's budget. In order to provide the best possible service to the community it is necessary to maintain well trained and highly motivated staff to make effective use of the resources of the library and to meet the demands of the community. Staff should be available in sufficient numbers to carry out these responsibilities. The management of library staff is itself an important task. All staff should have a clear understanding of the policy of the library service, well-defined duties and responsibilities, properly regulated conditions of employment and salaries that are competitive with other similar jobs.

THE SKILLS OF LIBRARY STAFF

The public library is a service aimed at all members of the community who will have varied and changing needs. Public library staff will require a range of skills and qualities, including interpersonal skills, social awareness, teamwork and leadership and competence in the practices and procedures of the organisation.

The fundamental qualities and skills required of public library staff can be defined as:

- The ability to communicate positively with people.
- The ability to understand the needs of users.
- The ability to co-operate with individuals and groups in the community.
- Knowledge and understanding of cultural diversity.
- Knowledge of the material that forms the library's collection and how to access it.
- An understanding of and sympathy with the principles of public service.
- The ability to work with others in providing an effective library service
- Organisational skills, with the flexibility to identify and implement changes.
- Imagination, vision and openness to new ideas and practice.
- Readiness to change methods of working to meet new situations.
- Knowledge of information and communications technology.

STAFF CATEGORIES

The following categories of staff are found in public libraries:

- Qualified librarians.
- Library assistants.
- Specialist staff.
- Support staff.

In some countries there is an additional category of library technician, or para-professional, with an intermediate level of qualifications. Staff in all categories may be appointed on either a full-time or part-time basis. In some countries two or more people share a single post, a practice known as job-sharing.

This provides the opportunity to appoint and retain experienced staff who may not be able to work full-time.

Qualified Librarians

Qualified librarians are professional staff who have undertaken a course of study in librarianship and information studies to degree or post-graduate level. A librarian designs, plans, organises, implements, manages and evaluates library and information services and systems to meet the needs of the users of library and information services in the community. This will include collection development, the organisation and exploitation of resources, the provision of advice and assistance to users in finding and using information and the development of systems that will facilitate access to the library's resources.

Qualified librarians will have regular contact with members of the community that they serve. In order to fulfil its functions staff with expertise in specific areas, for example, children's librarians, information officers and reference librarians should form part of the professional team. The following is a list of some of the duties of the qualified librarian.

This list is not exhaustive nor is it likely that the qualified librarian will undertake all these activities simultaneously:

- Analysing the resource and information needs of the community.
- Formulating and implementing policies for service development.
- Planning services to the public and participating in their delivery.
- Retrieving and presenting information.
- Answering reference and information enquiries using appropriate material.
- Assisting users in the use of library resources and information.
- Developing services to meet the needs of special groups, *e.g.*, children
- Creating and maintaining databases to meet the needs of the library and its users.
- Designing library and information services and systems to meet the needs of the public.
- Developing acquisition policies and systems for library resources.
- Managing and administering library and information systems.
- Cataloguing and classification of library materials.
- Promoting library services.
- Evaluating library services and systems and measuring their performance.
- Selecting, evaluating, managing and training staff.
- Budgeting.
- Strategic planning.
- Participation in planning the design and layout of new and refurbished libraries and of mobile libraries.

- Keeping up-to-date with current developments in librarianship and information services including the relevant technologies.

Library Assistants

The duties of the library assistant include routine circulation functions and operational library tasks such as shelving, shelf-checking, processing library materials, data entry, filing, secretarial support and basic level reader enquiry work. Library assistants are the staff the public will come into contact with most frequently. It is essential, therefore, that they should have a high level of interpersonal and communication skills and receive appropriate training.

Specialist Staff

Large public library services may employ specialist staff to carry out specific functions, for example, computer system managers, administrative, financial, training and marketing staff. Specialist staff may have a qualification in their specialism rather than in librarianship.

Support Staff

Support staff include caretakers, cleaners, drivers and security staff. They carry out important functions, which contribute to the smooth operation of the library service. They should be regarded as an integral part of the library's staff.

The Composition of the Staff

The composition of the staff should, as far as possible, reflect the make-up of the population it serves. Where, for example, there is a significant number of people from a particular ethnic group within the community, the library staff should include members of that group. This demonstrates that the library is a service for all members of the local community and will help to attract users from all sections of the public.

ETHICAL STANDARDS

Public library staff have a responsibility to maintain high ethical standards in their dealings with the public, other members of staff and external organisations. All members of the public should be dealt with on an equal basis and every effort must be made to ensure that information provided is as full and accurate as possible. Librarians must not allow their personal attitudes and opinions to determine which members of the public are served and what materials are selected and displayed. The public must have confidence in the impartiality of the library staff if the library is to meet the needs of all members of the community. Library associations in some countries have developed codes of ethics, which can be used as models to introduce similar codes elsewhere.

THE DUTIES OF LIBRARY STAFF

The operation of a library should be a team effort with a close working relationship between all members of staff. It is important, however, that staff are used primarily for tasks related to their skills and qualifications. It is a wasteful use of scarce resources, for example, for qualified librarians to regularly carry out routine circulation functions. For the same reason it is not necessary to have a qualified librarian in every library regardless of size or circulation rate. Small libraries open for limited hours do not require the continuous presence of a qualified librarian. They should however be under the supervision of a member of the qualified staff. All users should have the opportunity of access to a qualified librarian. Staff should have a written contract at the time of their appointment, which clearly states their duties and responsibilities. These should not be changed without consulting the member of staff involved.

STAFFING LEVELS

The number of staff required in each library service will be affected by a range of factors, for example, the number of library buildings, their size and layout, the number of departments within each building, the level of use, services provided beyond the library and requirements for specialist staff. Where some services are provided or supplemented by a regional or national central agency this will have an impact on the number of staff required at local level. The level of available resources is also a critical factor.

Allowing for these and other local differences the following basic staffing level is recommended:

- These are basic recommended levels, which will be affected by local circumstances. Where reliable population figures are not available staffing levels can be related to the size of the library, the range of its functions and the number of users. Another method of developing an appropriate staffing level for a library service is to carry out bench-marking with libraries of comparative size and similar characteristics.

EDUCATION OF LIBRARIANS

Qualified librarians will have undertaken a degree or post-graduate course in librarianship and information studies at a school of librarianship. To ensure that they remain in touch with the latest developments, librarians should maintain a process of continuing professional development on a formal and informal basis. It is important that public librarians maintain close links with the schools of librarianship in their country and are fully aware of course content. Whenever possible they should participate in the work of the schools, for example, by contributing lectures, assisting in interviewing of prospective students and other appropriate forms of co-operation.

TRAINING

Training is a vital element of the activities of a public library. There must be a planned and continuous programme of training for staff at all levels, which should include both full-time and part-time staff. The rapid developments in information technology make the need for regular training even more essential, and the importance of networking and access to other information sources should be included in training programmes. Specialist and support staff should receive induction training in the functions and purpose of the public library and the context in which it operates. In budgeting for the implementation of new systems, an element should be included for training.

In large library services a post of training officer should be created to plan and implement the training programme. To ensure funds are available for training a set percentage of the budget should be earmarked for this function. This level of funding for training should be maintained at times of budget reductions as the need for a well-trained staff is very important in such circumstances.

Mentoring

An effective and economical method of training is to introduce a system of mentoring. New staff work with a more experienced colleague who provides guidance and training. The mentor should be able to advise the new member of staff about issues relating to their work and employment. A checklist of the training provided by the mentor should be maintained to ensure that it is carried out effectively.

Contacts

In addition to in-service training staff should be given opportunities to attend short courses and conferences relevant to their ability to carry out their work. They should be encouraged to be active members of the relevant library association, as this creates links with other library staff and provides opportunities for an exchange of ideas and experience. It may also be possible to arrange staff exchanges with staff in other libraries, either in the same country or in a similar library in another country, which can be a valuable experience for all those involved.

Career Development

In order to motivate and retain skilled staff opportunities for career development should be available at all levels. A scheme of performance appraisal should be in place that provides staff with an evaluation of current performance and guidance in improving and developing their skills. It also presents an opportunity to review career progression.

WORKING CONDITIONS

All library staff should have satisfactory working conditions and the conditions of employment should be clearly stated in the contract given to the new member of staff when they are employed. Salaries should be at a level appropriate to the level of work being undertaken and competitive with other similar jobs in the community.

Health and Safety

The health and safety of staff must be a high priority and policies and procedures put in place to reduce risks.

Consideration should be given to:

- Good working conditions for staff.
- Ergonomically designed furniture and equipment.
- Availability of technical aids for employees with special needs and disabilities.
- The drawing up of evacuation plans and their testing on a regular basis.
- Identified health and safety risks being rectified at the earliest opportunity.
- Ensuring that all equipment and cabling conforms with recognised safety standards.
- The establishment of a staff health and safety committee.
- Appointment and training of staff as first-aid officers and fire wardens.
- Provision of safety devices for staff, particularly when staff work at nights or away from the library.
- Providing advanced driver training for staff who drive library vehicles
- Protective clothing when required.
- Limiting the weight of cartons and loads on book trolleys.

Public libraries are often open for long hours including evenings and weekends. In creating work schedules for staff every effort should be made to ensure that their working hours provide them with adequate time off at appropriate times for social activity. It is vital that good labour relations are maintained and fostered with staff.

Anti-social Behaviour

In any building freely accessible to the public, staff will occasionally encounter users who behave in an unpleasant and anti-social manner. Staff should be trained in how to deal with such situations and have alarm systems that can alert other staff. Senior staff should be immediately available to assist staff and full records of such occurrences should be kept. A support system involving other staff and people from other agencies, for example, social workers, should be developed to help library staff deal with these situations.

VOLUNTEERS

Where a library uses volunteer help from individuals in the community to assist library staff, a written policy should be in place defining the tasks of these volunteers and their relationship to the library operation and staff. Volunteers should not be used as a substitute for paid staff.

THE MANAGEMENT AND MARKETING OF PUBLIC LIBRARIES

A successful public library is a dynamic organisation working with other institutions and with individuals to provide a range of library and information services to meet the varied and changing needs of the community. To be effective it requires experienced, flexible and well trained managers and staff able to use a range of management techniques. This chapter deals with the key elements of public library management.

MANAGEMENT SKILLS

Management of a public library involves a number of different skills:

- Leadership and motivation.
- Maintaining effective relationships with governing and funding bodies.
- Planning and policy development.
- Building and maintaining networks with other organisations.
- Budget negotiations and management.
- Management of library resources.
- Staff management.
- Planning and development of library systems.
- The management of change.
- Marketing and promotion.
- Community liaison and lobbying.

Leadership and Motivation

The library manager has a vital role in advocating the value of public libraries as an integral part of an international, national and local infrastructure. He/she must promote public libraries to politicians and key stakeholders at all levels in order to ensure they are aware of the importance of public libraries and to attract adequate funding for their maintenance and development. The library manager must ensure that governing authorities are informed of new developments that may impact on public library services and are made aware that the library service is a key player in providing access to the delivery of new services.

The library manager is responsible for the motivation of staff and bringing energy, vitality and strength into the library service and its staff. The manager also plays a key role in managing the development of physical facilities and ensuring that the most effective use is made of resources, including information technology, to enable the library service to meet the library and information needs of the community.

Relationships with Governing and Funding Bodies

To achieve its goals the public library needs adequate and sustained funding. It is very important that the library manager establishes and maintains a close and positive relationship with the bodies that govern the library service and provide its funding.

The library manager as head of the public library service should have direct access to and involvement with the board or committee that is directly responsible for the library service. As well as formal meetings there should be regular informal contacts between the library manager and members of the governing body, and they should be kept well informed about the library service and current and future developments.

Planning and Policy Development

Planning ensures that:

- The library responds to the needs of the community.
- The governing body, management and staff understand what the library is trying to achieve.
- Community funds are spent in an effective and responsible manner.
- Continuity of service is maintained regardless of changes of personnel.
- The library expands the expectations of the community as new services are developed.
- The library is able to respond effectively to change.

The determination of public library goals, short and long term objectives, strategies and performance measurement is necessary to ensure equitable, effective and efficient library service provision with access for all sectors of the community. Strategic and operational plans require formulation, documentation and adoption. Planning should not take place in isolation but in conjunction with the governing and funding bodies, the library staff and the actual and potential clients served.

A strategic plan must be user-focused and should include the following elements:

- Review of achievements.
- Examination of needs.
- Identification of priorities and short term goals.

- Development of strategies for achieving goals.
- Identification of critical success factors.
- Budget allocation.
- Deployment of resources to achieve optimum performance.
- Measurement and evaluation of input and output performance.
- Reassessment of needs and policies.

Operational Planning

An operational plan is necessary to ensure that the activities of the library service are focused on achieving the priorities and goals identified in the strategic plan.

The plan should reflect the following elements:

- A focus on service to users.
- The implementation of the priorities and goals of the strategic plan.
- The formation of operational elements of the agreed strategies.
- The development of clearly identified goals with manageable and achievable time frames.
- The definition of achievable outputs for the level of inputs.
- The participation of library staff who carry out the activities.
- The allocation of responsibility to identified staff members for achieving outputs.
- A programme for monitoring, evaluating and amending the plan at regular intervals.

By-laws or local legislation, specific policies and procedures may be needed and should be properly formulated, documented and communicated to all those involved. Business and marketing plans, market research, community needs analyses and surveys of users and non-users should form part of the management process. Planning for the future should advocate positive change and flexibility and aim to minimize the impact of transition on services, staff and users. To achieve effective change, all stakeholders must be involved in the change process.

BUILDING AND MAINTAINING NETWORKS

The library manager must ensure that networks are developed and maintained at national, regional and local level, using information and communications technology wherever appropriate. This enables a very wide range of resources to be brought to the user at a local level. The library manager should also develop good working relationships with other agencies in the community, for example, schools, other local government departments and voluntary organisations for the benefit of the users, and to confirm the public library's role at the centre of community activity. The library manager should, wherever possible, ensure that the library takes an active and positive role within the corporate structure of the parent organisation.

FINANCIAL MANAGEMENT

Financial management and financial planning are vitally important to ensure that the library operates efficiently, economically, and effectively.

In order to achieve these aims the library manager should:

- Look for ways of improving levels of funding from national, state or local government or from other sources.
- Prepare 3–5 year business plans based on the library's long term plans, including bids for the required funds.
- Allocate funds to support activities identified in the library's policy statement and based on the priorities previously determined.
- Establish partnerships, where appropriate, for co-operative purchasing to maximize the use of available funds.
- Undertake activity-based costing to determine the cost of activities and programmes and to facilitate future planning.
- Maintain a policy for the sustainable renewal of plant and equipment.
- Evaluate and implement automated techniques, wherever appropriate, to improve efficiency and effectiveness.
- Introduce systems that will ensure that all staff with responsibility for any part of the budget will be fully accountable for the expenditure of funds for which they are responsible.
- Improve staff productivity and efficiency.

MANAGEMENT OF LIBRARY RESOURCES

A major element of a library's budget is expenditure on library materials. The library manager should ensure that these funds are spent properly and in accordance with the agreed priorities of the library and that the materials are maintained and made available so that they can be of maximum benefit to the library user.

STAFF MANAGEMENT

Library staff are a vital element of the library's resources and staff salaries are normally the largest part of the library budget. It is very important that the management of staff should be sensitive, consistent and based on sound principles if staff are to work most effectively and with high levels of motivation and job satisfaction.

The following are important elements of staff management:

- An equitable procedure for staff appointments. Job and person specifications should be drawn up prior to a post being advertised.

Interviews should be conducted in a way that is fair to all applicants. Appointments should be based solely on professional judgement and suitability for the post and not be prejudiced by any other factors.

- Good communication between staff at all levels. Managers should review internal communication systems regularly to make sure staff are well informed about the policies and procedures of the library service.
- The opportunity for staff to participate in the development of policy and operational procedures. Initiative should be encouraged to make the best use of the skills and experience of staff. By bringing staff into the decision-making process they will feel they 'own' the policies and procedures of the service.
- The principles of affirmative action, including the creation of nominated positions for special needs areas, may be adopted.

PLANNING AND DEVELOPMENT OF LIBRARY SYSTEMS

To make the most effective use of resources the public library will require a variety of systems, for example circulation control, financial management, internal communications. The library manager should ensure that appropriate systems are introduced, making use of specialist staff for their development where necessary. Staff must be given adequate training in the use of such systems, the effectiveness of which must be reviewed regularly.

THE MANAGEMENT OF CHANGE

In common with many other organisations public libraries are going through a period of unprecedented and ongoing change as a result of the rapid development of information technology and social and demographic change. This presents tremendous opportunities for the public library, as information provision is one of its primary roles.

It also presents challenges to managers and staff to ensure that change can be introduced with the maximum effectiveness and the least stress on staff and the organisation. Library managers must be aware of the issues arising from continuous and fundamental change and establish methods of dealing with them.

Planning for the Future

Library managers should be aware of developments both within and outside librarianship that are likely to have an impact on service development. They should make time to read and study so that they can anticipate the effect of changes, particularly technological, on the future shape of the service. They should also ensure that policy-makers and other staff are kept informed of future developments.

DELEGATION

The library manager in charge of the public library service has ultimate responsibility for the service, in conjunction with the governing body. However, all library staff with responsibility for any resources of the library, whether materials, staff or library premises, have a managerial role, and this should be recognised by the library manager and the member of staff concerned.

They should be given appropriate managerial training and participate in the policy development of the library whenever possible. Managerial responsibility should be delegated to staff at an appropriate lower level. It should be made clear what responsibilities are being delegated and what the reporting mechanism to senior managers is.

Staff must be given training to enable them to carry out the delegated responsibilities effectively. A planned system of delegation makes best use of the skills and experience of a wide range of staff and provides opportunities for professional development. It also increases the number of people fully involved in the development and operation of the library service, improves job satisfaction and prepares staff for promotion when opportunities arise.

MANAGEMENT TOOLS

A wide range of management tools can be used in a public library. Their relevance will depend on a number of factors, for example, the cultural context, the size and character of the service, the management style of other departments in the same organisation and available experience and funding.

The following are however important tools for public libraries in almost any situation:

- Community needs analysis.
- Monitoring and evaluation.
- Performance measurement.

Community Needs Analysis

In order to provide services that meet the needs of the whole community, the public library has to establish the extent of those needs. As needs and expectations will change, this process will need to be repeated at regular intervals, perhaps every five years.

A community needs assessment is a process in which the library collects detailed information about the local community and its library and information needs. Planning and policy development are based on the results of this assessment and in this way a match between services and needs can be achieved. In some countries the preparation of a community needs assessment is a legislative requirement of the local authority.

The information to be collected will include:

- Socio-demographic information about the local community *e.g.*, the age and gender profile, ethnic diversity, educational level.
- Data about organisations in the community, *e.g.*, educational institutions, health centres, hospitals, penal establishments, voluntary organisations.
- Information about business and commerce in the locality.
- The catchment area of the library, *i.e.*, where library users live in relation to the library.
- Transport patterns in the community.
- Information services provided by other agencies in the community.

This is not an exhaustive list and further research would be required to establish what information is needed to form a community needs assessment in each situation. However, the principle of preparing a community profile, which will enable the librarian and the governing body to plan service development and promotion on the needs of the community, is an important one whatever the local context. The assessment should be complemented by regular customer surveys to establish what library and information services the public wants, at what level, and how they judge the services they receive. Survey work is a specialist skill and, where resources are available, a more objective result will be gained if the survey is carried out by an external organisation.

Monitoring and Evaluation

As the library service moves towards its goals, management must be accountable in terms of financial control and the monitoring and evaluation of library activities. Management must continually monitor the performance of the library service to ensure that strategies and operational results are achieving the set objectives. Statistics should be collected over time to allow trends to be identified. Community needs and satisfaction surveys, and performance indicators are valuable tools in monitoring the achievements of the library. Techniques should be developed to measure the quality of the services provided and their impact on the community.

All programmes and services should be evaluated on a regular basis to ascertain whether they are:

- Achieving the objectives and declared goals of the library.
- Actually and regularly provided.
- Meeting the needs of the community.
- Able to meet changing needs.
- In need of improvement, new direction or redefinition.
- Adequately resourced.
- Cost effective.

Procedures and processes operating within the library also require constant evaluation and revision to increase efficiency and effectiveness.

Performance Indicators

The availability of reliable performance information is a necessary tool for evaluation and the improvement of efficiency, effectiveness and quality of service.

The collection of statistics related to resources, staff, services, circulation, activities, etc., will provide data for planning, show accountability and assist informed management decision-making. The following key performance indicators may be used to evaluate and monitor the achievement of the library's objectives.

Usage indicators:

- Loans per capita.
- Total library visits per capita.
- Membership as a percentage of the population.
- Loans per item, *i.e.*, turnover resources.
- Reference enquiries per capita.
- Loans per opening hour.
- Number of accesses to electronic services and other non-print materials.

Resource indicators:

- Total stock per capita.
- Provision of terminals/personal computers per capita.
- Provision of online public access computers (OPACs) per capita.

Human Resource Indicators:

- Ratio of full time equivalent (FTE) staff to population
- Ratio of professional staff to population.
- Ratio of full time equivalent (FTE) staff to library use.

Qualitative indicators:

- User satisfaction surveys.
- Enquiries satisfied.

Cost indicators:

- Unit costs for functions, services and activities.
- Staff costs per functions, *e.g.*, books processed, programmes.
- Total costs per capita, per member, per visitor, per service point, etc.

Comparative indicators:

- bench-mark statistical data against other relevant and comparable library services, internationally, nationally and locally.

In addition to the collection and analysis of input and output service statistics, the unstated needs of non-users should be established by carrying out market research including the use of focus groups and community surveys. Where reliable population statistics are not available it becomes more difficult to develop reliable performance indicators. Use can be made of estimated population totals, the comparison of costs with user and visitor statistics and bench-marking with other libraries with similar characteristics.

Performance Measurement

Performance measurement has been used in public libraries for some years. Measurements or performance indicators are established to measure the input to libraries, that is the resources devoted to the whole or particular services, and the output: what is achieved as a result of the activity being carried out. For example, the establishment of an enquiry service for users requires the input of staff, materials, equipment and floor space.

The output is the number of enquiries received, the number satisfied, the level of use made of the resources and the use of other services, for example, the reservation service, arising from the original activity. These measures can then be compared each year to see if the effectiveness of the library service is improving. Computer technology makes performance measurement a simpler task and enables sophisticated models of library use to be established and used in service development. Performance measurement should be a planned process carried out with consistency over a period of time.

Further information about library performance indicators can be found in ISO 11620:1998 *Information and documentation. Library performance indicators*. Another way of gaining a useful indication of the success of a library service is to compare key input and output measurements with other public libraries of similar size and characteristics. This is usually known as benchmarking and is a useful adjunct to performance measurements carried out internally.

MARKETING AND PROMOTION

Library managers can use marketing techniques to enable them to understand the needs of their users and to plan effectively to meet those needs. The library should also promote its services to the public to ensure that they are kept informed of the services provided to meet their library and information requirements.

Marketing and Promotion Policy

The library should have a written communications, marketing and promotions policy to enable it to undertake a planned promotion of its services to the public. The policy should include a marketing and communication strategy and methods of evaluating promotional programmes.

Marketing and Promotion Plan

To enable the library to achieve its marketing strategy, a coherent marketing and promotion plan should be developed based on the agreed policy.

It could include the following elements:

- Making positive use of print, electronic and communications media.
- Displays and exhibits.
- Effective interior and exterior sign-posting.
- Regular publications and the preparation of resource lists and pamphlets.
- Reading and literacy campaigns.
- Designing campaigns to meet the needs of people with physical and sensory disabilities.
- Book fairs.
- Library web sites.
- Links to and from related web sites and portals.
- Friends of the library groups.
- Annual library week celebrations and other collective promotional activities.
- Special years of celebration and anniversaries.
- Library listings in the telephone book and other community directories.
- Fund-raising activities and campaigns.
- Public-speaking activities and liaison with community groups.
- Special library publications, *e.g.*, history of the library, history of the community.

This list is not exhaustive and other elements can be added depending on local circumstances.

Working with the Media

Library staff should be trained to use communication media to promote the library service and respond to media enquiries. They should be able to write articles for local newspapers and prepare press releases. They should be familiar with the techniques of speaking and being interviewed on radio and television. They should also be able to promote the library and its services via computer and telecommunication networks including the creation of library web sites.

Community Support

The library managers must ensure that the community is aware of the importance of the library service. Municipal, regional and national funding bodies should be made fully aware of the important place that the library occupies in the community, and support its development.

Gaining Community Support

The library should have an agreed policy and a sustained programme for developing community support.

This can include:

- Maintaining a 'friends of the library' organisation for fund-raising and general support.
- Working with community advocates in support of major initiatives such as new buildings and services.
- Forming liaisons with community groups to enhance parts of the collection or strengthen specific services.
- Working with groups that wish to speak out on behalf of the library service and its development.
- Participation by library staff in activities aimed at increasing awareness of the variety and value of the library service.

The support of the community also depends on the library delivering the services it has promised to deliver.

Advocacy

The library should have established and adopted written policies that define its role in generating public support for the library service. A well informed public can provide valuable support for the public library service and actively promote it within the community. Getting people to talk positively about the library and its services is one of the most effective marketing tools. Lobbying involves interaction with decision-makers to secure specific objectives at an appropriate point in the legislative, policy-making or budget process.

Working with Governing Bodies

Library managers should meet at least annually with the library's principal governing and funding body to review the library's services, development plans, achievements and obstacles. Librarians should look for as many opportunities as possible to involve its governing body in its major activities. Events such as the opening of a new library, the launching of a service, the installation of public Internet access, the opening of a new collection and the inauguration of a fund-raising drive can be used for this purpose.

Participation in Community Life

One of the most effective promotional strategies is the participation of wellinformed library staff and committee or board members in community activities.

Examples include:

- Presenting book and activity reviews on radio and television.

- Working with adults and children's literature and cultural groups.
- Writing a newspaper column.
- Supporting literacy organisations and campaigns.
- Participating in the activities of local organisations.
- Assisting with school-based initiatives.
- Participating in local history and genealogy societies.
- Being a member of a service organisation, *e.g.*, Rotary.
- Visiting local organisations to promote the library service.

Evaluation

The library should carry out a regular evaluation of its marketing and promotion programme and ensure the results of the evaluation are taken into account when planning future programmes.

3

National Policy on Public Libraries in India

Pre–Five-Year Plan Period

The programmes executed by provincial and central governments since 1910 for the social and adult education of the populace have paved the way for the enactment of library laws and rules for grants-in-aid in the country. Hence, public library finance is part of the education budget. The level of literacy in 1941 being as low as 16 per cent, universalization of elementary education and eradication of illiteracy in the nation were the aims of the education policy of the government. To fulfil this goal, a variety of programmes were undertaken such as extension services, continuing education, social education, part-time education, refresher courses, non-formal education, and adult education.

In order to accelerate the pace of socio–economic development, the government considered public libraries to be an integral part of development projects. In 1948, the first public library bill was passed in the state of Madras, mainly due to the efforts of the eminent librarian S.R. Ranganathan. One of the earliest Advisory Committees-the Sinha Committee, appointed in 1957-recommended that public libraries be developed on the basis of a hierarchical network. The hierarchy should have the national central library at the apex, followed by state central libraries, district libraries, block libraries and panchayat libraries. This is the foundation upon which the public library system has been built.

First Five-Year Plan (1951–1956)

The first plan provision was ₹ 140 million for social education, physical education, and youth welfare, out of the total budget for education of ₹ 1.33 billion. Libraries were considered to be part of social education. ₹ 5 million was set aside for establishment of the national central library, but this sum was not used.Improvement of library services was mentioned in this plan for educational development. The essence of the scheme was to establish district libraries in each state, which were to be supplemented by a state central library. The government of India also initiated a scheme, "Integrated Library Service," with the support of the state government. The scheme targeted units in every area selected by the governments for intensive educational development.

The experimental project was meant to monitor the impact of a number of educational institutions in areas covering 100 villages. Each area was to have five model community centers, plus a main library with branches to distribute books to 20 villages. This pilot project was implemented in 29 areas in the country. Nine states made plans to open state central libraries, and some others were in the process of setting up district libraries in about 100 districts. This cost approximately ₹ 10 million, of which nearly two–thirds was contributed by the government of India. Thus, libraries were considered to be an essential part of the Community Development Programme that was launched during the first plan period.

Other important developments included establishment of the Delhi Public Library in 1951. The Central Reference Library in Calcutta was established in 1955. Connemara Public Library, in Madras became the State Central Library in 1950 under the provisions of the Madras Public Libraries Act of 1948; in 1955, it became one of the three depository libraries. At the end of March 1954, the country had 32,000 libraries with a book stock of about 7.1 million volumes; an amount of ₹ 9 million was spent on library services. By 1951, the level of literacy had risen to 18.33 per cent.

In 1954, the Delivery of Books Act was passed to include newspapers. The act obligated every publisher in India to deposit a copy of its publication with the National Library in Calcutta; the Asiatic Society Library, Bombay; Connemara Public Library, Madras; and the Delhi Public Library. On the basis of books received under this act, India has a national bibliography which is published by the Central Reference Library, Calcutta. The bibliography, however, does not include textbooks, musical scores, maps, and atlases.

Second Five-Year Plan, (1956–1961)

Of the ₹ 2.040 billion budgeted for education, ₹ 100 million was proposed for social education, physical education, and youth welfare. This plan contained the same provisions as the first plan, plus additional provisions for establishing integrated library service. There were three objectives. First, state and district libraries were to be set up in each state. Second, the library services were to be organized on the basis of legislation. Finally, district libraries were to form the link between the state central library and village libraries. As a result, nine states in India established state central libraries and 254 district libraries. But the national central library was still not established. In 1960, the state of Andhra Pradesh enacted library legislation.

During this plan period, a total of ₹ 2.040 billion was spent on educational development, of which ₹ 9 million was spent on library development. Even though ₹ 18.6 million was provided, the states only used 48.6 per cent of this amount. Thus, the number of libraries nearly doubled in 1964 as compared to 1951, and the expenditure on public libraries in this period increased three–fold. A UNESCO report published on the occasion of the Public Library Seminar held at Delhi in 1955, India had 24,086 public library service points at the time. The level of literacy in 1961 increased to 28.31 per cent.

The Advisory Committee for Libraries was appointed in 1957 by the Government of India, with K.P. Sinha as the chairman.

The committee drafted a Model Library Bill and drew up a 25-year plan. In 1959, the committee submitted a report with recommendations, some of which follow:

- Enact library legislation, in all constituent states, to establish public libraries;
- Build nationwide library service with detailed suggestions for financing through the state and central governments;
- Extend public library service to the blocks, panchayats, and villages; and,
- Create an independent Department of Social Education and Libraries.

Third Five-Year Plan, (1962–1967)

The amount of ₹ 5.6 billion was budgeted for education in this plan period, but the amount to be spent on libraries was not clearly indicated in the plan. Of this amount, ₹ 620 million was expected to be available for social education. During this plan period, the system of central government assistance to the states was changed, and funding for libraries was kept to a bare minimum.

Thus, it was up to the individual states to take the initiative and develop their public libraries. With the beginning of this plan period, the scheme to assist state governments in establishing state central libraries, district central libraries, and block development libraries was abandoned. The central government decided to let the states decide on the development; the decision was a major setback that hindered the development of public libraries.

During this plan period, four national libraries were to be established at Delhi, Calcutta, Bombay, and Madras. District–level libraries were to be established in all the states. A sum of ₹ 32.3 million was made available to the states for this purpose.

In 1962 the central government sent a model Public Libraries Bill to those state governments which had not adopted any library legislation, hoping to persuade these states to show an interest in passing the legislation.

A Working Group on Libraries was appointed by the Planning Commission in 1964. Group recommendations included:

- By the end of the Fifth Five Year Plan, set up libraries at block headquarters and in every village having a population of 5,000;

- Encourage the Programme of Adult Education to use the services of the public libraries to eradicate illiteracy.

As of January 1, 1965, according to the information received from the states by the Working Group:

- Twelve of 18 states/UT had state central libraries;
- 205 of 327 districts had district central libraries;
- 1,394 blocks of 5,223 had block development libraries;
- 28,317 villages out of 566,878 had village libraries.

Library legislation was passed in two states during this period: Karnataka in 1965, and Maharashtra in 1967.

Fourth Five-Year Plan, (1969–1974)

The education budget was estimated at ₹ 7.120 billion of which the social education component was ₹ 100 million. Thus, the tempo that had built for the development of library services slowed. However, ₹ 130 million was provided in this plan period for provision of information services, which included information centers, radio transmitters, film production, mobile cine vans, and other media.

The literacy level rose to 34.45 per cent in 1971.In 1972, the Working Group on Development of Public Libraries was constituted by the Government of India Planning Commission to make recommendations for library development. These recommendations were to be included in the Fifth Five Year Plan.

The group submitted detailed proposals for:

- Allotment of ₹ 310 million for the development of public libraries; but the amount actually provided was a meager ₹ 20 million;
- A network of libraries to cover the whole country, and other recommendations similar to those made earlier by the Advisory Committee.

Figures provided in 1973 concerned the number of public libraries, and read as follows:

- Fifteen of 21 states/UT had state central libraries;
- 235 of 376 districts had district central libraries;
- 1,500 of 3,100 sub–districts had sub–district central libraries;
- 50,000 villages of 566,878 had village libraries;
- 1,800 of 2,641 towns had town libraries.

In 1972, during this plan period, the central government established the Raja Rammohun Roy Library Foundation. The foundation was created as an autonomous body under the Department of Culture, controlled by the Ministry of Education, for the development of public libraries in India. This foundation matches the funds of the states for purchasing furniture and books, organizing conferences and seminars, and providing mobile library service to the rural areas. It also advises the central government on all matters relating to library development in the country.

Fifth Five-Year Plan, (1974–1979)

An adult education programme was the emphasis of this plan. The programme was to be supported by a network of libraries at the village and block levels, and various community centers. Thus, steps were taken to strengthen not only the village and block libraries, but also the central and state libraries, and the district libraries. The states were assisted by the Raja Rammohun Roy Library Foundation, which was established in 1972. During this plan period, the amount of ₹ 15.620 billion was allocated for general education, and ₹ 350 million was budgeted for social education.

The only state that enacted a public library law during this plan period was West Bengal, in 1979. In 1978, the government adopted the National Adult Education Programme, but it did not recognize the public library as an agency that could be assigned a role in solving the literacy problem. Rather, the public library was relegated to the role of post–literacy work. This view was also promulgated by the Draft National Policy on Education (NPE), 1979. However, the need for the rural public library system to play a role in continuing education in the villages and rural areas was recognized.

In 1979, the Ministry of Education in the Department of Culture established a library section under the charge of an under secretary. The goal: to promote development of public libraries in India. Since then, libraries have not been part of the social education budget. Instead, they have been included in the art and culture component of the budget.

Sub–Sixth Five-Year Plan, (1980–1985)

This plan emphasized minimum essential education of all adults, to be achieved by inter-sectoral cooperation and interand150; agency coordination. These efforts were to be supported by post–literacy, continuing education through a network of rural libraries as well as instructional programmes conducted through mass communication media. The amount allocated for general education was ₹ 21.622 billion. The art and culture component was ₹ 839 million.

During this period:

- Twenty–six states/UT out of 31 existing in 1982 had established/ designated state central libraries;
- Out of 401 districts, 291 had district central libraries;
- Out of 5,027 blocks, 1,798 development blocks had block libraries;
- Out of 575,936 villages, 41,828 had village libraries;
- Out of 2,643 towns, 1,280 had town libraries.

Of the 29 metropolitan cities with a population of 400,000 and above, only four — Madras, Hyderabad, Bangalore, and Delhi — have city public library systems with central libraries, branches, and deposit stations. Thus, it is estimated that approximately 20 per cent of the literate population has access to public library service.

A Working Group on Modernization of Library Services and Informatics in the Seventh Plan was appointed by the Planning Commission in 1983. In its 1984 report, the group recommended formulation of a National Policy on Library Services and Informatics in support of similar recommendations made earlier by other committees.

From its establishment in 1972, to 1982, the Raja Rammohun Roy Foundation provided funds of ₹ 250 million to assist 15,000 rural libraries. In 1982, the Delhi Public Library became a copyright library. The level of literacy increased to 43.56 per cent in 1981.

Seventh Five-Year Plan, (1985–1990)

During this Plan period, the Planning Commission's objective was to address the needs of 90 million people, ages 15–35, in the Adult Education Programme. The network of libraries was to play a role in the development of literature for neoliterates. Library systems were to be strengthened with specific attention given to improvement of facilities at the national-level institutions. The general education budget was ₹ 47,753 million; ₹ 4.821 billion constituted the art and culture component.

An important development during this period was the 1986 adoption of the National Literacy Mission, which emphasized the education of women and also the establishment of rural libraries.

In 1989, there were 7,180 main libraries and 18,000 service points. The collections of the National Library of Calcutta were increased significantly. The Central Secretariat Library started creating a database on the epic "Mahabharata." The Raja Rammohun Roy Foundation set up an "Integrated Research Cell-cum-Computer Unit" for promoting research in librarianship, and also started a database of public libraries in the country. A Committee on National Policy on Library and Information System was appointed in 1985 by the Government of India, Department of Culture. The resulting final report was submitted in 1986. This policy stressed the need to establish strong links between a village's community library and primary school. If the school lacked a library, the community library was to provide the children with adequate resources. Furthermore, a children's section was to be organized in every public library.

The National Policy on Education, 1986 barely mentions libraries. It states that a nationwide movement for improvement of existing libraries and the establishment of new ones will be taken up, provision will be made in all educational institutions for library facilities, and the status of librarians improved. The school library programme, "Operation Blackboard," was initiated with the provision of essential teaching and learning materials.

The National Book Policy–1986 also had an impact on libraries, as it recommended:

- Provision of reading material for children by all the agencies involved;
- That 10 per cent of the annual education budget of the governments be used to purchase books for libraries.

During this plan period, these states passed library acts: Manipur in 1988, Assam in 1989, Haryana in 1989, and Kerala in 1989.

Eighth Five-Year Plan, (1992–1997)

The money allocated for this period for general education is ₹ 168.133 billion; for art and culture, ₹ 7.276 billion has been allocated. Universalization of elementary education, eradication of illiteracy in the 15-35-year age group, and strengthening of vocational education in relation to emerging needs in urban and rural settings are the major thrusts of the plan. These goals are to be achieved by using formal, non-formal, and open channels of learning. The plan states that in those states with an advanced library system, rural libraries should become the focal points for post–literacy and continuing education programmes.

Book promotion is also emphasized in this plan, to be promoted by the organization of a National Centre for Children's Literature, which should produce 3,000 titles annually. Important books are to be translated into the various Indian languages, and books for neoliterates published. Publishers and voluntary agencies will be given assistance, and the school library programme, undertaken as part of the "Operation Blackboard" scheme of the National Policy on Education-1986, will continue.

Public libraries of national importance are to be provided funds for improvements/innovations such as the following:

- The Khuda Baksh Public Library proposed establishment of an Institute of Oriental Studies and open regional units for research on Indo-Islamic and comparative religion;
- The Rampur Raza Library would acquire sophisticated equipment for preservation of its collections;
- The Asiatic Society, Calcutta, is to open an art gallery, introduce a desktop publishing system, and construct a new building;
- The National Library proposed making microfilms available, producing a national union catalogue, and providing book production statistics;
- The Central Reference Library is to be reorganized into a National Bibliographical and Documentation Center with a computer center; and,

- The Delhi Public Library is to open two new libraries within its service area.

The Raja Rammohun Roy Foundation proposes assisting state central libraries in their quest to obtain reprographic equipment. The Foundation also hopes to assist certain libraries in the processing of rare books, and to provide assistance to rural libraries, and to those public libraries that have completed 100 years of service.

The Model Public Libraries Act is based on the national seminar on this subject, which was held February 14, 1990, in New Delhi. The seminar was organized by the Indian Library Association in collaboration with the Raja Rammohun Roy Library Foundation. This excellent document encompasses all aspects of legislation important to the establishment of public libraries.

The National Cultural Policy, 1993 is the new policy designed by the Government of India. It was created by merging the National Policy of Library and Information Science, the National Book Policy, and other related policies dealt with by the Department of Culture of the Ministry of Human Resource Development.

LIBRARY LEGISLATION

The Nature of the Problem

It would appear at first sight that provision and public maintenance of a system of public libraries would be an obvious step in any country where education and the promotion of literacy were considered important. Education, after all, is not an end in itself; the individual must not only have access to the printed word during his period of formal education, he must have the means of enlarging his experience after school and university, and this necessarily implies organized collections of printed materials. If a library is an essential adjunct to school or college, it is an essential adjunct in the world outside.

One would also think that the legislative base for such a system of public libraries would be a comparatively simple matter, and that those libraries would automatically be free for all to use. It is almost universally recognized that education should be compulsory, and that it should be free up to a certain level. True, cost can be a limiting factor but few countries today do not devote a large proportion of their resources to educational provision. Neither of these assumptions is in fact correct. Systems of public libraries, as against individual public libraries, have only recently been recognized as essential, even in advanced countries, and many countries, some with a secure basis of culture and education, do not have generally applicable public library legislation. Examples are France, Belgium, the Netherlands and Italy. Even where public library legislation has been long established, it can be seen from the examples studied here that, in the framework of the modern State, public library law is noticeably defective. The development of public libraries has probably been hampered by the paradox that they were in fact recognized as instruments of popular education and social welfare long before the conception of compulsory education and before the legal framework of the modern State was established. The concept of the public library has been essentially that of a local community project.

All countries have public libraries, buildings where books are provided for general reading, either free of charge or for a small subscription. They have been provided in thousands all over the world by charitable bodies, educational, social and religious organizations, by philanthropic individuals, as memorials to a person or to commemorate an occasion.

The public libraries in England and the United States in the early nineteenth century were typical, but they are not always a passing phase of development. The traveller interested in the phenomenon will come across examples almost anywhere: in Asia, for example, the Hardinge Library in Delhi, the Connemara Library in Madras, the Raffles Library in Singapore; in Africa, the King George VI Memorial Library in Tanga, the Connaught Library in Nairobi. Some become moribund. Some are being or have been incorporated by good fortune into a national or local public library system.

Some operate even today with some success. But they are not public libraries in the modern accepted sense, nor were they, for that matter, in the nineteenth century.

Edward Edwards, pioneer of the public library in Great Britain, summed up their built-in failure over a hundred years ago, in evidence to the Select Committee on Public Libraries of the House of Commons in 1849:

- Without some assured provision of the means of continued increase, as well as simple preservation-no man ever secured to posterity the true advantage of a public library. To those persons, therefore, who took thought of such matters, two principles to start with seemed plain. The one that new libraries should be formed in a catholic spirit. The other, that they should be freed from all dependence either in gifts or in current 'subscriptions', for their permanent support. The first principle involved the corollary that the new institutions and their management should stand entirely aloof from party influences in politics or religion. The second principle involved the corollary that the maintenance must be by rate, levied on the whole tax-paying community, and administered by its elective and responsible functionaries.

This statement quite obviously implied that a legal basis was necessary, if the public library was to be a permanent institution and on the implications of this statement most of the public library legislation of the nineteenth century and early twentieth century was founded.

In 1949, Unesco issued the first international declaration on the need and the functions of the public library, and in it was contained the same principle:

- This manifesto, by describing the potentialities of the public library, proclaims Unesco's belief in the public library as a living force for popular education and for the growth of international understanding and thereby for the promotion of peace.
- The public library is a product of modern democracy and a practical demonstration of democracy's faith in universal education as a lifelong process.
- Though primarily intended to serve the educational needs of adults, the public library should also supplement the work of schools in developing the reading tastes of children and young people, helping them to become adults who can use books with appreciation and profit.
- As a democratic institution operated by the people for the people, the public library should be: established and maintained under clear authority of law: supported wholly or mainly from public funds: open for free use on equal terms to all members of the community, regardless of occupa-tion, creed, class, or race.

The manifesto goes on to define the purposes and list some of the services of the public library. It did not, however, attempt to deal with a problem that was already engaging the attention of public librarians and those concerned with the spread of education and literacy, that there must not only be a legal base, but that that base must give equal opportunity to all citizens to use the services of public libraries. In other words, the legislation must be mandatory and cover the whole of the area falling within the scope of the legislation. The legislation must also provide for something more than opportunities for voluntary co-operation between libraries-it must provide for a nation-wide service, even though the public library remains a locally rooted institution. In 1953, Unesco organized its first seminar on public libraries in developing countries, at Ibadan, in Nigeria. Eighteen countries were represented, mostly in West Africa. Legislation was one of the primary subjects discussed, and in the general report of the seminar, the following statement of principles was included:

- Only legislation can empower the appropriate authorities to provide the service and ensure adequate financial support and efficient administration according to a national standard. Only legislation can define the functions of the providing authority, create the conditions in which it may fulfil those functions, and ensure development.

Library law for national schemes should include the following elements:

- General authorization of expenditure without fixing a maximum.
- Compulsory implementation whenever conditions become favourable. The basis of favourable conditions, it is suggested, is the possession

of necessary finance and all requisite material by the providing authority, the existence of a tested organization and the presence of trained and experienced personnel. Compulsory provision is never likely to precede compulsory primary education.

- The obligation to employ only qualified and trained personnel as librarians, and to authorize development only when professional librarians are available to administer the service.
- Service for the entire population in some form or other.
- The inter-lending of books between libraries so that the book resources of the whole territory shall be available to all.
- The book stock shall embrace every shade of opinion, without prejudice to anyone.
- The national scheme in all its parts shall aim at free service.

An addendum to this statement pointed out that there was great difficulty in arriving at a conclusion regarding compulsory legislation, since it was recognized that permissive legislation might well allow for a high standard to be set by enthusiastic authorities, which would act as an inspiration to others. This, and other proposals of the Ibadan seminar, were an act of faith at the time they were published, in view of the conditions of West Africa at the time, just beginning to emerge from colonial rule, with very few African librarians. But the statement was the beginning from which can be traced the rapid development of public library services in Ghana, Eastern Nigeria and Sierra Leone, based on simple but mandatory legislation. In 1955, the Public Libraries Section of the International Federation of Library Associations published a memorandum on the development of public library services, of which one section was devoted to legislation:

Each State should adopt library laws which will include the following provisions:

- Appropriate local authorities must be empowered to expend public funds for public library purposes.
- The amount of local expenditure should not be limited: local authorities should be able to expend as much as they are willing and able.
- The public library purposes for which funds may be expended shall be so defined as not to restrict development.
- Local authorities should be empowered to enter into arrangements with other local authorities for joint schemes for providing the whole or any part of the service, and to contribute to the cost of schemes for cooperation and mutual assistance.
- Each local authority should appoint a library committee directly responsible to the local council.

- Each local authority should have power to appoint staff who shall be employed in accordance with the conditions and regulations applicable to other local government officers.
- The use of all the services provided must be available to all inhabitants free of any charge whatsoever.
- Though each local authority provides services primarily for the use of its own inhabitants and those who work or study in its area, other persons living outside that area should be able to use those services if they wish... when adequate library services are provided generally in a country or region, however, they should be available to all, regardless of place of residence, without payment.

As soon as practicable, all appropriate local authorities should be legally obliged to maintain adequate public library services. The document was adopted as a statement of policy, with the recommendation that it be sent for study to all governments and appropriate agencies concerned. One further example may be given of the continuing concern with the importance of library legislation. In October 1955, Unesco organized a further seminar on public libraries, this time at Delhi, India, where a successful demonstration project had been founded. The seminar was held in the Delhi Public Library and twelve Asian countries were represented by forty-six librarians and educators. Again, public library legislation and its nature were under discussion, and the following proposals were accepted:

Over-all control and co-operation of development, to provide for a permanent and progressive national public library service, can be obtained only by legislation, which should provide for the following:

- Opportunity for the development of public library service which will be available to all people on the basis of free and equal access.
- An independent service, and not one attached to another department.
- The constitution of a governing body, to be referred to in this report as the central library board, or in a federal state a number of such bodies, subject to a national body with advisory functions.
- Provision for adequate public finance.
- The constitution of district library boards responsible for administration of units of public library service.

Other parts of the report pay tribute to the work done by private bodies in founding and maintaining public library services, but affirm that planned direction and control are now required, and that these cannot be achieved by subsidy to private organizations. On finance the report states: It is of fundamental importance that finance should be by public funds, whether national, state or local, or a combination of these... differences in the structure, powers and financial resources of government at local, state, and national level are such that a simple statement of general applicability cannot be made. It can be said however that sources of finance must be adequate for the support of the service established. The proportion of local funds to national or state funds is a matter for decision by individual governments.

On the unit of service:

- At an early stage in the establishment of a national public library service, the question arises of the convenient administrative unit. This may be defined as the smallest autonomous unit of public library service... the selection of this unit as the real basis for the development of public library service, is a matter of some importance. It should be a viable area as regards finance and administration, and should conform as for as possible to existing local government boundaries... for ideal development, the area chosen should contain both rural and urban districts.

It is illustrative of the complexity of the problem that these four authoritative statements on public library development, issued over a short period of time, should vary so greatly in their emphasis. The Unesco Manifesto concentrated on the value and use of the public library, but said nothing about its financial or legislative base. The Ibadan seminar defined as a first principle that only legislation could provide the necessary secure and permanent foundations. It said nothing about the administrative unit on which implementation must depend, or financial problems, but it did prescribe mandatory legislation under favourable conditions.

The IFLA statement, though it defined the nature of public library service, proposed what was in fact permissive legislation, and it did not make any proposals about central control, the size of the administrative area, or financial viability of local authority areas. Although it said there should be no upper limit on expenditure, it did not mention the vital problem of minimum expenditure. The Delhi seminar proposals, with the previous statements before it, went much further, and proposed legislation which would provide for over-all control, viable areas and financial support at national and local level. But it found itself in difficulties when it attempted to define the nature of the viable area. Any acceptable general statement must be vitiated by the enormous differences between countries in national administrative and executive structure, local government and its relationship to central government, the powers existing at different levels of government, and above all, the financial capacity of these different levels.

The stage of educational and technical development of a country must also be taken into account, but this is possibly not quite as important as it may appear. While literacy is obviously a primary requirement of public library use, most countries now have an extensive programme of primary and secondary education, and in many countries, too, advanced technology exists side by side with primitive standards of living in some areas. It should also be remembered that in the last century, in some countries, notably the United Kingdom, public library legislation actually preceded general legislation on education. It would be a mistake, also, to assume that the problems of public library legislation are confined to the developing countries. If there is one thing that emerges quite clearly from this study of public library law, it is that the problems of an adequate and effective library law are just as great in the more advanced countries as in the developing ones, apart from the fact that some advanced countries do not yet have a general public library law.

In some countries, such as the United Kingdom, the United States and Canada, the problem is primarily one of reshaping law which is defective and inadequate to meet the need of the user of the public library in the twentieth century, who requires access to the enormous and increasing flood of printed material, numbered in books by the hundred thousand, and periodicals by the thousand. These requirements create in their turn a need for more and more specialized and trained personnel. The search is for a legislative base for viable units which can meet the readers' needs, and provide not only the material, but the technical services, equipment and staff required.

In other advanced countries, such as Norway and Denmark, the problem is not one of the viable unit, which in fact cannot be provided, but of compulsory co-operation to give the same results.

The problems facing the developing countries may be different, but not so very different. It has often been stated that in social legislation, some African and Asian countries are at the stage others had reached in the nineteenth century. This is only superficially true. We are all living in the twentieth century. If the legislation of the nineteenth century is to be repeated, there is a long road to travel. Not only long, but unnecessary. The example of the past is to be learned from, not repeated.

Basic Principles and Practical Considerations in the Framing of Legislation

Assuming for the purpose of this chapter that new legislation is being considered, the first consideration in the framing of legislation is, of course, the nature of the State itself and the place that legislation takes in its structure. Particularly in social legislation such as the establishment of public libraries, which has primarily a local impact, account must be taken of the nature of the authority by which national government passes on its responsibilities, the basis of taxation at local and national level and in a federal State, the constitutional rights of established organisms within the State. Even where there is no general legislation, in countries where the doctrine of ultra quires does not apply and organs of local government may establish any service they are not specifically forbidden to do, public libraries may exist perfectly legally by local legislation, and this in turn will cause difficulties in framing a general law.

This is the case in the Federal Republic of Germany, and to some extent in the Netherlands and Belgium. Apart from this, there are patterns in the relationship of local government to national government which must be taken into account. H. F. Alderferl in his study of local government in developing countries, identifies four basic patterns, which are established in developing countries either through adoption or by passing on of previous colonial development. The French pattern, which exists in a large part of Africa, carries the doctrine of ultra vires much further than in England or the United States. Local government has no powers not granted to it by constituted authority.

Local government also is subject to executive jurisdiction which is independent of the administrative and legislative branch to a great extent. Generally, he states, French local government is characterized by centralization, chain of command, hierarchical structure, executive domination and legislative subordination. The English pattern, as defined by Alderfer, is characterized by decentralization, with local decision-making bodies with more or less independent powers, as against concentration, in the French pattern, where all power lies with the central government with local units acting as agents.

The English pattern generally implies also legislative dominance, the committee system and voluntary citizen participation. The Soviet system is one of 'democratic centralism', with all organs as links in one continuous chain of governmental power. Communist Party direction and leadership exist at all levels, and local agencies are not law-making or executive bodies in their own right, but subject to correction not only at the next higher level but at other levels. The 'traditional' form of local government is non-Western, though in Western forms there are traditional residues. The pattern is one of a chief or local leader, or a group of people, having jurisdiction over a village or group of villages. Essentially the form is non-urban, but it has deep roots and cannot be ignored as a working unity.

The Indian panchayat system of local government is an example of a traditional form being incorporated into the local government system of a modern State, organized generally on the English system. The clash between two systems, and the different types of law that may be produced, was illustrated in Africa when, at a UNESCO seminar at Enugu in I961, the question of a model Act for African countries was discussed. The Act proposed was on the English model. This was simple and mandatory, giving almost unlimited authority to an independent board, subject to central government control. It was this type of legislation which has been successful in practice in Ghana, Eastern Nigeria and Tanzania.

The delegates from the French-speaking countries could not accept this since it was not an acceptable type of legislation for their countries, and they proposed a different model Act for their purposes. Without quoting this in full, it can be said that it was at once more detailed and less specific. Though it set up a directorate attached to the Ministry of Education, and advisory bodies, it could be said to be rather a statement of intention than a legislative instrument. Subsequent decrees in the various territories have similar structure. Thus, the decree for the Ivory Coast goes into some detail on expenditures and staff required, but does not provide for means of raising the necessary funds or an organization charged with continuous development.

The differences may be more apparent than real, given a determination to create a public library service, but it does seem that in Europe, the Scandinavian countries, the United Kingdom and Ireland have been more successful, through planned co-operation between local and national government, than for instance, in France. A recent survey in Le Monde of the public libraries of Paris showed enormous variations in expenditure on libraries in the various communes, with seemingly no co-operation or standards imposed centrally. A generous system of subsidies for building is offered by the central government, but there does not appear to be any way of forcing local authorities to take advantage of them if they do not wish to provide their share.

There are other, important factors to consider in pre-consideration of legislation. Some investigation must be made of the practical problems, and a body of facts built up. While the survey is important, it must be a practical move towards action, and not an end in itself or a means of delaying action. One of the most successful librarians in charge of a library service in a developing country has said that until a service is provided it is impossible to say what sort of service is needed. A careful analysis at grass roots level involves a detailed statistical examination of a community-its growth rate, its educational levels, its literacy rates; it involves the testing of different types of reading materials and a survey of existing places for reading and studying.

Such an approach overlooks the complete lack of basic statistics on which to base the survey. And above all, it ignores the sense of urgency which permeates any developing country trying to pull itself into the twentieth century by its bootstraps. I am sure that these critics would produce a magnificent report. . . and that report would probably conclude that the contemplation of any form of library service was premature.

By the time it appeared it would have been overtaken by events, such is the speed of development of Africa today. This may be overstating the case against survey, but it is true that a survey should be made after decision-to discover specific problems and how they might be overcome.

These problems can be summarized as follows:

- *Educational Situation:* The provision of libraries depends on adult literacy, and is also concerned with the provision of primary education. Literacy rates based on averages are deceptive-for instance, the adult literacy rate in India is less than 20 per cent, but in Delhi in 1954 it was nearly 40 per cent and is now over 50 per cent. The Government of India report of 1959 did not consider that a literacy rate of 20 per cent was any barrier to a nationally organized public library service, but of course one would assume that a low average literacy rate would suggest concentration on urban areas. In terms of cost relative to use, there would be no point in providing for an elaborate system of mobile libraries to serve rural areas.

- *Language and Book Production:* The number of languages in use and their relative importance is a factor in pre-consideration. Allied to this is the matter of book production. Lack of book production in the national language is an extreme limiting factor, though the establishment of public libraries may well stimulate production and in fact has done so in some countries. But it must be observed that the success of public library development in some African countries has been due largely to the fact that English is the established language of communication, thus giving immediate access to an abundant source of material.
- *Population Density and Concentration:* It goes without saying that a rural and scattered population is more difficult to provide for than an urban one. The problem therefore is not one so much of over-all density as of concentration, and this can well affect the unit of administration
- *Communications:* This also affects the matter of the unit, and administrative arrangements. Decentrali-zation may well be necessary. This may be a problem of organization rather than legislation, but it must be considered.
- *Income and tax structure:* This affects the time factor during which legislation can be expected to come into effect, and also the proportion of cost to be met from various sources.
- *Existing Legislation:* This may exist nationally or locally, and consideration must be given to its possible incorporation in new legislation. In some countries, Ceylon is an example, effective public libraries exist in some areas through local legislation, and a new library law must take into account their existence and their legislative base.
- *'Trained Librarians and Training Facilities:* While most countries will have trained librarians, though not in public libraries, pre-consideration must take into account the availability of trained librarians to implement legislation. Opportunities for training abroad must also be considered. While it is an important consideration, the availability of trained librarians is no more than a temporary limiting factor, since there is little point in training unless there are opportunities for

employment. In India and Pakistan, facilities for training and qualification are in advance of employment possibilities in the public sector-not only bad planning but wasteful public policy.

These are some of the major items For pre-consideration and survey. The objective is to determine what a country can afford, how great is the need, what structure is required, and how legislation can assist rapid development, without placing too great a burden on financial ability or the administrative structure. None of them should be over-emphasized. The objective remains the same; the limiting factors affect how it is to be attained and at what speed. In this connation, the object by E. M. Broome repays careful study. Nearly all these limiting factors were present, but none of them deterred the Government of Tanzania from passing legislation and implementing it with determination and success.

As was reported at the Delhi seminar:

- In all countries represented at the seminar, public library service is already being provided in some degree, and the time is ripe for further development. In no country do the material difficulties appear to be unsurmountable, nor is a low literacy rate a decisive adverse factor. The rate of development may vary with the speed of overcoming these problems, but the basis for public library services should be laid now. The major deficiencies in present provisions are: lack of over-all control, and the existence of small unco-ordinated units; lack of, or deficiencies in, existing legislation; lack of sufficient funds and government interest; and lack of trained and experienced librarians.

Practical Considerations in Framing Legislation

It has been said that it is easier to pass a law than it is to change it, and this is a lesson to be learned from existing legislation. In the United Kingdom, for nearly seventy years only minor amendments were made to the enabling legislation, despite the fact that under the existing law there was no means by which county councils could set up public library services for rural populations.

Legislation should therefore be flexible and allow for changes in social conditions, in local-government structure and in the tax base. It should be capable of immediate application, but with progressive application. Study is made of the comparative merits and defects of existing legislation, but certain basic problems can be enumerated for primary consideration.

The Public Library as an Independent Service or Part of a National Library Service

In any country which can even consider the foundation of a public library service, there will already be in existence many libraries of high standard: university libraries, libraries of institutions, government departmental libraries, technical libraries and almost certainly a national and probably state libraries. It is tempting to think that there is an advantage in creating an integrated library service of which such libraries are a part. But it must be remembered that public libraries are for the whole community, whereas all other libraries are designed to serve a section of the community for a special purpose, and that purpose must be their prime consideration. Techniques are similar, but basic purposes are different. Uniting all libraries in one piece of legislation at an early stage is hardly practical, since not only would it tend to stifle the growth of the public library, but it would also entail bringing independent libraries under the legislation, and this would undoubtedly be resisted.

At the same time, there is an obvious need for provision for cooperation and some co-ordination, probably best organized around the national library. Bibliographical and interloan functions should be of value to all libraries. The national library could therefore be usefully linked to the central public library authority.

The Central Authority

The need for a central authority charged with carrying out the provisions of legislation is clear. Should it be an independent body or one linked to, or subordinate to, a government department? This is a matter for decision at governmental level. There are advantages in making the central authority part of the department of education, with a department for libraries and controlling body, which should have more than advisory functions. The central board or authority is a modern device of government much used in developing countries, and experience of its past success in other circumstances will affect legislation for public libraries. But the implementation of legislation should not be left to any other body but education, and if education is chosen as the implementing and organizing department, then a section including trained librarians is essential, with advisory and inspecting functions.

Permissive or Mandatory Legislation

It has been shown that permissive legislation is of limited effectiveness, even when accompanied by financial inducements. Legislation should therefore require action to be taken, wherever the ultimate source of action. But provision should be made for progressive implementation at a rate to be determined by resources.

Relationship Between Local and Central Authority

It is generally accepted that the public library is a local community service. In fact, this becomes less and less true with the explosive growth in production of information material and technical developments in library organization. The answer must be sought in the local government structure of the country concerned. In some countries, a nationally controlled public library service has been created, with provision for some devolution to local government at later stages. The existence of federally organized states also presents some problems. But it must be stated that local interest is desirable and must be stimulated. This implies the passing over of some authority, or the creation of local advisory bodies.

The Size of' the Unit

Assuming that local authority interest is essential, the question then arises: what unit, what size and with what authority? The lbadan seminar, speaking for the situation in Africa, concluded that since recognition of local authority was only beginning, the sole public authority should be the national or state agency. At the same time, the appropriate local authority must eventually be given a responsible place in any national scheme of book service. The roots of the service must be in the local community rather than in the state, regional or national headquarters.

The size and authority of the local unit are important questions, even when there is a suitable urban authority. An urban authority should never be the sole local unit, since its economic and social catchment area is equally important for public library purposes. The requirements for a viable unit, as we have seen, were well stated in the report of the Delhi seminar, but it is already clear, fifteen years later, that they are expanding. In developed countries for example, much larger units than previously thought necessary are now postulated, and the basing of a service on too small a unit can be disastrously hampering in later development. Apart from size, there are other considerations. Whatever the attachment at national level, it is generally conceded that at local level the public library service should be executively independent of other agencies, whether education or other departments such as cultural affairs or social education.

The public library serves all, but is not solely a part of any, SO it should remain independently governed and administered. The question of policy control is a matter of the form local government takes. There is much to be said for the board system, independent but responsible to the local-government system, but this is not always legally possible. But it should be possible at all times to bring into consultation persons of knowledge and goodwill.

Finance

It is generally now accepted that financial support for public libraries should come from public funds, that is, taxation. It is also generally recognized that the service should be free to the user, though this is not always the case in practice. In most developing countries, this means major support at national level, with assistance at local level so far as practicable, having regard to the limitations of local taxation in most developing countries. The acceptance of this principle has been a major limiting factor in public library progress, even in advanced countries, as will be demonstrated in study of existing legislation. It follows, therefore, that any unit at local level must be a tax-raising body, and provision for funds from taxation at a national level must be written in to any legislation. In a federal system, of course, another stage of financial support will be introduced.

Various calculations of the cost of a public library service have been made, but they are of little value in view of changing needs, and could not sensibly be included in basic legislation. No one would expect a public library service to spring armed and ready from the ground, like Jason's dragons' teeth, and financial provision must depend on the rate of implementation of legislation. The Government of India report of 1959 postulated a period of twenty-five years for the creation of a full service, but its calculations as to cost are already completely out of date. Given progressive implementation, standards of service required are also a matter for progressive regulation, and not a suitable one for inclusion in legislation. The power to make regulations on standards and other matters should, however, be given.

Other Considerations

There are several other considerations which may have to be taken into account in framing legislation, but their importance will vary according to country. In some countries, there will be a problem of fitting in private or subscription libraries to the system. There must also be some provision for co-operation between libraries, but this again will vary with the primary decisions already taken. If a linkage with the national library, for instance, is envisaged, or if the unit of service is the whole country, then these provisions can be taken care of automatically under regulation. But if existing resources, as provided by various agencies, are to be fully utilized, then some provision for co-operation and inter-lending must be made. Although university and institutional libraries may not be fully integrated, their resources, after their first priorities are met, should be circulated generally. Whether library education, or the encouragement of library associations, should be incorporated in legislation is a moot point.

It could be fairly argued that if opportunity for employment of qualified people is given by the provision of a public library service, then educational institutions will provide the necessary further education facilities for training librarians and technicians, without any legal requirement to do so. Library associations, also, should not be too dependent on legislative assistance. Again, the provision of a service will itself exert the necessary stimulus for the creation of an active body of professional librarians. And if such associations are to encourage further progress and technical improvement, they should be independent. All these problems and others applying to particular countries will need to be closely considered before framing suitable legislation in terms which will create a permanent, expanding public library service available to all people, whatever their age, status or geographical situation.

The way in which the problems have already been approached and the answers embodied in legislation is the subject of the next stage. There are many lessons to be learned, and the gap between intentions and results is often a depressing commentary on how the goodwill of legislators can be frustrated by circumstances unforeseen or unsuspected. Government and legislation are, alas, by no means an exact science. But in the framework of the modern State, legislation as an instrument of authority is necessary. In the case of public libraries it can truthfully be said that no successful public library system can exist without legal authority, but that many devices have been necessary to get round defective legislation. Public libraries happen to be the subject of this study, but no doubt authorities on law and government could produce better examples of problems caused by legislation rather than solved by it.

The Pattern of Legislation Comparative Solutions

The main body of this study consists of summaries of the existing legislation in fourteen countries, and taking into account the federal countries, twenty Acts are considered, with others mentioned in passing. More could have been chosen, but in fact, not more than thirty countries have effective general library legislation, less than a quarter of the independent nations of the world. Of the countries chosen, four are developing countries, two are countries with centrally planned economies and three are federally organized.

This, therefore can be considered a reasonably representative sample, ranging from the most advanced countries, where coverage is complete and basic standards established, to a country which has only just become independent, Botswana. They all have one thing in common; in none of them is legislation, even now, entirely satisfactory and effective, in that it encourages development to the point of greatest efficiency and maximum results. All have problems to some degree, despite the fact that in most of the countries considered there has been revision of law in the last ten years. The advanced countries, most of which have had public library legislation in some form for many years, but with varying effectiveness, have no great problem of financial ability to provide a nationwide system of public libraries, if that ability can be brought to bear.

The problem is rather one of an inadequate and unsuitable local-government structure, and the supplementation of local resources, or in some examples, replacement of local initiative, by central-government intervention. A pattern clearly emerges in nearly all recent legislation, first of a search for a larger and more viable unit of service, which must be both geographically and financially able to deploy larger resources for public library service, and second of the creation of a central advisory body to encourage improvement of public library service. One can see similarities in the solutions adopted, but there are also wide variations.

It is proposed in this chapter to show by comparison the major similarities and variations of the law as it stands in advanced countries. There are important lessons to be learned by the developing countries in framing their own legislation, and it appears that the advanced countries could also learn from their neighbours. In making these comparisons, it must of course be borne in mind that though public library law is evolutionary in character, it cannot be separated from the general body of law of a country, and it must be set in the executive, social and geopolitical structure of the country concerned.The fact that some countries with a high educational and cultural standard have not so far been able to enact general mandatory legislation on public libraries proves this to be the case. Permissive legislation has been replaced by mandatory legislation in most countries. The appropriate local authorities are now required rather than permitted to provide a public library service.

In some countries, notably the United Kingdom, Finland and Sweden, mandatory provision is not necessary, since coverage is already complete. In Norway, obligatory provision is laid down in the Act, and in Denmark a date is set for all communes to provide public libraries. In Canada and the United States, though provision is not mandatory, the problem is no longer one of provision but of viability, and this could be said generally of all the countries considered, except the countries having centrally planned economies, where the law has nothing to say on this. But it would appear that in Hungary, at any rate, there is complete coverage.

Central Government and Advisory Bodies

In all countries, the intervention of the central government, either at state or federal level, or both, has led to the setting up of a central body to guide future progress, and this is the most common feature in all recent legislation. These central bodies may take many forms, either advisory or executive. They may be independent, or responsible to a department of State. Their membership may be drawn from organizations or individuals. Their constitution and powers can be summarized as follows:

Czechoslovakia

The Central Library Council is an advisory body in the Ministry of Education and Culture. There are two bodies, one for Bohemia-Moravia and one for Slovakia. Membership consists of representatives of authorities and expert librarians. All proposals concerning libraries are submitted to them, and they have the right to initiate proposals themselves.

Denmark

The Library Council consists of sixteen members representing all sections of the Danish Library Service. They are appointed by the Minister of Cultural Affairs, are consulted in all matters of importance to the working of the Libraries Act, and have the right to initiate representations. The chairman is the Library Director, head of the State inspectorate.

Finland

The library delegation is an advisory body responsible to the Central Board of Schools. There are twelve delegates, representing the Department of Education, local authorities, library training and other organizations working for libraries and adult education. The delegation can take the initiative in submitting proposals to the Central Board of Schools.

Hungary

The National Council for Library Activity, responsible to the Ministry of Culture, has a section for public libraries. It has also a working organization, the State Institute of Libraries, similar in some respects to the State inspectorates of Scandinavian library systems. The functions of the National Council are advisory and technical, but being a direct organ of central government, it obviously has great prestige.

Ireland

The Library Council has as its main purpose the operation and supervision of the Irish Central library, and a secondary purpose of assisting local library authorities to improve their services. Its membership is by nomination, and a majority of the members are nominated by universities or the National Library. The powers of the Library Council are considerable, since it considers applications for grants from local authorities and its functions are much more than advisory. In view of the form of local government in Ireland, it can be said to be an executive body with potentially great powers. In fact, the original secondary function has become the primary one.

Qntario

The Provincial Library Council is an advisory body responsible to the Minister for Education, and it consists of nine members appointed by the minister, and one for each regional system. It has certain functions under the Act and may also make recommendations regarding development and co-ordination of library service.

Quebec

The Quebec Public Libraries Commission is responsible to the Minister for Cultural Affairs. Its membership is six persons nominated by the minister, whose qualifications shall be their interest in the development of public libraries, and the Director of Public Libraries of the Province. The powers and duties of the commission are wide, in that it is generally charged with the study of the best means of developing public library services, and it must report every three months on its findings regarding the working of the Public Libraries Act.

United Kingdom

The Library Advisory Councils, set up by the Minister of Education under the 1964 Act, one for England and one for Wales, have no set number of members, nor any stated qualifications for membership. They are nominated directly by the minister, and actually the representatives are drawn from local authority members, university and public librarians representing all the major interests of local government and various sizes and types of library. The function of the councils is purely advisory, and their main work is in connexion with the achievement of standards and the general working of the Act. But by their existence, they have become the advisory bodies for libraries in general, and on such matters as librarianship training.

Washington State

The State Library Commission is an executive commission appointed by the Governor, and responsible for administration of federal and state funds for improvement of public library services. It operates through the state library and appoints the state librarian, who acts as secretary to the commission. Though its main functions are executive, it also has advisory responsibilities. The functions of these bodies are mainly advisory, and as will be seen generally from their constitutions, are intended as a source of expert opinion on public library development.

They are useful bodies, but equally important, their existence creates a secretariat, and that secretariat, whether clearly laid down in legislation as in Quebec, or not, as in England and Wales, inevitably assumes supervisory functions. Those functions can be of inspection and control, as in Finland and Denmark, or they can be limited to advice to the appropriate minister and the right to ask for regular reports and give advice to individual library authorities. Even where there is no central coordinating body, there is invariably a central coordinating government department.

In Norway, the State inspectorate is recognized by the Act, and the State Inspector is a direct appointment of the Crown, though responsible to the Ministry of Church and Education. In Sweden, there is a Library Section of the Central Board of Education, and its functions include supervision of State grants, approval of building plans, and supervision of the School of Librarianship. With the change in local government law, its functions are now more limited, being more advisory than supervisory. In the United States, in addition to the state departments concerned with public libraries, now established in most states, there is an office in the Department of Education in Washington charged with supervision of the very substantial grants under the Library Services and Construction Act. Except in Scandinavia, where they have been in existence for many years, the emergence of these bodies and the departments attached to them is comparatively recent, and their influence on public library development is bound to increase.

It will be noted that the usual attachment of the library councils and their civil-service bureaux is to the Ministry of Education, in some cases to the Minister of Culture. But this attachment at central-government levels does not necessarily imply any attachment of public libraries at lower levels of government to any particular department.

Provision for Co-Operation

In most countries, legislation shows a marked preference for the provision of public library services within the existing local-government framework, and an equal reluctance to interfere with those existing agencies, even when they are clearly not viable. The only exception to this in recent legislation, where smaller authorities are required to give up their powers, is in England and Wales, where there is provision for the compulsory surrender of library powers by authorities of less than 40,000 population.

Even here, the clauses have not so far been used, since a major local-government reform is expected to make them unnecessary. Local-government reform in Sweden and Denmark is also making the problem less urgent, though it will still exist. Failing the forcible creation of larger public library authorities, the search for the larger unit must take the form of co-operation, and recent legislation is characterized by the creation of a superstructure of co-ordination, often at two or three levels, either mandatory or permissive. Library authorities are either to be persuaded to join with others in a library system, or a superstructure of co-operation is created above them, in which they have the opportunity, or are compelled, to take part. Financial assistance is usually given. Some examples of this kind of provision are as follows:

Denmark

A number of suitable libraries are designated as county libraries, serving a district. Their functions are to assist the local libraries in the district by lending or obtaining for them books and other suitable materials they cannot provide themselves, and by giving advice and technical assistance. In the present legislation, the Library Director recommends which libraries shall be recognized as county libraries, and the minister shall ensure that the district served is of a suitable size and that the county library is able to carry out its functions. In the past, it is thought, too many county libraries were designated, and the districts were too small. The provision is mandatory, that is to say, all libraries must join a district, and an advisory committee is formed to direct the work. National grants are made to the county libraries, and the county or counties must also contribute at rates laid down. The communes themselves do not contribute directly.

Norway

The system of regional central libraries is similar, except that the designated libraries have wider functions in super-vision of their local libraries. The problems of establishment, and suitable areas, are very great in Norway, and though nineteen regional libraries have now been established, they vary greatly in resources. Again the inclusion in an area is mandatory, and grants are made to meet the cost, with supplementary grants from the areas covered.

Sweden

In addition to the establishment of county libraries on similar lines to Denmark and Norway, a further superstructure has been added of three inter-library loan centres, which lend to the county libraries and receive grants for their services from the State. It must be emphasized that in the Scandinavian countries, the aid-giving libraries are the larger libraries in their area, and though they may establish special departments for their additional functions, in no sense, except in a limited way in Norway, do they administer or supervise the other libraries in their area.

Quebec

The regional libraries in Quebec are quite different from others, and serve a different purpose. They are intended, not to superimpose an additional system, but to encourage the provision of public library service in those sparsely populated areas which cannot provide for themselves, even with grant aid. The system is fully described in the appropriate section, but briefly, when a minimum area containing 25,000 inhabitants can be defined, an ad hoc committee is formed. The kind of service depends on the size of the area and other factors, but generally, grant is 85 per cent of the total cost. Such a system is only required under extreme adverse conditions, but the similarity to the Norwegian system in its northern area is obvious.

Ontario

The Ontario method of creating larger areas is in effect a three-tier system. In a county, a combined library system can be formed at the request of 75 per cent of the authorities in the county, then a county library service is formed, and a separate public library board set up. But it is only responsible for that part of the county which has asked for inclusion. The system has obvious defects, but it does have the effect of helping some at least of the smaller authorities to combine. Superimposed on this system of county libraries and independent libraries is provision for regional library systems, working roughly on the Scandinavian pattern, and having similar responsibilities. Substantial grants are available from state funds, but regions are not necessarily inclusive of all the libraries in their area since, throughout the legislation of Ontario, there are no mandatory powers.

United States of America

There are no mandatory powers in the United States, and most recent legislation, both federal and state, has written into it an injunction that the independence of the community library is to be respected and preserved.

The creation of the larger unit therefore is by the voluntary amalgamation of independent libraries into 'systems', in which service is often provided by contract between one library and another. It is interesting to note that current thinking puts the minimum viability of a system at 150,000 population.

United Kingdom

A voluntary system of co-operation has existed for many years, with member libraries paying subscriptions usually on a per capita basis. The country is divided into fourteen regions for this purpose. The 1964 Act legally recognizes this system, and provides for compulsory membership by all library authorities, and for amalgamation of the regions where necessary.

Two of the largest regions, comprising London and the south-east of England, have already amalgamated, with the authority of the Ministry of Education. The purpose of the regions is principally inter-library co-operation, and for this purpose provision is made in legislation for bringing into the system other than public libraries.

LIBRARY LEGISLATION IN INDIA

India became an independent republic in January 1950. It is a federal union of states, there being seventeen states and ten union territories. The form of government is democratic, with a president and two Houses of Parliament. The Upper House, or Council of States, is indirectly elected, the members being elected by the legislative assembly of each state. The Lower House, or House of the People, consists of 500 members directly elected by adult suffrage. Each state has its own legislature, directly elected.

Certain legislative powers are retained by the central government, but education, the most important function so far as libraries are concerned, is reserved to the states, though there is a central Ministry of Education with co-ordinating powers, including that of making grants for specific purposes.

These powers have been increased by the very large sums made available under successive Five-year Plans. The area of India is 1,262,275 square miles, and its population approxi-mately 5II million.

Local Government

Local government is in the hands of some 2700 municipal authorities which have primary functions relating to their own areas and frame their own budgets, though usually, however, these require approval at state level. For rural areas there is a three-tier system of panchayats, or local councils-at village, block and district levels.

Generally speaking, the block panchayats consist of groupings of village panchayats, but this does not apply to the whole of India, There are nearly 4000 block panchayats, and some 212,000 village panchayats. The district is the taxing authority below the state. The system is virtually complete and one can therefore say that local administration proceeds from state to city, district or municipality, and right down to its roots in the villages.

Education

The literacy percentage is approximately 24 - men 34.5, women 13. Despite this very low rate of literacy, very great progress has been made in education, and the rate has been improved by 8 per cent since 1951. Over ₹5,000 million were spent on education in 1964 and over 750,000 primary and secondary schools were in operation. The official national language under the Constitution is Hindi, but under the Official Language Act of 1963, English will continue to be used as an official language for an indefinite period alongside Hindi. The regional language of the state is also taught at various levels. There are fourteen officially recognized regional languages.

Library Provision

In the light of the facts the problems of public library provision are very great. India is a very large country with a predominantly rural population, a small per capita income and a number of recognized languages. There are other problems, arising from the local-government system and the relations of the central government to the states. India is a federal State and, as in Canada and the United States, provision of public libraries is reserved to the states and is their sole responsibility. Even grants under the Five-year Plans, given specifically in the past for public library development, were changed under the third plan to block grants to be spent at the discretion of the states. The central government has therefore no coercive powers to enforce legislation by the states, or to dictate the form of such legislation.

The legal powers to take over the many private or association libraries are also limited. To bring them into the public sector would require separate legislation which is unlikely to be voted. In view of the numbers of such libraries, this is important. Given a government determined enough to create a nation-wide public library system, the position could, of course, be changed.

There is a national Ministry of Education, and it could be given coordinating functions. In fact, the Advisory Committee of I 959 proposed this in the form of an All-India Library Advisory Council, with an executive committee nominated by the Minister of Education, and a secretariat consisting of a division of libraries in the Ministry of Education.

It also suggested that the Government of India should contribute to the library funds of the state an amount equal to funds raised by property tax. Presumably, these proposals would require legislation at national level. Despite many obstacles, India has a strong and continuing literary tradition, and there is a thirst for knowledge which is evidenced by the fact that over 10,000 periodicals and newspapers are published in India. Book production, although its organization is chaotic, flourishes and there is not in fact, any shortage of libraries. Very few Indian towns or even large villages are without a library of some sort, provided by a charitable foundation, by an educational organization or by executive action on the part of state, municipal or district authority.

Very few of these institutions are well endowed, many are little more than reading-rooms. In this connexion, the statement by the Advisory Committee on Libraries, which reported in 1959, is of value in estimating the true position:

- In India the phrase 'public libraries' is used in a very loose sense. It is used to denote any library which permits members of the public to use its material for reference or borrowing on payment of fees or rent. In this sense, all kinds of libraries, national, university, schools and subscription libraries, etc., would be public libraries. Because of the loose connotation of the term, it would appear from the statistics published by Unesco in 1956 that India leads the world in the number of public libraries, which is given as 24,086. The statistics are flattering; they express the aspiration rather than the achievement of the country. The internationally accepted definition of a public library is that it is a library which is:
  - Is financed out of public funds;
  - Charges no fees from readers and yet is open for full use by the public without distinction of caste, creed or sex;
  - Is intended as an auxiliary educational institution providing a means of self education which is endless;
  - Houses learning materials giving reliable information freely and without partiality or prejudice on as wide a variety of subjects as will satisfy the interests of readers. Were such a definition adopted, the number of public libraries in India could not be counted by tens, let alone by hundreds or thousands.

A framework of library provision does, however, exist, and it has been expanded by grants under successive five-year plans, at national level. In the first five-year plan, 1951-56, a scheme of improvement of library service was included calling for a network of libraries to be spread over the whole country. The kernel of the scheme was the establishment of district libraries, which would circulate books throughout the district. These were to be supplemented and supported by a central library for the whole state, or for a whole linguistic region. A supplementary scheme to set up integrated library units was also commended to state governments in connexion with the areas selected for intensive educational development. Under successive Five-year Plans, the schemes have been developed but have not so far been backed up generally by a legislative base, despite strong recommendations by the Advisory Committee in 1959.

These recommendations were for a comprehensive state library law, which would provide for free library service for all. Funds would be provided by a library rate on property tax, the income to be covered by a matching State grant. The unit of library service would be the district. Proposals were also made for legislative action by the Government of India to collate the various Copyright and Book Deposit Acts and to make them viable for a national library service. The Act should also provide for assistance to state governments for public library service. Since provision of public libraries by executive action is an important feature in public library provision in developing countries, a typical example in India, that of West Bengal, is worthy of brief examination.

West Bengal Library System

West Bengal not only contains the largest city in India, Calcutta, but also India's National Library. Its population is over 65 million, and the principal language is Bengali. The literacy rate is 30 per cent. The first public library was opened in Calcutta in 1836 and it was followed during the nineteenth century by the founding of many other libraries on a subscription basis. After independence, small grants were made by local authorities and from state funds, and in 1950, about 1,000 subscription libraries were receiving small grants. In 1956, a coordinated scheme was sponsored by the state government, with financial assistance on a 50 per cent basis from the Government of India.

In 1969-70 a sum of ₹4,313,000 was given in annual grants. All the districts of West Bengal now have a district library and much progress has been made in the provision of buildings, furniture and equipment. A reasonably coherent library system has now been established, with a state central library in Calcutta, over 68 district and area libraries and 579 rural libraries, with total staffs of over 1500. Many of the libraries are still subscription libraries, and grants in fact are still given to many subscription libraries outside the system. While it is a source of satisfaction that public library service has been created, it cannot be denied that it is far from ideal. Since the entire service is under the Department of Social Education, district librarians have no real executive powers, and there appears to be little co-ordination of book stocks. Above all, the lack of a legislative and tax base necessarily makes for uncertainty in future planning.

The Delhi Public Library

Another example of executive action is the Delhi Public Library. This was founded by joint action of the Government of India and Unesco as a demonstration project applying Western concepts of book provision, furniture and equipment in a developing country.

In the final terms of agreement between Unesco and the Indian Government, the terms of reference for the project were set out:

> "It shall provide a public library service for the people of the City of Delhi and shall be a model for all public library development in India, and in all other countries where similar development of public libraries can be undertaken. The library shall be designed to carry out the policy of the Unesco Public Libraries Manifesto and to serve the needs of popular education."

The organizers of the library had, therefore, to plan for a library which would have complete open access to the shelves, which would make no direct charge to readers, and would be organized not for preservation, but for use by readers of all ages and all levels of education. These concepts were not new to India. They had been propagated by the devoted work of Dr. Ranganathan and his disciples. But between concept and execution there was still a wide gap, and the Delhi Public Library was the first in India, and probably the first in Asia, to apply these principles.

The library was opened in 1951 by the Prime Minister, Mr. Nehru, and the present author was consultant to the project during the first year of its life. The government of the library is by the Delhi Library Board, an autonomous body acting on behalf of the Ministry of Education.

It is a well-balanced body, now with fifteen members. The Ministry of Education, the Finance Ministry, the Delhi Municipal Corporation, the Delhi Administration and the New Delhi Municipal Committee are all represented and four experts with technical qualifications or library experience are co-opted.

The director of the library is secretary of the board and ex oficio member of it. Finance was jointly from the two sponsoring bodies in the first two years, but is now the sole responsibility of the Indian Government, with small grants from the municipal bodies. The story of the Delhi Public Library has been told many times, and it is not proposed to repeat it here. From its inception it was an enormous success, enrolling over 10,000 members in the first few months and lending over 70,000 books.

In 1966-67, membership had increased to 136,000 and annual issue of books to nearly 2 million volumes. Book stocks have increased from 14,000 to 350,000. It is still, in the words of a recent Indian writer, 'the only public library in India worth the name.' In 1955, the author was invited by Unesco to make a detailed evaluation of the project. This was published by Unesco in 1957. In 1956, the Government of India notified its acceptance of this evaluation, the preamble of which began with the statement: 'During this period of five years the library has made gratifying progress and it has, therefore, been decided to place it on a permanent basis. ' After twenty years of existence, this statement is still the only basis on which the library operates.

Its functions have never been more clearly defined than in the original terms of reference as a pilot project, and it is still not a statutory body. More curious still, though it spends over I million rupees a year, by far the greatest expenditure of a single Indian public library unit, it still has not been given over-all responsibility for providing public library service in Delhi.

In 1964, a further evaluation of the library was made by the board itself, which has this to say about the area of the library's responsibility:

> "A rather peculiar feature of the situation regarding public library service in Delhi is that in addition to the Delhi Library Board, three other bodies, *viz.*, the Delhi Administration, the Delhi Municipal Corporation and the New Delhi Municipal Committee operate a few libraries and reading rooms, and the New Delhi Municipal Committee proposes to open small lending libraries in the area within its jurisdiction. There is no co-operation at all between the several authorities administering these libraries. The fact is stated here because of a possible wasteful duplication of effort and money."

The fact that Delhi is the seat of government and has no state administration possibly accounts for the perpetuation of this rather odd situation. But one would have thought that a short enabling Act would have been possible giving the Delhi Public Library responsibility for providing all public reference and lending services in the Delhi area. Nevertheless, the Delhi Public Library has shown and continues to show that a modern public library can exist and can flourish in India.

Model Libraries Bill

In 1960, following the recommendations of the Advisory Committee on Libraries, the Government of India appointed a committee for drafting a library bill. This was submitted to the Ministry of Education in 1963 and in 1964 the ministry circulated the bill for comments to the various state governments and professional organizations. No further action has yet been taken. The bill is intended for adoption on a nation-wide basis. It would therefore need to be adopted by each state and presumably general legislation by the Government of India would be necessary to define the rights of the citizen to access to libraries, similar to those he has to education, to provide for some form of co-ordination of the various state library services and to provide for financial assistance for the state public library services as envisaged in the Model Bill.The exact form of such legislation, in view of the states' rights, is difficult to foresee, but a similar problem was solved in the United States with the Library Services Act. A long process of legislation is therefore obviously involved, and an equally long process of organization. The integration of the present systems of public libraries provided by executive action will in itself present certain problems.

State Legislation

The Model Bill has been discussed at length because it is presumably the basis on which future legislation will be founded for all the states. But four Indian states have already passed legislation: two, Madras and Andhra Pradesh, before the publication of the Advisory Committee Report and the Model Bill, and two, Mysore and Maharashtra, after the publication of the Model Bill.

Madras Act

Madras State (capital: Madras) has a population of 37 million. The literacy rate is 30 per cent. Tamil is the principal language. Madras was the first state to pass legislation to create a public library system, in 1948. This was largely due to the unremitting efforts of Dr. Ranganathan, but the bill was watered down in its various stages to make it acceptable and it is generally agreed that in its present form not only is the Act defective but that its implementation has been unsound.

In the words of S. K. Mookerjee:

> "The Madras Act and its implementation in the sphere of library organization have taught us all a very good lesson. It has shown how completely the intentions of the legislature can be flouted and the public needs neglected when such implementation is entrusted to the wrong agency."

The main provisions of the Madras Act are as follows: A state library committee is formed for the purpose of advising the government. Its membership includes the Minister in Charge of Education, who is to be president of the board, representatives of universities and local library authorities and three persons nominated by library associations in the state. But the Director of Public Instruction is named as being ex officio Director of Public Libraries and a 'Special Officer' assisting the director in the administration of the Act is secretary of the committee.

It is quite clear that it is not intended that the special officer shall be a librarian and there is no place in fact in the Act for a state librarian with technical qualifications.

It has been stated that the 'Special Officer', not a librarian, was in fact appointed with some haste. The Director of Public Libraries is charged with managing the State Central Library, superintending the work of local library authorities and superintending and directing all matters relating to public libraries in the state. The Act creates local library authorities, one for the City of Madras and one for each district, each district authority being given full powers of management of libraries within the district.

This is a much more sensible arrangement than the one in the Model Bill, in that it creates, in theory at any rate, more viable authorities. There are thirteen districts in Madras, so the average effective literate population of a district is around I million. The powers and duties of district library authorities do not, however, include provision for the appointment of a librarian, and there is no provision for a librarian on the committee.

The power to make regulations also includes clauses: to 'provide for the admission of the public to public libraries in its area on such conditions and on payment of such fees as it may specify'; and 'requiring from persons desiring to use such libraries any guarantee or security against injury to, misuse, destruction or loss of the property of such libraries'.

These sections of the Act do, of course, nullify the whole function of public libraries if acted on, although they are permissive. Each local library authority is empowered to levy a library cess in its area, of six paise per rupee. This can be increased by an authority with sanction. The principal defects of the Act, apart from the omission of a requirement for trained staff with some status and the out-of-date provisions for access to the libraries, are that the Act does not in any way create a system of libraries. The State Central Library has no duties in relation to the district libraries and the district libraries have no duties in relation to each other. A parallel system of libraries is also created under the Act, since one of the duties of the director is to declare what libraries are eligible for government aid.

In the rules made under the Act, the director is to maintain a register of such libraries and conditions are laid down for eligibility for grant. There appear to be no provisions, as in the Model Bill, for eventual merging of these libraries within the public libraries administered by district authorities. Despite the defects of the Act, and its slow implementation, in recent years the public library service has obviously made some impression.

In 1965, total expenditure reached over 7 million rupees as against I,685,000 in 1957, and of this sum I,897,000 was raised in library cess. Over half the total expenditure in 1965, however, was by special grant, under the five-year plan, and it is not known whether this has been maintained since. Book stocks are reported as being nearly 2,500,000, visitors to the libraries nearly 18 million.

But one notes with surprise that there are in the whole state only 15,000 registered borrowers and only 143 trained library staff, of whom only I have full library qualifications. But however suspect some of the statistics, and it must be noted that criticism of the Madras library service by Indian librarians has been very severe, it is undoubtedly true that some progress has been made which would not have been made without a legislative base.

It is to be hoped that the efforts of Dr. Ranganathan and others to improve the Act will eventually bear fruit and that Madras may then emerge as not only the first, but also the foremost, Indian state with a tax-based, legally founded, public library service.

Andhra Pradesh

Andhra Pradesh was a linguistic state formed from Hyderabad and parts of Madras State. A Telugu-speaking area, it has always had a strong library and literary tradition. In the words of an Indian librarian, 'the library movement has had a vast influence on the social and political life in Telugu land'. The population is over 40 million. When the new state was formed, there was already an Act in force for Hyderabad, while the parts of Madras taken over were covered by the Madras Act. In 1960 an integrated Act was passed for the entire state. In many ways the Act is similar to the Madras Act, in the provision of a state library committee, the constitution of local library authorities, the levying of library cess and the matching of the funds raised in this way by grants from the state government. But generally the Act is a great improvement on the Madras Act, and corrects many of its defects.

The Act creates a separate department of public libraries, although the Director of Public Instruction may be the director in charge of the department. But the librarian of the State Central Library has a place on the State Library Committee. In the provisions for the district authorities and the city authority it is laid down that the District Librarian and the City Central Librarian shall each be secretary of the respective committee. The amount of library cess is fixed at four paise, which may be increased to eight paise at the discretion of the district authority. It is prescribed in the Act that no fees for admission to any public library shall be charged, but it is not clear whether a fee can be charged for borrowing of books. Again, a parallel system of libraries is formed, since under the definitions, a public library can be 'a library established or maintained by any local body or co-operative society and declared open to the public', or 'a library declared to be eligible for aid and receiving aid from the Government or from the Library Fund'.

The duties of the Director of Public Libraries also include a declaration of what libraries are eligible for aid and under the rules of the Act conditions for such aid are laid down. It is clear that these are libraries outside those provided directly by the library authority, but there are no provisions, as in the Model Bill, for taking them over. The Act has been rapidly implemented, and appears to be working fairly satisfactorily.

Mysore Act, 1965

This Act has taken features from the Madras Act, the Andhra Pradesh Act, and the Model Bill and is a great improvement on all of them. Mysore is a Kannada-speaking State formed under the States Reorganization Act. The capital is Bangalore and the population is approximately 27 million. The literacy rate is 25 per cent (36 % males). The preamble of the Act states that it is:

'To provide for the establishment and maintenance of public libraries and the organization of a comprehensive rural and urban library service for the State of Mysore.'

The State Library Authority includes a member representing the State Library Association, but the State Librarian, though *ex officion* secretary of the authority, is not a member. A department of public libraries is formed under the Act, with the State Librarian at its head.

This clause takes the administration of the public library out of the province of the Department of Education. The State Librarian is also specifically stated to be a whole-time officer with qualifications to practise as a librarian. All posts in the Department of Public Libraries are to be filled by appointment of persons employed by the state library service. This may seem supererogatory, but is obviously intended to prevent appointment of persons already in other departments of the civil service. It is one of the grievances of Indian librarians that posts are often filled by people without library qualifications, coming by promotion from such departments as social education and community development.

Local library authorities are specified for cities and urban areas with populations of more than 100,000, and for each district authority. The chief librarian of the city or district is *ex officion* secretary of the local library authority. Development plans are to be prepared for each district and advisory committees formed by branch libraries and mobile libraries under the plan. The library cess is not confined to a levy on property, but is also levied on other taxes in city areas. It is limited to three paise in the rupee, subject to increase at discretion, with an upper limit of six paise. It will, of course, raise much more money, though the rate is the same, than property tax.

The grant from the state to districts is met from land revenue tax, at the rate of three per cent. In addition the whole of staff salaries in the library authority is met by the state. The State Central Library has, among other functions, the task of providing facilities for the blind. This is not mentioned in any other Act. The Act also specifies a number of public libraries owned by societies which are to be taken over under the Act. Whether this is by prior agreement or not, it is an immense step forward. The Mysore Act, it will be seen, is in many respects an improvement of the Model Bill, particularly in its creation of an independent library service and the widening of the tax base for urban libraries. The provision that all staff are employees of the state library service and paid by the state creates, for the first time in any of the Indian legislation, an integrated library system with the State Central Library at its head.

Maharashtra, 1967

Maharashtra, a Marathi-speaking State has a population of 46 million. Literacy is 30 per cent (males 42%). The Maharashtra Act, passed in 1967, has some of the features of the Mysore Act in that it creates a state library council, with a director of libraries who is a member of the council, acts as its secretary and must be a qualified librarian. A department of libraries is established and a state library service with staff salaries to be paid from state funds. There the resemblance to the Mysore Act stops.

A state library is to be established and a divisional library for every division. But provision for library service in a local area can only be made if the director is not satisfied that a local authority, society or trust is willing or competent to provide a public library service. No such library however shall be established without an opportunity being given to the local authority, society or trust to show because why the state authority should not establish a library. The Act gives no powers of taxation; the Library Fund is made up solely from general and special grants, and central government grants. The general state grant is to be not less than 2,500,000 rupees, not a large sum. It is difficult to see from this how the Act can work satisfactorily, even though a functioning department and qualified staff are provided for.

SUMMARY

The Indian position has been dealt with at some length because of the variety of existing legislation and the fact that for the greater part of India there still is no legislation. This is not for want of trying. There must be few countries where there has been so much effort, so many reports, such unremitting lobbying of politicians. Dr. Ranganathan has devoted a lifetime to the problem, as well as gaining an international reputation for his contributions to librarianship, and nearly every Indian state has been in consultation with him at one time or another over legislation.

All states have active and persistent library associations, hampered by lack of funds it is true, but making up for it in publications and conferences. The will is there, the sympathy is there, but results have been more than disappointing. The main problem is, of course, one of taxation. The states' governments are reluctant to pass mandatory legislation that will increase the tax burden; the rural and urban areas have not sufficient potential revenue to provide library services; and the states themselves have a limited amount of revenue to disburse.

Finally, the central government, although it has distributed large sums for libraries under successive five-year plans, is reluctant to make permanent commitments. But eventually the problem must be solved by central government contributions to make up the deficiency in the states. It has been suggested that 5 per cent of the amount spent on education should be aimed at as the total. This would not provide expensive buildings and equipment, but it would provide a basic public library service. The difficulty is that the longer the central government hesitates to insist on mandatory state legislation, the more difficult it will be to provide this basic service.

A start must sometime be made on bringing the many semi-public libraries into a system and possibly channeling and consolidating the small sums they spend. Grant-in-aid to them altogether must amount to a respectable sum and a large part of it is wasted so long as these libraries are independent, using untrained staff and decrepit premises. The attitude is that they are better than nothing, but this is not true if they give the impression that they are a library service. There is also a danger that more states will pass defective legislation, and the more that do, the longer it will take to bring them into line.

The only Act which is reasonably acceptable so far is the Mysore Act and it is the only one to create a state-wide service. It is now nearly ten years since the Advisory Committee reported and gave a comprehensive view of the situation. It is surely time for the Government of India to make a definite move, if only because otherwise they may be faced with a series of defective and conflicting Acts by the states.

4

Intellectual Property Rights

INTRODUCTION

Computers and the concomitant capability they have provided for making copyrighted works available in digital form in networked environments have created many new kinds of expressive opportunities. Computer technology together with communications technology has enabled authors to create digital libraries and hypertext publishing systems. Active development of such systems is now underway. While some difficult technical problems must be solved to build these systems, technical obstacles are thought to be surmountable. Less clear, however, is what kind of intellectual property scheme can be used to make digital library or hypertext publishing systems commercially viable.

An intellectual property system works well when it embodies a reasonably accurate model of how people are likely to behave. Copyright law is based on a relatively simple and straightforward model of author and reader behaviour. Authors are motivated to produce interesting and valuable texts and to make these works available to others by copyright's reassurance that authors can control the sale of copies of their works. Readers are motivated to purchase the texts, or to urge institutions such as libraries to purchase the texts, so that they can have access to the work.

Authors have generally had little control over what uses readers make of the copies after the first sale of the work to the public. Commentators on U.S. copyright law have sometimes regarded this lack of control over uses as a virtue. But while it can be said that the absence of copyright control over uses has promoted the dissemination of knowledge, the truth is that in the print world it is infeasible to maintain meaningful control over uses anyway. Copyright should be accounted a great success at modeling author and reader behaviour, for the basic framework of this law has lasted nearly three hundred years.

During this period, copyright industries have flourished and copyright law has broadened to include a wide variety of intellectual products besides those manufactured by printing presses. While the copyright model is being utilized for all manner of texts in digital form, the behaviour of authors and readers is being changed by the new digital technologies. It is becoming increasingly likely that some adjustments will have to be made in the copyright model to make digital libraries and hypertext publishing environments as commercially viable as the print industries have been. But few new models have yet been constructed, and work in this direction has only just begun, After a brief discussion of some characteristics of informational works in digital form that challenge existing intellectual property systems.

It will then try to foresee how such rights might be handled if digital libraries become, as some in the technical community foresee they will, hypertext publishing systems (that is, systems in which users can become authors by linking portions of the digital library's contents-with or without any additional content contributed by them-whose link-based work can be published within the digital library). The most innovative and well-developed model for how intellectual property rights might be dealt with in a hypertext publishing system is that proposed by Ted Nelson (a hypertext developer and visionary—indeed the person who coined the term hypertext for which a whole field of endeavor is now known) in his book Literary Machines.

This book describes the Xanadu hypertext publishing system designed by Nelson, which was to have been commercialized by Autodesk, a software publishing firm. Although the object ultimately concludes that the Xanadu intellectual property rights model is flawed because it does not accurately reflect how authors and users would likely behave, it praises a number of aspects of Nelson's model and the innovative concepts it embodies. The authors hope this critique of the Nelson model will aid in the formulation of a new conception about how intellectual property rights can be dealt with so that digital libraries and hypertext publishing systems can become commercially viable.

DIGITAL MEDIA AND INTELLECTUAL PROPERTY LAW

Six characteristics of works in digital form seem likely to change significantly the contours of intellectual property law, especially copyright. The ease with which such works can be replicated and the ease with which they can be transmitted and accessed by multiple users are the first and second of these characteristics. These characteristics would seem to create strong incentives for copyright industries to move away from their traditional focus on the sale of copies, and towards greater control over uses of protected works. That it is now feasible to control uses through controlling access to computer systems containing works in digital form will also affect this trend.

A third characteristic of digital works is the ease with which they can be manipulated and modified. While this plasticity offers users some important advantages over the print medium (printed works are sometimes too fixed to be maximally usable), copyright law is more geared towards dealing with works that are permanently fixed. The law may need to be adjusted to cope with the new benefits and new problems that this plasticity will entail, such as providing guidelines for circumstances in which plastic uses of digital information are permissible.

A fourth characteristic is the breakdown of copyright distinctions among different kinds of works when they are in digital form. The copyright statute identifies seven categories of protected works, each of which has somewhat varying degrees of protection, Is a hypertext version of Mozart's Magic Flute that contains the music, the libretto, textual commentary, pictures of Mozart, and other media a "literary work," a "musical work," a "sound recording," a "pictorial work," or an "audiovisual work'? The answer to this question under copyright law cannot be all of the above—even if it really is.

Copyright's classification scheme, oriented as it is towards the appearance of works and the medium in which they are embodied, seems in need of adjustment if the statutory differences are absent from the digital representation. Because so many of the exclusive fights and special privilege provisions in the copyright statute depend on the category of the work, they will need some refinement to deal with digital multimedia works. A fifth characteristic is that digital works are virtually invisible to users/readers. Works in digital form are stored as a sequence of high and low voltage signals in computer memory. They cannot be perceived or read by humans except with the aid of a user interface.

One cannot tell from viewing one portion of such a work on a computer screen how large the work is, nor can one navigate through the text unless navigation aids have been specially constructed in software to permit this. Fortunately, the sixth and final characteristic of digital media is that they allow new kinds of search and linking activities to be achieved. This characteristic has given rise to new classes of protected intellectual property products, including hypertexts.

Intellectual property protection for innovative aspects of new kinds of digital works, such as software user interfaces and hypertext navigation aids, has been a subject of significant controversy, both on copyright and patent fronts, and seems likely to remain so for the foreseeable future. Despite repeated Supreme Court rulings that algorithms are unpatentable and evidence that practitioners believe strong protection by copyright and patent will have a negative effect on the software industry, the U.S. Patent Office has been issuing many software patents in recent years, some of which are for functions and user interface features for hypertext systems.

Some court decisions have taken such an expansive view of the scope of copyright protection that reuse of almost anything but very high level abstractions in software would seem dangerous, although other decisions have taken a far narrower view, seeming to confine "expression" to that which would readily be viewed as expressive in traditional categories of works. Some decisions have recognized that computer software is difficult to fit in the traditional copyright mold.

MODELS OF AUTHOR AND READER BEHAVIOUR IN RECENT ELECTRONIC INFORMATION SYSTEMS

Some clues about how authors and readers might behave in digital libraries and hypertext publishing systems can be perceived by looking at how people currently use computer bulletin boards, computer data bases, and other information services and electronic mail systems. Instead of viewing these systems as technical precedents, it is instructive to consider them as experiments in developing appropriate models for intellectual property and reader/user/author behaviour that might be adapted for more ambitious applications such as Xanadu.

PRODIGY AND CompuServe

Prodigy and CompuServe are commercial services that provide a variety of bulletin boards, electronic mail, infor-mation services, and entertainment. They embody significantly different models of user behaviour, and their pricing strategies are markedly different. Prodigy targets the consumer and home markets, and treats its users as relatively passive information consumers who do not interact much with each other. Prodigy offers users access to many different kinds of information, as well as bulletin boards, electronic mail, and some entertainment. Its services are made available for a fixed monthly fee.

Usage-insensitive pricing is made possible by the paid advertising that Prodigy presents along with nearly every screen of information displayed to users. When Prodigy imposed a usage-pricing scheme for sending electronic mail, many users felt that their contract with Prodigy, as well as their "free speech fights," had been violated. In contrast, CompuServe has been oriented towards business and professional users and always had usage-based pricing based on connect time.

CompuServe information services are specifically focused, organized into a complex hierarchy of bulletin boards and data bases, many of which are moderated by an expert, who in some circumstances is compensated by CompuServe. This finer-grained categorization enables CompuServe to impose sur-charges for supposedly more timely or valuable information, but its user population is presumably used to paying for information according to its value. Users engage in heated electronic dialogues with one another on bulletin boards, commenting on and criticizing one another's postings. Both Prodigy and CompuServe place some limits on user downloading.

Some materials, such as shareware or public domain software from both sources, can be downloaded without restriction, but other materials are restricted. The two systems differ, however, in the locus of restrictions. Prodigy is a centralized service which means it sets and enforces the downloading policy. CompuServe, by contrast, has a more decentralized policy because it is essentially an umbrella organization for a number of information services, and these services often have their own downloading policies. Quite recently, however, both Prodigy and CompuServe have expanded user opportunities to download materials, although this adds to the cost of the service.

THE INTERNET

The Internet is a vast network of networks that inter-connect thousands of computing sites in government, industry, and academia. The Intermit has evolved from primarily providing electronic mail services to become the infrastructure for significantly broader services of information exchange and collaborative work. Like CompuServe, the heart of the Internet is a vast collection of newsgroups in which participants from around the world post and comment on messages. Some people take on the role of newsgroup moderators, but the overwhelming majority of newsgroups are unmediated.

Author and reader behaviour on the Internet are largely governed by norms or "netiquette" that have evolved over time and that are enforced both by system administrators and by the informal but effective sanctions of "flames" (critical messages) directed at violators. Included in these norms are rules about selecting newsgroups in which to post messages, sensitivity to authors of posted messages when citing or responding to them, and other matters that affect both authors and readers. Users of the Internet vary greatly in their perception of intellectual property laws as they apply to this new kind of publishing system. Some users, especially new users who are college students, act as if the Internet services and the information that can be had by exploring the Internet are completely free.

In fact, each host machine that serves as an Internet site has to pay a fee for the privilege. Institutions recoup these fees as well as other costs associated with use of host machines by passing them on, even if the costs are not immediately evident because they may be borne by a particular unit of the institution, rather than directly by those who use the machine for Internet services. Those who post information not authored by them on Intermit bulletin boards or in electronic newsletters delivered by Internet sometimes do so with a conspicuous notice that it is being posted without copyright permission, thereby asserting the poster's view of an appropriate scope of fair use.

But some who post materials on the Internet explicitly assert copyrights on the messages that they post. And it has become increasingly common for electronic journals distributed on the Internet to contain a notice that those who contribute items to the journals are responsible for obtaining whatever copyright permissions might be needed. Although "net" users generally regard it as fair to download items from the bulletin board for one's personal use, and even to send a copy to a friend who might otherwise not see the item, it is considered bad manners (or worse) to redistribute more widely someone else's posting without its author's permission.

Still, it is worth noting that because "the net" is so vast and the number of its users so large, it can be extremely difficult to police it for copyright purposes. Authors who distribute works on the Internet are generally not paid to publish, and receive no royalties. Nor do readers generally have to pay to read items on the Internet. But it is fair to state that many Interact activities are being paid for (or at least subsidized) by Interact participants' employers. Hence, it can be argued that anything posted on the Internet that is work-related is the intellectual property of the employer who provides access to the Internet by paying for the computers and telecommunications infrastructure.

Employers may feel that the value of the information their employees glean from the Internet outweighs the costs of the time to obtain it, but it is unlikely that many employers explicitly make this analysis. In addition to electronic mail and newsgroups, the Internet now supports several innovative services that enable it to function as a distributed digital library with vast holdings. If an Internet site chooses to make some of its information publicly available, a user on another site can use the anonymous FTP (file transfer protocol) mechanism to retrieve it.

Other experimental services, some with fanciful names like Archie, Gopher, and World Wide Web, build upon FTP to provide users with a worldwide index so that they can find sites that offer the information they seek. The WWW service allows users to retrieve what they want even if they cannot directly connect to the site that stores it. These new services are being enthusiastically embraced in the academic and research communities of the Internet, but they pose even more problems for intellectual property rights because they erode the boundaries between public and commercial information sources.

LEXIS ARM WESTLAW

Lawyers have had access to digital libraries of legal materials for well over a decade, thanks initially to the farsightedness of a paper manufacturer, which perceived a market opportunity for providing electronic access to judicial opinions, statutes, regulations, and other legal materials. This manufacturer formed Mead Data Central, whose Lexis data base lawyers use regularly. Like so many other print publishers, the major legal print publisher, West Publishing, did not see the market opportunity for electronic information services until after Lexis had become a major success.

Although a late entrant to the business, West has succeeded in designing a digital library of legal materials that offers some services, particularly the key numbering system that West had long used in print, that give it some competitive advantage. The initial pricing scheme employed by Lexis and by West was similar to that used by CompuServe: usage-based pricing based on connect-time. This pricing strategy worked particularly well because lawyers could typically pass these charges on to clients. Over time, both services developed pricing strategies for institutions, such as law schools, where connect-time charges could not be passed on.

Both services also now permit downloading of electronic versions of legal materials as well as printouts of selected materials. No special charges seem to be levied for these services, although usage-based charging would absorb the costs through connect-time, and institutional subscription pricing would be based on a predicted quantum of such uses. There is no technical reason why these two digital libraries could not become hypertext publishing systems. Their considerable financial success might suggest that this extension would be a natural one, and indeed, at least one author has tried to make them become so.

Professor Peter Martin of the Comell Law School sought to bring about this kind of expansion of legal data base functions by creating a hypertext treatise on Social Security Law on the Lexis system. Because Lexis had no particular incentive to promote its use, Martin eventually negotiated an arrangement by which he could "port" the treatise to a CD-ROM so it could be commercialized. Professor Henry Perritt of Villanova Law School has also proposed hypertext publishing systems built on top of digital libraries of legal materials as a way to produce electronic casebooks.

But except for the work of a few pioneers, such as Professors William Andersen of the University of Washington Law School, William Boyd of the University of Arizona Law School, and Ronald Staudt of the Chicago-Kent Law School, hypertext has yet to come to the field of law. The richly inter textual nature of law makes it a natural field for hypertext applications, and perhaps ways can be found to create them on top of a digital library of legal materials such as Lexis or Westlaw, and make them commercially viable.

THE INTELLECTUAL PROPERTY SYSTEM IN XANADU

The most complete proposal for making digital library or hypertext publishing systems commercially viable has Ted Nelson. For over two decades, Nelson has been writing and talking about a proposed system called Xanadu, which he envisioned as a vast digital library containing all of the world's literature. Because Xanadu would allow users to create new and derivative documents via links, Xanadu is also a hypertext publishing system. Xanadu can usefully be understood as an attempt to create an institution that will be writing environment, publishing environment, library, and bookstore in one. Despite his visionary reputation, Nelson is practical enough to realise that the commercial success of the Xanadu proposal critically depends on the way it deals with intellectual property issues. The intellectual property system in Xanadu has sometimes been summarized in writings about the Xanadu system in popular magazines, but has been subject to little serious analysis. After a brief description of how Xanadu would deal with intellectual property rights issues, this Part will discuss some respects in which the Xanadu proposal differs from that which is reflected in the existing copyright system.

Xanadu contains some interesting ideas about how to solve certain problems with digital library and hypertext publishing systems, but some aspects of the Xanadu model of author and user behaviour may be unworkable. Nevertheless, Nelson's analysis suggests some respects in which intellectual property systems might have to adapt to make digital libraries and hypertext publishing systems commercially viable.

XANADU'S REVENUE SOURCES AND MECHANISMS

Nelson envisions revenues being generated in Xanadu from two sources: first, from authors who would pay fees for renting space for their documents in the Xanadu system, and second, from users who would pay fees based on their usage of the system. Nelson expects that authors will want to put their documents into the Xanadu system because once the documents are in the system; authors will be able to earn royalties whenever users make use of their documents.

Between ten and twenty per cent of usage fees would go to authors whose documents are accessed by users; the rest would go to the system to recoup costs and make profits. Nelson intends for usage fees, and consequently the royalties as well, to be set on a per byte delivery basis for administrative convenience.

Nelson expects that people will pay to use the Xanadu system, because not only will it contain as much of the world's literature as Nelson can get into it, but there will also be legion opportunities in the Xanadu system for users/browsers/readers to make money by adding value to the system through their creative uses of the system. There are two main means by which Nelson intends to let users make money in the Xanadu system. One is by making derivative works of documents already in the system. This would include creating new versions of other authors' documents, creating compound documents consisting of portions of a number of different documents, or creating commentaries on other documents in the system.

By creating derivative documents, users would become system authors themselves, and thereby become able to earn royalties when other users access their derivative documents. No special permission would be needed to make derivative documents from other authors' documents, for Nelson will make it a condition of storing documents in Xanadu that authors agree to allow others to make whatever derivative uses they want of published documents in the system.

Nelson relies on two factors to motivate authors to agree to allowing derivatives to he made of their documents. One is that they will then be able to do to others' documents what others can do to theirs. But more importantly, when a third party accesses the derivative document on Xanadu, the author of the underlying document, as well as the author of the derivative document, will earn a royalty, because the derivative document will be connected to the original document; bytes from both will be called up when third parties access the derivative document.. Hence, both authors will receive royalties.

The second way for users to generate revenues when using the Xanadu system will be by creating links between or among documents in the system. Nelson expects some links to be very elaborate, such as a specialized index to certain classes of documents in the system. Other links may be modest, such as a connector between two documents. User links between documents, in effect, become new documents in the system. Each time other users traverse a set of links, the link author will receive a royalty, as will the authors of the documents on either end of the link.

Although Vannevar Bush was the first to perceive that information trailblazers would be needed for computerized information systems, Nelson deserves credit for recognizing the need to give incentives to information pioneers to cut paths through the invisible contents of a digital library. Nelson's scheme would also provide authors with the opportunity to store private as well as published documents in the Xanadu system. Authors would be able to decide who could have access to private documents and under what conditions. But Nelson envisions that authors of private documents would generally make them available for linking.

Private documents could be withdrawn without difficulty from Xanadu by their authors. The same will not be true for published documents because of the effect withdrawal would have on the interests of authors who have linked to or otherwise built upon the foundation of the published document. Nelson attempts to create a strong incentive for authors to publish their documents ill the Xanadu system by making system royalties unavailable to authors for private documents, even those with unrestricted distribution (*i.e.*, from which derivatives can be made, and to which links can be constructed). Because publication imposes obligations on the Xanadu operator and the author, publication of a document in the Xanadu system is a formal event, requiring a signature of the author on a form affirming the intent to publish the work.

COMPARING XANADU AND THE COPYRIGHT SYSTEM

Nelson refers to copyright in a positive way in a number of passages in his book, and takes care to establish a plausible case that nothing in Xanadu violates existing copyright law. Xanadu gives authors new ways to generate revenues from their works—even some that copyright might not provide—and so aims to create incentives to authorship, revealing a predisposition in keeping with traditional copyright incentives.

But the Xanadu system is more different from copyright than might be apparent from a cursory examination.

Compensatian based on Uses, Rather than Distribution of Copies

One difference between the Xanadu intellectual property system and traditional copyright is that Xanadu aims to derive revenues for authors by charging for each and every use of their documents, rather than, as has traditionally been done in copyright industries, on the sale or other commercial distribution of copies of copyrighted works. Many commercial computer data bases do much the same thing. Such arrangements seem likely to become increasingly common for works in digital form.

Blurring the "Idea" and "Expression" Distinction and Eliminating "Fair Use"

A more novel set of differences from copyright flow from Xanadu's treatment of links. Fundamental to the copyright regime is a distinction between "ideas" (which are unprotected by copyright law) and "expression" (which copyright protects). Under the copyright regime, authors generally do not expect remuneration whenever other authors comment on, quote from, use ideas from, or make reference to their work. The statutory fair use provision has been interpreted as allowing even literal copying of copyrighted text if the amount taken is relatively small, especially if the taking is for research, educational, or critical purposes.

Only if other authors take a fairly hefty chunk of "expr-ession" from the protected work do copyright holders expect compensation. In Xanadu, information can be included in a document by linking.

Because of this, Xanadu draws a different line than the print world would about what information to count as a single work. Even if Xanadu had a fair use provision, the lack of separateness among documents would complicate the determination of what constitutes fair use. But Xanadu allows no fair use copying.

Authors in the Xanadu system will get royalties based on how many bytes were linked to-merely for being linked to.

This aspect of Xanadu prefigures an intellectual property system that compensates authors without regard to whether chunks of expression have been appropriated. In time, this would seem likely to undermine the "idea/expression" distinction that has been a staple part of the copyright system.

Treating Linking as Authorship

Nelson's decision to treat linking as a kind of authorship-that is, as an intellectual activity that should not only be encouraged, but should serve as the basis for earning royalties when users traverse the links-also seems to diverge somewhat from the traditional copyright model. While an extensive set of links, such as an index, might readily be protectable by traditional copyright law as a compilation, many of the kinds of links that Nelson would treat as works of authorship might be unprotectable under traditional copyright law.

A link between a passage in document A and a passage in document B might, for example, be considered a "discovery" that thc statute says copyright cannot protect. Traditional copyright law would also not regard it as a compensable use of a copyrighted work for readers to traverse the links among documents referred to in a printed article. Yet link authors in Nelson's scheme would be compensated for others' traversal of their links.

Use Rights vs. Rights to Exclude

Nelson, like many others who are not lawyers, finds it natural to think of intellectual property rights in terms of what uses of works should give rise to author compensation. This intuitive "rights to do" framework is used by Xanadu. The law tends to define intellectual property rights in a somewhat different way. The law focuses on what rights owners have to exclude other people from doing certain kinds of things with the protected work. Copyright law defines the ownership rights of authors by saying what kinds of activities they can stop unauthorized people from doing.

Chief among copyright's exclusive rights are these: controlling the making of copies and derivative works of the protected work and distributing copies or derivative works. The only exclusive right Xanadu seems to contemplate is whether or not to put a document into the Xanadu system in the first place. Xanadu is more like a compulsory-license system than an exclusive-rights system. While U.S. copyright law does contain some compulsory-license provisions, compulsory licenses are generally an anathema to owners of intellectual property rights because the license fee generally bears little or no relation to the price obtainable if the issue were left to the market.

Unlimited Duration

The Xanadu system seems to contemplate no end to the duration of author rights. As long as authors (or their heirs) continue to pay for storage on this system, Xanadu will continue to pay royalties for uses of the documents. Under the U.S. Constitution, copyright can only be granted to authors for limited times. Upon expiration of the copyright, the work is in the public domain. While Nelson may not have conscio-usly rejected this aspect of copyright in the Xanadu system, his description of the system reveals that he does not intend to reduce usage fees for accessing public domain materials. Royalties from them go into the "author's fund" over which he undoubtedly will exercise some control.

Making Publication an Important Formal Event (Again)

Publication is an important formal event in the Xanadu system. Under previous U.S. copyright laws, authors generally only "copyrighted" their works when the work was published. A formal copyright notice had to appear prominently in all publicly distributed copies of the work, or the claim of copyright would be forfeited. The Copyright Act of 1976 permitted inadvertent omissions of copyright on a small number of copies of the work to be remedied, but extended protection to all original works of authorship from the moment of their first fixation in a tangible medium.

In 1989, in order to bring U.S. copyright law into compli-ance with requirements of the Beme Convention, the notice requirement as a precondition to protection of published works was dropped. Copyright notices are now important only for incidental purposes, such as foreclosure of a defence of innocent infringement. Publication used to be a very important event in U.S. copyright law, but more recently, this law has made publication into a virtual nonevent. By making publi-cation into a significant event, Nelson's scheme resembles "old" copyright more than "new" copyright.

Nelson's decision to make publication a formal event in Xanadu is necessary because publication in Xanadu would create a contract between the Xanadu system and the author to guarantee the existence of the published document for a period of time. This provides an integrity to links and citations generally absent in the print world, where only law reviews, with their armies of student citation-checkers, assure the reader that the cited document exists and supports the proposition for which it was cited.

Contracting to Permit Derivative Works

Yet another respect in which the Xanadu system diverges from the standard copyright model is in proposing to contract with all authors whose works would be stored in the Xanadu system so that users could make derivative documents from documents in the system. Varying the "default setting" of copyright by contract is not, in itself, a novel thing.

The motion picture industry is an example of a copyright industry that has historically depended for commercial success on contract-based distributions of copies, rather than on the outright sale of copies that has typified most copyright industries. Nelson's scheme is novel in proposing to use a contract-based scheme for commercial distribution of written texts, the prototypical subject matter of copyright, and in seeking to permit the widest derivative uses of documents in the system. Copyright, by contrast, has become rather stingy about derivative uses of anything but abstract ideas from protected works.

A CRITIQUE OF XANADU'S MODELS

CONCERNING ITS MODEL OF AUTHOR BEHAVIOUR

One question raised by Nelson's proposal is whether authors, particularly good ones, will be willing to pay to publish their works in Xanadu. In the print world, some authors do pay to have their works published by "vanity presses," but this represents a small percentage of publications. There might be some authors who would pay to publish documents in Xanadu out of misplaced confidence in the value of their work, just as some authors now post messages of dubious information content to CompuServe or Internet newsgroups. Such authors would get negative feedback at the end of the first rental period when no royalties were credited to their account, and perhaps decide not to renew.

However, some authors might decide not to renew their document rental space in Xanadu if no one linked to them during the first rental period, even though if they had stayed in the system, their documents would eventually have been discovered and made them a fortune. Still other authors might lack confidence in their work or might be too poor to afford the rental fee, which might cause them to withhold from the Xanadu system documents that would have been widely utilized if published there.

Xanadu might benefit from a scheme by which authors could solicit sponsors willing to subsidize the inclusion of their works in Xanadu in exchange for some portion of the royalties. Authors may not, in other words, behave in the way Xanadu's designer might expect them to behave. Authors may prefer the print world's system, which does not require them to pay directly for the privilege of being published. Authors may feel it is quite enough to have had to work hard to write the text in the first place. Some of the trick of authoring is writing something that publishers are willing to risk their capital to publish.

A system that would make authors pay to get published may end up either deterring authorship or sending authors in search of another digital library/ hypertext publishing system in which to place their work. Nelson may also have under-estimated how reluctant many authors may be about giving other people unlimited rights to make derivatives of their work. Although authors might have no objection to letting Xanadu users link to their documents, many may feel quite differently about allowing any Tom, Dick, or Susan to make new versions of their works. It will be little consolation to such authors that they might get royalties when the revised version is accessed by Xanadu users.

Authors often regard their writings as expressions of their personalities. Any tampering with their texts may be viewed by such authors as a "mutilation" of the work, as objectionable as if someone had the effrontery to walk up to you and cut your hair without your permission. In many countries, authors are expressly granted "moral rights" in their intellectual products, one of which protects the integrity of the work. In the United States, the derivative work right of copyright owners protects authors' economic interests in controlling adaptations of their works, although sometimes unauthorized adaptations affect economic rights of authors as well as moral rights. Nelson, like many in the technical community, seems to have a very positive attitude about the acceptability of making use of someone else's work and building on it to create a better modified version. Nelson seems to have assumed that this attitude is more widespread in the authorial community than may, in fact, be true.

CONCERNING ITS MODEL OF USER BEHAVIOUR AND INCENTIVES FOR USERS TO BECOME AUTHORS

The Xanadu intellectual property system also reflects a certain model of user behaviour. Nelson proposes a number of incentives for people to make use of the Xanadu system for a wide variety of purposes, from research to entertainment to hobby to full-time occupation. Probably his most creative idea about user behaviour is in contemplating the transformation of the digital library part of Xanadu into a hypertext publishing system, and incenting users to become system authors through linking and other derivative uses of documents in the system. The royalty mechanism in Xanadu, however, may create some unfortunate, unintended incentives.

The system would seem to give a special premium to those who are first to mention a particular topic in the Xanadu system, even if the first treatment of the topic were shallow or wrong. This may create incentives to rush documents into the system rather than to craft them to be deeper and more accurate. An example will illustrate one such problem. Suppose a journalist attended the first conference of scientists concerning the just-formed Human Genome Initiative (HGI), that he was an avid Xanadu user, and that at the first break in the conference schedule, the journalist authored a document for Xanadu describing in a shallow but intelligible way what HGI was about.

By virtue of being the first to mention HGI in Xanadu, this journalist's entry might be, for a time at least, the most frequently linked to source on HGI in Xanadu, which would make him the most compensated author on the topic. A naive user of Xanadu, when faced with a decision whether to access the journalist's HGI description or a later much deeper one by a scientist who was a founder of the HGI, might see that the first had been linked to a thousand times, whereas the scientist's document had been linked to only five times in the time it was on the system.

This might cause the user to choose the more frequently cited source over the better but less frequently cited source, again causing more royalties to flow into the journalist's account, and incenting rushed documents over considered documents in the system. In the print world, the shallow first treatment on a topic will tend to be ignored by later authors, but in Xanadu, the first document to mention a subject might always be called up on a user search, and not until the user reads the shallow document (and hence pays the author royalties on it) will the user know to ignore it.

Even creating a derivative document advising users to ignore the underlying document will result in royalties to the author of the underlying document. Suppose further that the journalist's Xanadu document on HGI contained some errors.

Other Xanadu users might well notice the errors, and make derivative documents containing the needed corrections. Although this would correct the error, an inadvertent result of the scenario would be that the journalist might make a lot of money from putting out an erroneous document, for every time someone linked to his document or created a revised version of it, the journalist would share in the revenues.

The more and more noticeable the errors in the document, the more Xanadu users would be likely to notice the errors, to link to the journalist's document, and/or to revise it, which once again would generate more revenues for the journalist. This would seem to over-reward the journalist for rushing to get his document on HGI into the Xanadu system and not to deter entry of erroneous information.

Usage-based systems, such as Xanadu, may also have the disadvantage, at least for price-sensitive users, of making those with the most curiosity and tenacity in research pay the highest cost. They are the ones who will presumably use Xanadu for longer periods of time. One might argue that this is fair because those who use the system the most are those who pay most. But some may conceive the issue differently, and think it one of the great virtues of the library systems of the print world that scholars do not have to pay more than casual users for access to the library.

Society has an interest in encouraging deep scholarship. By not making scholars or other deep users pay more for their use of the library, the print world encourages scholarship. Digital library and hypertext publishing systems may also need to find ways to encourage good scholarship and curiosity without making it prohibitively expensive. But a more serious problem perhaps than this may be figuring out how to motivate users to be persistent and creative in their use of the Xanadu system.

When people use traditional libraries, they can walk around and browse until they find something to interest them. In Xanadu, the clock will be ticking and the price will be rising as one browses. Also, digital libraries, because of their invisibility to the user, may be too abstract to be enjoyably browsable. Once again, Nelson may have mistakenly modeled the Xanadu user in terms of his own persistence and creativity, which others may not share.

QUESTIONS ABOUT PRICING INCENTIVES

Perhaps the single most questionable element of the Xanadu intellectual property scheme, in terms of economic incentives, is pricing. If one looks at the universe of copy-righted works in the print-dominated world, one immediately observes that copies are priced according, more or less, to what the publisher/distributor and author/creator think the market will bear for the number of copies that might reasonably be sold or licensed. Xanadu posits a flat fee for Xanadu connect time and a fixed royalty for authors based on per-byte delivery for usage of their documents. This is like mandating that all books are to be priced according to the number of pages they contain and all pages must be priced at the same amount.

The CompuServe example seems to suggest that differen-tial pricing of information is necessary to encourage the development of specialized markets. Unless Xanadu were the world's only digital library and hypertext publishing system, which remains Nelson's vision but which is unlikely', Xanadu will lack the negotiating power to compel authors to accept fixed pricing per byte of their information. People who own copyrights in very valuable intellectual properties simply will not use a system that does not let them make market-based pricing decisions.

The only options authors of very valuable intellectual properties would have in the world Nelson envisions is to put the work in Xanadu as an encrypted private document and contract with users for access to the document, or to withhold the document from Xanadu altogether. While encryption might allow market pricing to occur, Xanadu does not facilitate these transactions. They must be dealt with by private negotiations between the parties, but if Xanadu does not facilitate the transactions, it is difficult to see how they can occur.

The transaction costs of individual negotiations that would have to occur without Xanadu's help in order to access an encrypted document in Xanadu might be inordinately high. Another question we have about Nelson's Xanadu economic model is whether it overemphasizes author and user incentives and underemphasizes the need for some of the value-added services that publishers in the print world provide, particularly as to the promotion of sales of the work, whether by advertising or otherwise. Nelson wants people to use Xanadu, for that's how the system makes money. But Xanadu is indifferent to what they use. The lack of a promotional system for works in Xanadu may lead to underutilization of the system, which in turn may affect its commercial viability.

CONCLUSION

Whether digital library or hypertext publishing systems can be made commercially viable will depend on how they deal with intellectual property rights issues. The traditional copyright model will require adjustments in order to facilitate these new kinds of institutions. Ted Nelson offers one model of how such adjustments might be made. While Nelson's intellectual property scheme for the Xanadu system is bold and innovative, there are a number of respects in which his system can be questioned.

The most uncertain aspects of the Xanadu system are the accuracy of the Xanadu model of author and user behaviour, and the adequacy of financial incentives for authors to put their most valuable copyrighted works in the Xanadu system. A generation of exposure to tape recorders and VCRs—and a raft of new digital technologies for scanning, frame grabbing, and sampling—are making it harder to predict how people will understand and relate to intellectual property.

What is legal, and what is merely technically possible to copy? What constitutes "fair use" of copyrighted works in digital form? Laws that were suited for traditional kinds of copyrighted works no longer seem to fit. More work is needed to develop new models of author and user behaviour and the economics that will yield the right level of incentives for creation of digital library and hypertext publishing systems. The law can be made to conform to these new models, but only after we figure out what the right ones are.

5

Laws of Library Science

LIBRARY RESOURCE SHARING LIBRARY NETWORK

India, the largest democracy in the world with an estimated population of 114 millions has more than 1,00,000 libraries comprising academic libraries, public libraries, special libraries and libraries attached to the research and develop-ment institutions, government departments and ministries, etc. There is no denying the fact ICT has brought a paradigm change in the functionality of the libraries in the country but this technological change pattern is not seen uniformly across the wide-section of the libraries in the country.

On one hand the country is proud to have the most sophis-ticated libraries with ISO certifications and the implementation of modern tools and technologies, on the other hand, we do encounter the challenges of providing a better infrastructure in the form of PCs and Internet connectivity in the libraries that are still striving hard to get the necessary hardware and Internet connectivity in their libraries from their managements. The adoption of standards, retrospective conversion work, the adoption of suitable library software packages continues to remain as the major areas of concerns for the libraries and the library and information science professionals.

In such constraints and hostile conditions, DELNET has been able to establish itself as an effective, operational resource sharing library network in India. The network whose journey started as a city based library network in 1988, emerged as a major operational library network not only in India but in South Asia, connecting more than 1597 libraries in 30 States and UTs in India and seven other countries.

The network is growing from strength to strength, with escalating resources of union catalogues, the wider coverage of libraries from varied disciplines, the growing number of users and the horizontal and vertical expansion in its services to its members. This paper highlights the incredible and pioneering work being done by DELNET-Developing Library Network which is a non-governmental, non-profit making organisation with inputs from the Ministry of Communications and Information Technology, Government of India and located in its own building in the well-known academic environment of Jawaharlal Nehru University at New Delhi.

I would like to reiterate that DELNET do not receive any government funding and is based on a self-sustainable model, it is considered as a role model for the library networks especially of the developing nations. A survey has also been conducted by the author to assess the utilisation of DELNET resources among the member-institutions and is reported in the article. The questionnaire technique was used to get the inputs from the member-libraries. 147 libraries responded to the questionnaire.

THE GENESIS OF LIBRARY NETWORKING IN INDIA

In India during the late 1980s and 1990s there was a move-ment to establish city and regional-based library networks by NISSAT (National Information System for Science and Technology), a body under Dept of Scientific and Industrial Research (DSIR), Government of India. It provided some financial assistance for the setting up of these library networks.

This has lead to the mushrooming of various city library networks in India including:

- BONET (Bombay Library Network),
- CALIBNET (Calcutta Library Network),
- DELNET (Delhi Library Network which later became Developing Library Network in 2000),
- PUNENET (Pune Libary Network).

The University Grants Commission (UGC) has also developed INFLIBNET (Information and Library Network) in 1991 to network the University Libraries in the country. Only a few networks were able to work on the self sustainable model and continued to exist after the initial phases of implementation and functioning. DELNET, started as a project in 1988 became a national library network in India by the year 2000. UGC continued funding INFLIBNET to provide the support to the University Libraries in the country. The remaining city library networks due to the lack of planning for developing the networked resources and its functions soon perished from the networking scene of the country.

DELNET-DEVELOPING LIBRARY NETWORK

DELNET-Developing Library Network is a major operational resource sharing library network in India connecting more than 1597 libraries in 30 States and UTs in India and seven other countries. DELNET was conceived as a city based library network in Delhi in 1988 and was known as Delhi Library Network, networking the libraries of the Delhi region. It got registered as a society in 1992. With the availability of DELNET services on the World Wide Web, the accessibility soon was transformed from the local dial up connectivity for the Delhi region institutions to the global access through the Web.

This gave a great boost to DELNET and soon DELNET crossed the geographical boundaries within the country and also became accessible outside. It was on 13th September 2000 that the name of DELNET got changed from DELNET-Delhi Library Network to DELNET-Developing Library Network. The main objectives of DELNET is to promote resource sharing among the member-libraries by collecting, storing and disseminating information and by providing networked services to the researchers and scholars to supplement their research activity.

FIVE Cs-FUNCTIONAL PARAMETERS OF DELNET

We would like to mention the five Cs of the Library Networking which is essential for an operational library network and governs its functionality.

These five Cs are:

1. Connectivity;
2. Cost;
3. Computers;
4. Client; and
5. Content.

Connectivity

The connectivity is a life line for the smooth functioning of a library network. There is an availability of the leased-line, wireless, broadband, VSAT and Wifi connectivity in the libraries. The DELNET services are accessible through the World Wide Web by the registered member libraries. The DELNET databases are hosted on Basis Web server and are connected with a 11 mbps RF link offered by National Informatics Centre, Ministry of Communications and Infor-mation Technology, Government of India. The network remains functional on 24/7 basis. The web tracking software installed at DELNET servers gives a day to day picture of the usage of the DELNET services by the member libraries.

It is quite heartening to note that the access to the servers hosting the databases are being made by the researchers and scholars of the member libraries at different times starting from midnight to early morning besides the usual peak hour network access.

The survey conducted among the member libraries have shown very encouraging figures regarding the availability of the dedicated links in the libraries. ninety per cent of the respondents have confirmed the availability of the dedicated Internet facility in their libraries.

The University Libraries have the largest availability of the dedicated Internet facility with 95.2 per cent affirmed the availability of the dedicated link, followed by 90.7 per cent in Institutes, 89.7 per cent in Research/Special Libraries and 86.7 per cent in the Colleges. The survey results shows that Internet has been able to penetrate well among the organisations in the country and the libraries have the Internet bandwidth availability with them. It is found that in 97.3 per cent of the organisations, the faculty has Internet facility at their own desk. It is quite essential to have the direct internet access in order to utilise the library network's resource and services to the fullest.

Cost

The cost of membership to the library network and the resources provided through them are important for the sustainability of a library network. DELNET membership charges are quitc nominal, it is T 7500 per annum for the libraries in India and SAARC nations, the non-SAARC members pays USD 500 per annum. The membership fee is kept same for all Institutional Members whether it is a University, an Institution, an R&D organisation, a specialized library or a school library. The democratic approach, an unbias one, helps in promoting the resource sharing. Also it leaves an impression of being equal in their participatory roles in a network for resource sharing.

It is worth reporting that some of the library networks in India could not grow and sustained themselves due to the exorbitant membership charges rates and different categori-zation of the members on the basis of their collections, etc. DELNET charges for the actual courier charges for sending the books on Interlibrary loan and the member-institutions and their researchers finds it an affordable one. In a developing country like India, Cost of getting the desired material plays a crucial role. Herein, the researchers and scholars for higher research are not being helped financially to a reasonable extent through scholarships, grants, etc. contrary to their counterparts in the Western world.

Computers

In order to facilitate the optimum use of the library network resources and services, the researchers, scholars and faculty of the member institutions should have adequate availability of the computers. Through the survey conducted, it was found that 43.2 per cent of the libraries have upto 10 computers in the library whereas 59.1 per cent of the University Libraries have more than 20 computers in the library and only 32.2 per cent of the respondents have more than 20 computers in their libraries. It is quite evident that the libraries are not better equipped with the availability of the computers in their libraries though there may be separate computer labs or the computer departments but they are not the part of the libraries.

Client (Member-Libraries)

The more diverse the library network has the coverage, the more effective would be the resources of such a library network. In DELNET, the participating libraries are from various disciplines and they pool their resources together and share them across the network. I would like to mention the fascinating scenario of resource sharing wherein a technical book required by a S&T Library will be available in a library specialising in Commerce discipline rather than being available in the best technical libraries.

The resources and the collections becomes more trans-parent for the act of resource sharing. The survey results have shown that 92 per cent of the member-libraries are aware about DELNET services and 61 per cent are the frequent users of the DELNET services. It would like to mention that DELNET organizes one day orientation programmes in member-institutions located in various parts of the country. This enables in better promotion and spreads awareness about DELNET and helps in popularizing the services among the users, faculty and researchers of the member-libraries.

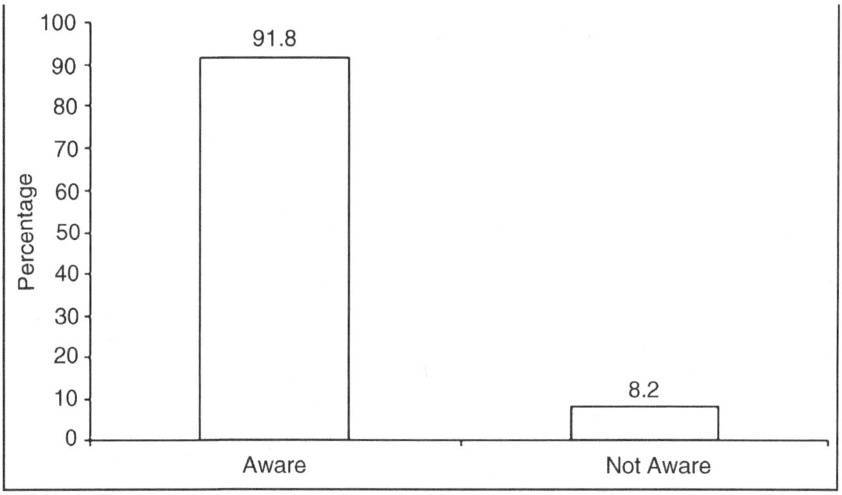

Fig7. Awareness about DELNET Services among the Library Users.

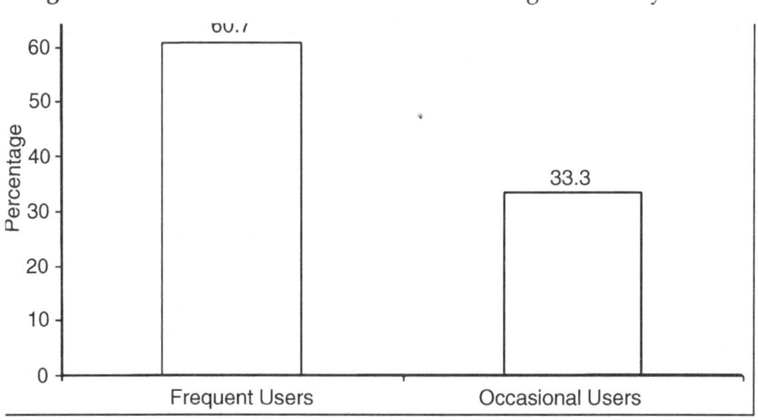

Fig. How Often do you Use DELNET Services.

Content

Content is a major resource of a library network. The greatest concern for a library network is the consolidation of the resources lying scattered across the member-libraries. This ensures a wider access to information to the information seekers. Since inception, DELNET is actively engaged in developing the union catalogues and union lists which are the major resource strength for any library network. The records in the DELNET databases are growing in size and more and more resources are becoming accessible to the member libraries. These resources are the major source for resource sharing as they carry the locations data wherein physically the information may be available.

The database are collected through the electronic transfer of the exported records through the online facility, e-mail, ftp protocols; the data is physically sent in CDs by the member libraries. I would like to mention that in a country like India, the cooperative cataloguing or cooperative collection building is still not in existence. There is a lot much of duplication efforts in the libraries for cataloguing the same titles in different libraries. The various libraries in the country are using various software packages which ranges from the commercial software packages (Libsys, Alice for Windows, Virtua, etc) which may be adhering to international standards to the inhouse developed software packages developed with the backend on SQL, Access, Excel, Oracle, Sybase, etc.

DELNET collects the records from the member libraries in the default exported format and the conversion programs are being developed to convert the base records into the standard ISO 2709 format before they are finally being merged in the Union Catalogues. I would like to mention that the information is also collected from the prominent libraries of the country who may be non-members since they can always be approached for getting the desired references. There is an online facility for uploading the machine readable records to DELNET by the member-libraries. The bibliographical databases do not strictly adheres to the international bibliographic formats and the library professionals are not much familiar with MARC 21 cataloguing.

DELNET DATABASES AND THEIR SIGNIFICANCE

Union Catalogue of Books

DELNET provides access to more than 8 million biblio-graphic records of books in English language available with various member libraries located in and outside the country. The databases can be accessed by any of the desired fields including Title, Author, Subject, Date of Publication. The Boolean operators can also be used for refining the search queries. The sorting can be done on the searched results. The searching using Phrase searching, Any Words and includes can be used. The records can also be retrieved using the specific indexes including Title,

Author, Subject, etc. The database size grows with each passing day as more and more data from the member libraries are being merged in the centralized union catalogues.

DELNET has developed its own modules on Basisplus software, an RDBMS. The member libraries availing to the Interlibrary Loan facility can place the requests online through the system itself for getting the books on loan. The Interlibrary Loan is one of the most popular services of DELNET, the resource sharing is done not only between the libraries located in India but also outside India. It is quite heartening to note that DELNET has evolved a very successful functional model of Interlibrary Loan/Document Delivery services. Through these services, the users, faculty, researchers and scholars of the member libraries are able to get and refer to the books which are not readily available in their own libraries.

At times the books are out of print and are not even available with the book publishers themselves. The Reference books are also lended out though for fewer loaning period. It is worth mentioning that certain libraries in the country which are reference libraries like Central Reference Library, Delhi University, Indian Institute of Advanced Study, Shimla does lend out books to DELNET. It is only possible due to the mutual cooperation and benefit the libraries generates from the process of resource sharing.

It demonstrates a win-win situation. DELNET charges only for the nominal courier for sending the books on loan and it is the responsibility of the borrowing Institution to return back the book at their own cost. In India wherein the users and also the libraries have the limited resources, through the resource sharing the needs of the information users are fulfilled in most economical ways. I would like to mention that DELNET also serves its member-libraries outside India. DELNET has also created a database of E-books which are available in the public domain.

Union List of Current Journals and E-journals Consortium in India

The journals are a vital source of current information for the scientific research. The information about the availability of the current journals is of great help for the document delivery services. DELNET is maintaining an online union list of current journals available in the fields of Science and Technology, Social Sciences and Humanities. This database has more than 25,000 unique titles of current journals available in member as well as the non member libraries of DELNET. The database is updated continuously by receiving the list of currently subscribed journals and this database contains the information about the journals not only available with the member libraries but also with the major reputed libraries in India which are the non members.

The photocopies of journal articles are arranged from the libraries and are supplied to the requesting libraries. It is also one of the most popular services.

In India a major E-journals consortium was formed in 2000 named "INDEST (Indian National Digital Library in Science and Technology Consor-tium" with a financial contribution of ₹200 million by the Ministry of Human Resource Development (MHRD), Govern-ment of India. All India Council for Technical Education (AICTE) has also contributed ₹37.5 million to this. Thirty Eight centrally funded government institutions including the IITs, NITs and NITs and few others are the core members of INDEST.

The private Institutions are self supported. Under the consortium, an access to more than 6500 journals from various publishers and aggregators are provided. The UGC Infonet E-journals consortium covers 4453+ejournals and provides access to nearly 100 Universities of the country. It has been noticed that private institutions who are not able to afford being the member of the consortium is greatly utilizing to the DELNET Document Delivery Services.

Moreover, at times the members of the Consortium also approaches DELNET for the delivery of the journal articles since the desired journal may not be the one covered under the access or the desired specific issues are not available online. There is lot much of speculation about the extent of utilization of E-journals in the Institutions and a large number of studies have been carried out to know about the pattern of accessibility. Moreover it has been noticed that if a Institution ceases to be a member of the Consortium because of the non availability of the digital archiving, the users are deprived to browse the issues for which the Institution had paid to the consortia.

Union Catalogue of Journals

DELNET has also created a database containing the holdings data of the journals available in the member libraries besides containing the other bibliographical information about the journals. At present the database contains 19,289 records of the journals. It is a good resource for tracking down the articles from the rare, old issues of the journals dating back to late 19th and early 20th century. DELNET does receive a number of requests from the libraries for locating the journal articles from the very old issues of the journals. It is a good resource for locating the articles from the rare old issues of the published journals.

Database of Journal Articles

There are a number of libraries, though not many on the network who are involved with the articles indexing in the machine readable form. A large portion of the library budget is annually spent on subscribing to the journals, either in print or in online mode by the libraries but the libraries lack the access to the databases containing the bibliographic details about the journal articles.

For the researchers and scholars it is very essential to know about the latest articles getting published in their specific fields of discipline. This specific database contains more than 800,000 records and is growing in size. For journal articles, the concerned users, researchers send the requests with their bibliography through e-mail and DELNET arran-ges for the full text delivery. DELNET also helps in providing the list of articles through various other networked sources and the fulltext copies of the selected articles are provided on demand.

Databases of Non-print Materials

DELNET does maintain the databases of CD-ROM, Video recordings and sound recordings available in the member libraries. The non-print materials can not be loaned out from the libraries, however the video recordings and sound recordings are being taken on loan in special cases though for a lesser period of time. The CD-ROMs are used for keyword searching and the concerned bibliography containing the abstracts are provided to the requesting libraries. There are 2,281 records of CDs available with member libraries, 748 sound recordings and more than 5,000 videorecordings listings in the respective databases.

Database of Thesis and Dissertations

This database contains around 45000, Thesis and Dissertations submitted to the various Universities and Institutions. This database contains bibliographic information and since thesis and dissertations are the reference materials available in the libraries, the researchers and scholars use this database to know about the works being carried out in their specific fields.

There has been some projects in India concerning the digitization of the Thesis and Dissertations by INFLIBNET and University of Mysore (Vidyavahini project), but the project has not taken off due to the copyright restrictions.

USEFULNESS OF DELNET UNION CATALOGUES

The access to Union Catalogues created and developed by the library networks remains the most highly used resources by the member-libraries. The locations data available in the union catalogues helps the respective users to find out the availability of the documents in their own regions, state and in different locations of the country and outside.

It is a very effective resource discovery tool and is a great boon to the scholars and researchers of the country. The survey results have highlighted the fact that 85.7 per cent of the member-libraries finds DELNET Union catalo-gues useful and 86.3 per cent of the library users are getting benefited.

While 78.9 per cent of the Postgraduate students, 62.5 per cent of the faculty and 53.7 per cent of the graduate students are getting benefited from the DELNET services. The content available through the union catalogues are very selective in nature since the libraries purchase the titles through a strict selection process.

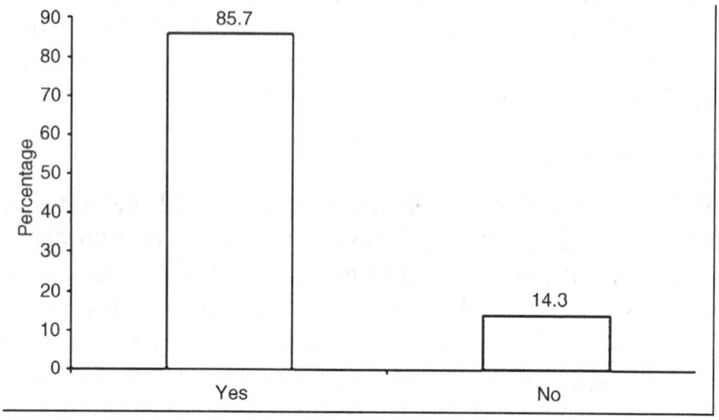

Fig. Do you Find DELNET's Union Catalogues Useful.

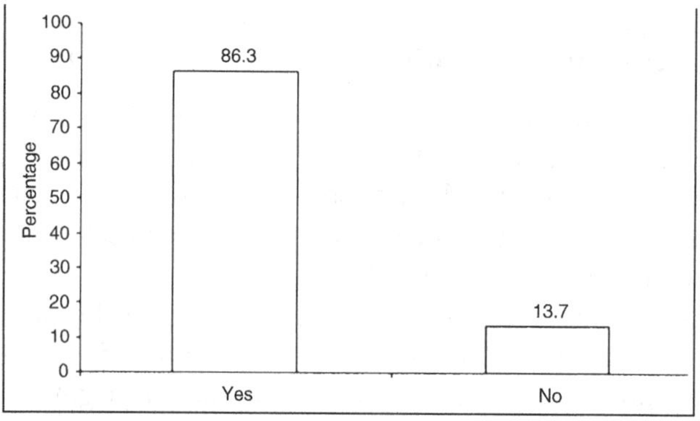

Fig. Do you Feel Library Users are Getting Benefited.

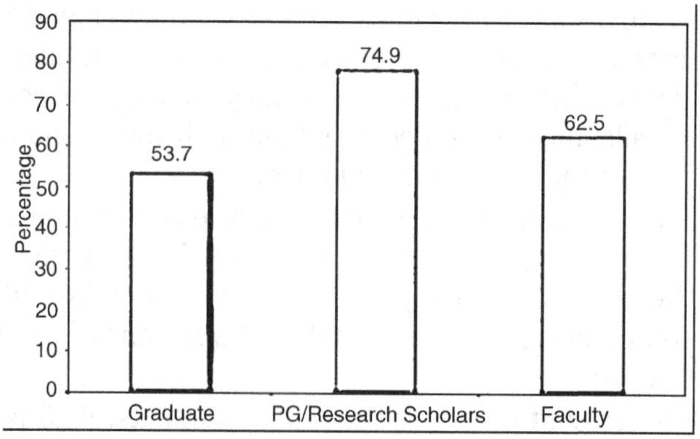

Fig. Kind of Users Getting Benefited from the DELNET Services.

DELNET SERVICES AND ITS UTILISATION

INTER LIBRAY LOAN (ILL) AND DOCUMENT DELIVERY SERVICES (DDS)

The DELNET's ILL and DDS services are one of the most popular services among the member libraries located in different parts of India as well as outside the country. The requests for the supply of books on Interlibrary Loan or the requests to arrange for the journal articles are received by DELNET through various modes including DELNET Online System (options are available through the online databases), E-mail (one of the most prevalent method used by the member libraries), also through fax and at times through post also.

DELNET promotes the electronic communication since it is more faster and interactive and it facilitate the process of quick and safe delivery of the ILL/DDS items. DELNET has a separate ILL tracking system wherein each and every transaction is recorded and status about its date of dispatch, date of retun, etc. are well recorded.

DELNET is able to reach out to the users of the member libraries located in far-flung, remote parts of the country apart from those from the main stream cities. The material is sent through the insured courier services. It is worth mentioning that DELNET not only provides the ILL/DDS to its member libraries located in various parts of the country but is also engaged with International Interlending.

DELNET sends the books on Interlibrary Loan to the member institutions outside India like Baha Social Sciences, Kathmandu, Nepal and Caledonian College of Engineering, Oman; Waljat College of Science and Technology, Muscat. Also the photocopies of journal articles are provided to the member libraries to NILIS, Sri Lanka, IRRI, Philippines, etc. DELNET is also working towards the implementation of ISO ILL protocols.

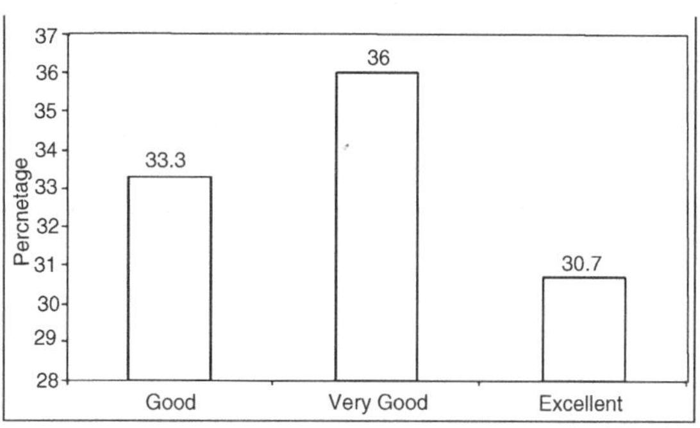

Fig. Response Time of ILL/DDS Services.

The member libraries saves a lot of revenue by availing to the Interlibrary Loan and Document Delivery services of DELNET. It is of great boon to the faculty, researchers and scholars since the expensive, reference books and also out of print titles are made available to the member institutions besides other titles. The DELNET ILL/DDS services are the heart-line of DELNET. There is a great sense of satisfaction among the member-libraries availing to the services. The timeliness factor is crucial in library services. The survey results supplements the fact that 30.7 per cent of the respondents find the response time of ILL/DDS requests as excellent, while 36 per cent rate it as very good and 33.3 per cent finds the response time as 'good'.

Regarding the overall impression of DELNET services, 35.3 per cent consider it as 'good', 31.9 per cent founds it to be 'very good' and the rating of being 'excellent' was given by 23 per cent and 2.72 per cent considered the services as poor.

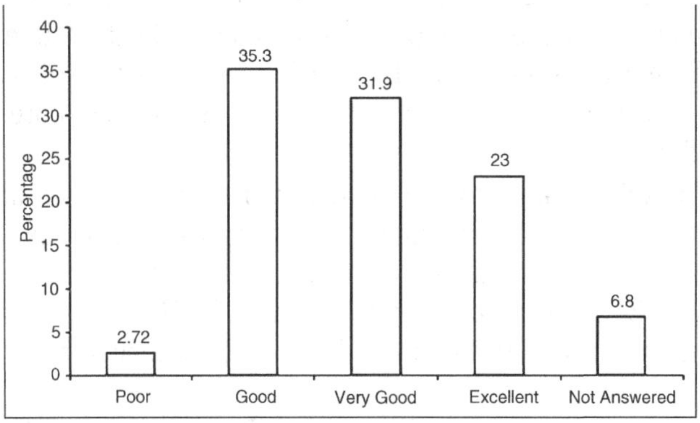

Fig. How do you Rate DELNET Services.

DELNET has also opened up a coordination units in Southern part of India i.e in Bangalore (Karnataka). The unit coordinates for the ILL/DDS services as the nation wide catalogue of the member libraries are available on the DELNET system and these it deals on day to day basis with the respective libraries of the region for the ILL/DDS.

Reference Services

DELNET receives a large number of reference queries every day through various modes. DELNET maintains a referral centre which provides reference services to the researchers, scholars and users from and outside India. DELNET is planning to start a national referral centre wherein the reference queries will be saved and accessed by the users on anytime, anywhere basis. It will be based on the question-answering technology.

NETWORKING AHEAD: NEW CHALLENGES

The new challenges posed by the growing Knowledge economy is the need to network knowledge more vigourously and dynamically. DELNET is also chalking out its plans to move with the needs of the time and to gradually move into the knowledge sharing model.

We have listed below some of the immediate plans of DELNET, though they are full of challenges but with its strong networking capabilities in the country, it is confident of moving ahead with the time in a self-reliant manner:

- DELNET intends to network both libraries and knowledge in the integrated network model. National Knowledge Commission of the Government of India has identified DELNET as one of the major library network in India which will network more than 25,000 libraries in the near future in India.
- DELNET is interested to help the libraries in tapping the tacit knowledge available in their Institutions and to contribute for the development of the Knowledge Repositories and networking the knowledge resources.
- DELNET is supporting the establishment of Knowledge Centres in India. The plans are under consideration for establishing a Central Institutional Repository for the member-libraries in order to tap the tacit knowledge available with the researchers, scholars and the faculty members.
- DELNET is interested to open shortly the State Centres in different parts of India and also the Regional Centres in order to provide training to the library professionals, promote the usage of network resources and also to help the local libraries in the development of the digital content.
- DELNET is wanting that more libraries especially specializing in South Asian studies from different parts of the World should become a part of the network and utilize the services and resources created for their researchers and scholars at much affordable cost.
- DELNET is wanting to implement the social networking tools in order to enhance the user interaction. The DELNET Helpline support is also offered through the YMS. The users of the member-libraries of DELNET interact with the official of DELNET in an interactive mode and it brings the end users closers to DELNET.
- DELNET is launching the Technical Support System for Koha-the Open source ILS in order to help the Indian Libraries for adopting the open source software. An online portal will also get launched soon by DELNET wherein the online audio/video learning material for implementing Koha, including tutorials on MARC 21 will be offered. It will be operational on 24/7 basis against a nominal registration fee.

LIBRARY MOVEMENT IN INDIA

India has a glorious history of 5000 years with a rich heritage of philosophy, language, religion, art and culture. The Nation has 428 languages with 1600 dialects out of which 13 are extinct. These languages have several classical scriptures in their Scripts. These scriptures are scattered and preserved in different libraries of the country. Creating a digital library of available classics and establishing federated look-ups to these collections are burning issues of the day. The Indian Digital Library Initiative (IDLI) has been triggered out of Digital Library Initiative (DLI) of United States. Both the Indian collections and the environment are totally different from the one United States has. A fresh look to the existing problems should be given.

ISSUES WITH INDIAN DIGITAL LIBRARIES

Though there is a huge thrust in India for establishing digital libraries, there are several reasons due to which the whole movement is fallen behind.

Behavioural Issues

The Government of India must look forward to pool the knowledge base of the country. Phase-wise pooling of available knowledge resource of various libraries in the country must be encouraged. This requires funding to various libraries for digitizing the documents of their collection. So far, much of the funding for the purpose is made through United States through Million Book Project.

Though, the project has been initiated with novel interest, unfortunately, keeping control over the whole project appeared little difficult. Besides, many of the technological challenges specific to Indian context are new to the American environment need to be addressed. It looks better to initiate test-beds in first phase with the objective to demonstrate technological capabilities.

Some centres can be identified from different language speaking states and accordingly funded for developing technical capabilities in a limited time frame. Unfortunately, the present growth of digital libraries in the country is unplanned which has resulted in bad models or instances with just scanned images.

The first phase of the National Digital Library Movement could have been better utilized only to understand the underlying difficulties and the possible solutions. The second phase of the project could have been funded for building the live digital collections for use and receive feedbacks.

The required changes and modifications could be further implemented nationwide. There are several libraries with unique collection of its kind. With the third phase such collection can be digitally preserved as well as universal access to the documents could be insured. It has been observed that many of the libraries having unique and rare collection are scared of going online because they think of loosing the physical presence of users in the library. This behavioural difficulty must be addressed in order to ensure universal accessibility including the digital preservation at national level.

Conditional Issues

A multilingual country like India has several conditional constraints hindering the overall growth of digital libraries in the country. There are representation in the literature from all states and languages. It is easy to map the script due to common origin from Brahmi but it is equally difficult to convey the meaning in different languages. It can be easily observed that in different parts of the country people know more than one language with having one script. For example, it is very common to see Brahmins reciting hymn in Sanskrit (a language) written in their mother script.

In such cases mapping of characters can be very handy. Since writing is known to Indians from 3000 BC and paper is invented only in AD. 104. Apart from that the printing technology reached very late to India. Hence, it was very late when Indians started using paper. Many of the ancient writings are on stones, leaves, clay tablets, tree barks, cloth etc. Anything before, AD 1600 is hand written which is difficult for machines to read. Some of the objects are so brittle that they can only be handled using special means. There is abundance of such material in the country.

Technological Issues

World has witnessed impeccable technological advancements. There are digital library suites can be used directly for creating digital collection. But much of the development is in English and European languages as the computer was first used by them only. But off late, market for other scripts is also felt by IT giants and hence Unicode as character representation standard is introduced. Unicode is still being evolving as it promises to cover all the world scripts and signs. The country has a big share in IT industry of the world. But little has been done for the languages and scripts of India.

An Optical Character Recognitions (OCR) software in any Indian script is yet to be developed. The tests are on the way at Indian Statistical Institute, Kolkata and Centre for Develop-ment of Advance Computing (CDAC), Pune. A product named Chitran-kan by CDAC, Pune is available for use in Devnagari but the product has limited variety of font support and is still in testing phase. The Indic scripts are off child of Brahmi script which is not in practice anymore. The derived scripts of Brahmi like Devanagari and other Indic scripts have complex rende-ring principles when it comes to representation of characters in machine.

Complex character glyphs are rendered depicting features like bidirectional and dynamic composition. It is difficult to create rendering engines of this kind for all the Indic languages but major work has been done in this area. The work is in progress to integrate rendering plug-ins with web browsers for creating websites in Indian scripts. With Devanagari and other major scripts the task has been achieved and now-a-days one can see many websites in regional languages. One of the important problems Indian IT community facing today is about sorting the words of one language. There are scores of examples of same kind in Sanskrit. It is because of these reasons it is very difficult to generate index for any Indic document.

Besides, there are no good corpora available in public domain which can be taken as sample for experimentation and testing. This has also influenced the search algorithm. Unlike search algorithms of English, search algorithms in Indian languages are yet to be evolved. What is available today as Indian language search is only pattern matching. The work is still at preliminary level because of the complexity of the languages. It is easy to work with Sanskrit for the purpose as it has morphological rules for construction of words but addressing the same is difficult with other Indic languages (Hindi, Oriya, Tamil etc.) as they don't have such kind of rules for word construction.

The Stemming algorithms like Soundex and Metaphone are yet to be developed by any of the Indian languages. To get a feel, if one searches for Hindi word (correctly spelt as means Back) in Google, gets only the former Hindi string in search result.

An application of stemming algorithm would have brought the correct later one in the search results. Similarly, there are n-gram techniques of string search which are warranted to be tested with Indic text.

Though the metadata is not a potential problem but due to uncontrolled growth there is lot of disparity in use of metadata standards. Many of the libraries have drafted their own metadata set not confirming to the International standard. This has happened in the case of distributed digitization centers at the initial stage. Though, an awareness has been aroused among the professionals to use International standard, but, still it is very difficult to convert non-conforming one's to the standard form.

With the use of codified data a standard metadata scheme can yield an efficient cross-lingual information retrieval. This technique of cross-lingual information retrieval has been demonstrated in the system named "Brass" developed at Documentation Research and Training Centre. Such infor-mation retrieval systems can supplement automatic translation projects to some extent, as there is not significant development in machine translation of Indic languages.

INDIAN SCENARIO

India is witnessing a strong move for developing digital libraries around the country. Some are in public domain like LDL of Documentation Research and Training Centre, Bangalore and Digital Library of India. Some are with restricted access like, Nalanda Digital Library of National Institute of Technology, Calicut. As far as, the English literature is concerned there are editable text available over web but when it comes to Indian language only scanned images of the documents are available for display supplemented by metadata. The experiment has been done with many of the Open source software and results are positive.

Some test beds can be found at Documentation Research and Training Centre site but still much has to be done.

LIBRARY LEGISLATION IN INDIA

The present information explosion and the direct relation of information to developments in all walks of life emphasizes the need to give greater priority to the planning of systems which give library and information services to the people. Such systems can only be planned at national levels, if the total information resources of the nation is to be pooled together in a federal country like India, and shared between the cons-tituent states to make it available to all the users who require it in an equally and unbiased way at optimal cost.

Such library and information systems are to be founded upon sound legislation, if they are to attain their objectives the Society's information need has become so imperative that, many of the national and international library organizations has started to stress the urgent need for national library systems working together and sharing their services and materials at international level to provide better services to the people. Better can be defined here in quantitative and qualitative terms. Such national level and international level networking and resource sharing between library systems make possible service at lower cost, convenience of access, access to more materials and more rapid availability of materials.

THE MODEL ACT OF S.R. RANGANATHAN

To attain these objectives Dr. S.R. Ranganathan had framed the first model public libraries Act in 1930 which he placed for discussion at the Educational Conference at Banaras. Before framing the Act, this internationally reputed library scientist had travelled through most countries of the world where library legislation existed and had evaluated them and in many countries his ideas helped them to improve the systems.

In his Library Development Plan which he submitted in 1947 to Government of India he had included a union library bill and a revised state library bill also which envisaged the national public library and information system according to the most modern principles. Another model library Act was drafted in 1963 by a committee under the chairmanship of D.M. Sen on behalf of the Ministry of Education, Government of India. In 1966 the Library Legislation Sub Committee of the Planning Commission also prepared a model bill. The library Acts that came into existence in Madras, Hyderabad, Andhra, Karnataka and Maharastra totally or partially accept the ideas of Rang ana than as reflected in his Model Acts and bills. These States became the laboratories where the ideas evolved by Ranganathan were experimented and observed.

In the light of these observations and suggestions contained in the other model bills and Acts, Ranganathan has improved his model Act by rectifying the clauses found to be defective in working and by adding new provisions that seemed essential. This model libraries Act was published in 1972. This is the latest and most advanced Model Act. Ten States out of the 25 States and 7 union territories have enacted library legislation. They are Madras 1948, Andhra 1960, Karnataka 1965, Maharastra 1967, West Bengal 1979, Manipur 1985, Kerala 1989 and Haryana 1989.

Others are Goa and Mizoram. But none of them are considered perfect or efficient. So in this comparative analysis of the essential aspects of State Public Library Acts, the Model Public Library Act, 1972 of Dr. S.R. Ranganathan is taken as the measuring rod or ideal situation with which the State Act is compared.

Whenever some notable additional provisions or improvements are found in other existing Acts the same is discussed at the concerned contexts. The Kerala Act to which stress is given in this study and Ranganathan's Model Act of 1972 will be referred herein after as KPLA and Model Act respectively.

PREAMBLE OF STATE ACTS

The preamble of a Library Act should summarise and state the aims and objectives of that Library Act. Even though the preamble of KPLA went on to explain the existing situations and the intentions with which the Act was initiated in an elaborate and vague form, it has given what is to be in preamble just before the preamble in precise and clear words as a long title ofthe Act. This summary or long title of the Act which we have to consider as preamble contains the basic concept of modern public library service which the actual preamble failed to state and the KPLA in its totality failed to support.

Like the Model Act, this summary provides for the establishment and maintenance of a system of public libraries and for the comprehensive development and organisation of all kinds of library and information services required for the people. The long title that follows the title of the Act in KPLA states, it is: An Act to consolidate and unify the library laws in the State and to provide for the reorganisation of the entire library system in the State of Kerala with a view to the develop-ment and maintenance of a comprehensive rural and urban library service and for matters connected therewith or incidental thereto.

Ranganathan has laid clear emphasis on legislation for public library service and for the organisation of a comprehensive library system. But all other Acts except KPLA provides for establishment and maintenance of public libraries only. They all cling to the obsolete concept of treating public libraries as independent units in their collection and services. So in this statement of the purpose of the Act, KPLA has accepted the most modern concept of Public

Library legislation and the statement is a distinct improvement over those in all other existing State Acts.

STATE LIBRARY AUTHORITY

The concept of the *State Library Authority* (SLA) underwent an evolution from State Library Committee to Minister of Education or Libraries; everywhere in the world. The Model Act recommends that for the purpose of promoting and organising a library system in the State the Ministry for Education of the State shall be the SLA. It shall be the duty of the SLA to provide; for an adequate library and information service in the State and, for the progressive development of the institutions devoted to the purpose and to secure the effective execution by *Local Library Authorities* (LLA) of the national policy for providing adequate library service to the people in every locality.

In the existing' State Acts only Karnataka Public Library Act, 1965 provides and clearly names SLA. Section 3 of the Act provides for the constitution and composition of the SLA.6 SLA shall be a body corporate having perpetual succession and a common seal with power, to acquire, hold and dispose of property and to contract and may by the same time sue and be sued. It consists of twenty members from the fields concerned with information creation, organisation and services, with Minister for Education who shall ex officio be the President and State Librarian who shall ex officio be the Secretary of SLA.

But it is desirable to make only one person, instead of a corporate body to be the supreme authority for providing this very important service, for that gives a unified command from administrative points of view. And this person should not be any person less than the Minister for Education, because he is directly responsible to the legislature and his term of office being limited to a period of five years he is ultimately responsible to the people. Hewit who made a study of the library legislation in India; it will be observed that two kinds of supreme authority are favoured in existing legislation and in the drafts of the model bills framed in India.

One is a body of persons *i.e.,* State Library Councilor Committee and second is a Minister of State. He suggests the second as the better of the two, mainly because a Minister is responsible to his legislature, and through it, to the electors and many be called to account therein. A body of persons even though a Minister may be President or Chairman thereof is not so easily questioned. In any case; so important an activity as the provision for public library and information service to the people fully justifies direct representation in State Legislature.

So all the studies on library legislations and the evaluation of existing legislations throughout the world and especially in third world counties, like that of Gardners's study comes to the conclusion that providing up of a body or a person as SLA and clearly naming and defining its powers and functions is certainly essential for the successful working of library Acts. But KPLA is very vague in this aspect and it fails to name a person or body as SLA.

STATE LIBRARY COMMITTEE

The Model Act provides for a *State Library Committee* (SLC) for the purpose of advising the SLA on all matters arising under the Act. All existing State Acts and Model Bills enacted or drafted in India provide for appointment of such a Committee or Council. KPLA names it as Kerala State Library Council. All Acts of the states except Kerala's have prescribed its membership on somewhat similar lines. All Acts provides that this body will be headed by Minister for Education. Despite differences in nomenclature and composition the function of this committee or council envisaged everywhere is basically the same *i.e.,* to advise the SLA or State Government in all matters arising out of the Act.

Kerala State Library Council (KSLC)

A careful analysis of the Kerala State Library Council (KSLC) in comparison with the SLC as provided in the Model Act or other State Acts will reveal that it is not a councilor committee of advisory nature as SLCs are. KSLC is an SLC and at the same time an SLA by itself. Naming it as a council is a difference in terminology only. Instead of appointing a Minister as SLA as in Mysore it appoints a body as SLA. But the Act fails to name it as SLA. The duties, powers and functions assigned to KSLC is inclusive of all those assigned to SLA and SLC in Model Act.

Sub-section 1 of the Section 3 of KPLA dealing with the constitution and composition of KSLC states9; KSLC shall be a body corporate having perpetual succession and a common seal with power, to acquire hold and dispose of property, both movable and immovable and to enter into contracts and shall by its name sue and be sued. This is an adaptation of the class related to Karnataka State Library Authority of Karnataka Act. No other Act including Model Act has so clearly defined the nature of this body and assigned so much powers as this like the Acts of Kerala and Karnataka. The powers and functions assigned to KSLC includes both the advisory functions of the committees and councils provided by Model Act and other Acts and the duties assigned to SLA by Model Act and Karnataka Act.

Sub-sections of section 8 of KPLA provides that the KSLC may:

- Advise the government of all matters connected with the administration of that Act and . . . the overall library policy of the State.
- Co-ordinate the working of the District Library Councils and Taluk Library Unions and...supervise and direct all matters relating to library service in the state.

- Establish one or more State Libraries . . . at such place or places in the State as may be considered necessary.
- Appoint and control such officers and servants as may be necessary for the efficient performance of its duties and functions under this Act and the rules made there under.
- Give to the District Library Councils and Taluk Library unions directions in the performance of their functions under this Act and . . . they shall not in-the discharge of their functions under this Act depart from directions given by the KSLC.

While we consider these classes and compare them with the parellel sections of the Model Act or other Acts it becomes clear that the classes which assigns the duties, powers and functions of KSLC is a distinct improvement from all others. KPLA has identified most of the functions and duties expected from such a body and very clearly assigned them to it without giving space for doubt and vagueness.

Composition of KSLC

If KSLC is to become able to fulfil such duties and functions expected from it, the composition of the body should be done accordingly. Membership of such a body should include persons who have contributed to the growth of knowledge, who has evolved or developed methods and techniques for collecting, organising and disseminating information and who have wide experience in related fields of activity. It is not the method of representation but the quality of representation that will make possible the efficient functioning of the system.

The sections which prescribe the membership of SLA in Karnataka Act and SLC in Model Act and other State Acts prescribe their membership on somewhat similar lines. Prof. P.B. Mangla in his study of library legislation opines that it should be a body having representatives from various institutions, organisations, government etc. interested in and connected with the growth and development of library and information services in the State.

The Model Act, the opinion of experts and recommen-dations of committees set for studying library legislation agrees that such a body should include among its members; the Minister for Libraries if there is one, otherwise Minister for Education, then Minister in charge of Local-Self-Government, Director of Libraries, State Librarian, sufficient number of representatives from State Legislative Assembly by election from among themselves, Secretary to Government for Education, representatives elected from Local Library Authorities by rotation to limit size of the body, representatives of associations of library profession and experts with specialization in library and information services and represen-tatives of Universities of the State.

It would be essential that the Minister in charge of Libraries should act as *ex-officio* chairman and the Director of Public Libraries or State Librarian should act as ex-officio secretary of the committee.

The rationale behind such a composition of this body is that it is a body which is to advise the government and discuss continuously on a most important responsibility of the government, that is organisation and dissemination of information required by the society. But disregarding all these principles KPLA provides for constituting a body of members who were not suitable to undertake this work.

The section 3 sub-section (2) related to the composition of the KSLC in KPLA provides: The KSLC shall consist of one member each from Taluks, elected by the general body of the District Library councils, and five members of whom one shall be a librarian, another a person belonging to the scheduled caste or scheduled tribe and another a woman nominated by the government. Library and information service is an intellectual service. It goes without saying that this body as provided in KPLA will not be able to fulfil satisfactorily the purpose for which it is intended.

In these days of information explosion and flooding of vast and varied types of books and other printed materials that originates every minute without wide familiarity of all spheres of knowledge and expertise in handling their information in most effective way at minimum cost the body which heads such a system will be having a mere formal and useless existence. As we have seen in section 8 of KPLA the most important function of KSLC is to advise the government on all matters connected with the administration of this Act and overall library policy ofthe State.

It is not clear how this committee will be competent to render such expert technical advise when it has only persons as members, who has come through election without expertise or knowledge about information work and without even any educational qualifications. Library and information service to the people if provided efficiently will be the continuously active service of government and will require expert advise everyday on many matters.

The KSLC's inability to provide such expert advise will make government's efforts futile and to overcome this, govern-ment will be forced to create a continuous chain of Advisory Committees which is also not very practicable. While no hard and fast rule can be laid down about the size of this body it is generally felt that it should not have more than twenty members. The KSLC may remain a supreme body in name only for real powers of the council have been passed over to a smaller body which is the executive committee. But it also becomes an unwieldy body with membership of 25 persons.

Thus KSLC has acquired all the defects existing in SLAs and SLCs into one body. This Executive Committee is a new addition in our library Acts. But the findings of Ashok Mehta Committee and various committees appointed by many State Governments to study Panchayat Raj Institutions advise us against such an elected body like KSLC for organising important service as library and information service to the people. Instead of adopting the constitution and composition of SLA and SLC provided by the Model Act or followed by the other State Acts KPLA gave legal sanction to the organizational set up of an association that was already existing there, that is Kerala Granthasala Sangham.

The constitution and composition of KSLC and its Executive Committee is the same followed by Sangham for its general body and Bharanasamithi. In all other provisions KPLA follows the same pattern of Sangham with some minor alterations. For more than half a century Sangham was pressurizing the Government to give legal sanction to Sangham to be the SLA and to accept its system as it is,as State's Library System.

But experts have continuously pointed out during this period the futility of such a system for library and information service. But Sangham objected government's all other attempts to enact a modern library system legislation and at last come out successful in legalizing its own system. But this in fact totally prevents the State from having an advanced library legislation and developing its library and information services in conformity with the requirements of the time.

LOCAL LIBRARY AUTHORITY

Library and information service is to be rendered locally by thousands of service points spread throughout the state. The State as a whole in view of its large size is not suitable for being considered as a single unit for organizing these services. So it becomes essential to organize this service system on a decentralized pattern. The units of responsibility at different levels, their nature, functions and relation with other levels should be clearly specified in the Act. In the Model Act Ranganathan recommended two types of Local Library Authorities; District Library Authority in a district and City Library Authority in a city.

The KPLA improves the scope of decentralization of services; providing a three tier system that is after State level at District and Taluk levels parallel to Government's Administrative machanism. The District Library Councils (DLC) and Taluk Library Unions (TLU) are miniature forms of KSLC.

Their constitution, composition, powers and functions are all the same as KSLC; limited within the geographical area of its coverage. DLC and TLU shall elect their Executive Committee which will elect the office bearers very much like in KSLC. All the defects of KSLC are reflected in these bodies also. The Act does not provide for City Library Authorities. It is the duty of the Taluk union to organize and administer the library and information service to the people living in cities and villages.

DEPARTMENT OF PUBLIC LIBRARIES AND OFFICIALS

It is generally emphasized that in order to develop a system of public libraries in a State or country on proper lines, it is essential that a separate department of public libraries be created at par with the department of education and that the former should not be a part of the later or any other' department. The Acts of Andhra, Maharashtra, West Bengal and Karnataka prescribe for the creation of separate department of Public Libraries.

Director of Public Libraries

Most of the recommendations related to public library system legislation emphasizes that the department of Public Libraries should be headed by a Director of Public Libraries (DPL), whose rank must be equivalent to that of Director of Education. He must be a person with qualification and experience in Library and Information Science.

Emphasis on his being a professional is laid because it is he to whom the whole public library system in the State would look for guidance and inspiration and his professional outlook would normally greatly help the development of the system on desired lines.

The first public library Act in this country; the Madras Public Library Act, 1948 provided for the appointment of DPL. Andhra, Maharastra and West Bengal also prescribes for the creation of DPL. In Madras and Andhra the Director of Public Instruction is made the ex-officio Director of Public Libraries also.

The disadvantages of such an administrative set-up are quite obvious. The Department of Public Libraries becomes an additional burden to the Director of Public Instruction. This new department will be looked upon as an uninvited guest. A. R. Hewit has rightly pointed out that many of the duties of Director of Public Libraries would require technical knowledge and skill in librarianship. So professional experts only can undertake this responsibility efficiently.

State Library

All the Acts except KPLA which is not providing for these offices, combines the responsibilities of developing and managing the State Central Library Superintending and directing all matters related to the State library system in a single person called State Librarian or DPL.

The Model Act also recommends this pattern. But the Sinha Committee report suggested the creation of two separate posts for this purpose when it said "The DPL may have the overall responsibility to organize develop and supervise the public library system as the Head of the Department of Public Libraries.

The State Librarian should have the responsibility to manage supervise and develop State Central Library and should be the Chief Technical Advisor of the DPL, with no responsibility for the administration of the service in the State. This responsibility should be entirely that of DPL. But in KPLA there is no provision for appointing a Director of Libraries or State Librarian. While the class by class discussion of the Bill was going on in Assembly Mr. V.M. Sudheeran; member presented an amendment to add a new clause in the Act providing for appointment of a Director of Libraries. But was not considered.

Administration

For the administration of public libraries all the State Acts have created a department or directorate of public libraries. It is put under the charge of Director of Libraries or State Librarian who is to be the *ex-officio* Secretary of SLA. The functions of these posts as prescribed by all Acts including the Model Act are: to supervise and direct all matters relating to public libraries, to direct and control the working of LLAs, submit reports to Government and deal with schemes and plans relating to libraries. Many of the highly technical and specialized works of State Central Library also is to be supervised by them.

So it is clear that these posts which are carrying heavy responsibility concerning various matters-financial, advisory, administrative, technical, supervisory and so on-under the Act would require technical knowledge and skill in library and information service. So the Secretary or High Officer of this body should be a whole time officer having the prescribed qualifications to practice the library profession. Disregarding all the facts KPLA assigns all these duties and powers to a Secretary elected by members of the Executive Committee ofKSLC.

Section 3 sub-section (5) of KPLA provides that the elected members of the Executive Committee shall elect a President, Vice-President, Secretary and Joint Secretary from among themselves to be the President, Vice-President, Secretary and Joint Secretary respectively of the State Library Council and of the Executive Committee. Their term of office will be for three years.

KPLA assigns to the Secretary of KSLC the duties and powers which other State Acts assign to State Librarian or Director of Libraries. Section 9 Sub-section (1) States: the Secretary of the State Library Council shall be Chief Executive Authority of KSLC.

The nature of the office of Secretary of KSLC requires professional knowledge and experience as well as continuity of office for the successful operation of the Act, so it is inevitable that this provision will prevent KPLA from fulfilling the objectives for which a modern library legislation should exist. This serious defect of the Act has been pointed out by many members during the discussion of the bill.

Dr. M.Kuttappan has brought to the notice of the Assembly that such an important system like that for library and information service requires qualified government officials as their secretaries at State, District and Taluk levels. The period of an elected non-official member may be over by three years and if he misappropriates government fund allotted for library development it will not be possible for the government to take action on him. Sri Ishac Kurikkal suggested an amend-ment to the Bill to provide that the Secretary of the SLC shall be appointed by the Government on the advice of the Kerala Public Service Commission.

Another member Sri Kodiyeri Balakrishnan opined that the Secretary of KSLC should be appointed by Government and the Act should specify the qualifications and method of appointment for this post. Sri Ramesh Chennitthala presented an amendment to add the following sub-clause in KPLA namely: The Secretary shall be a person not below the rank of a Joint Secretary to Government appointed by Government from among persons qualified and competent to hold such post. But all these suggestions were rejected and principles were disregarded to maintain a democratic system for constituting the SLA.

State Central Library

The existing State legislations and the Model Act provide for a State Central Library (SCL) as an integral part of the Public Library Service. The SCL is normally the copy right collection. It should collect as far as its resources allow, expensive work and literature published abroad, material for which the local public library would have little need and could not afford. All the countries of the world possessing adequate library systems, have national library systems and all have national central library as distinct from the other libraries in the system, but is accessible to all through any library of the system.

The same role of National Central Library to the National system is done by SCL to the State system. Usually the library legislations designate the biggest collection available in the State as SCL and makes its resources and services available to the system. Even though various Acts and Model Act give different names to SCL like State Service Library, etc. in a public library system only one such library will be maintained and its resources will be shared by all participating units. Maintaining more than one SCL is unnecessary duplication of work and waste of resources.

Most of the State Acts and Model bills drafted, designate the biggest public library existing in the State as SCL and adopts it to the system and shares its resources among participating units. But instead of designating Trivandrum Public Library, the oldest and biggest collection in the State as SCL, the KPLA deems it to be one of the many State libraries it will establish.

The Act provides for no SCL in its system. Instead it provides that KSLC shall establish one or more state libraries at such place or places in the State as may be considered necessary. The relation of State libraries with other state libraries and different level service units and the purpose of more than one such institution is not defined in the Act.

Library Co-operation

To make the best possible use of the document resources not only in the public library system but also in other types of libraries in the State such as universities, special libraries etc, a system of inter library co-operation needs to be developed in the state as a whole. It would also be useful and economical if centralization of different aspects such as acquisition programme, technical processing etc. of documents should be introduced at State level or at different levels of the system. The KPLA gives no such provision for co-operation or centralized processing and the institution which is to give leadership in such activities that is SCL is absent in KPLA.

State Library Service

State Library Service brings the manpower of the State in one pool and thus avoids the waste of time and money involved in filling up posts that would otherwise involve, if every Local Library Authority were to appoint the staff independently. A State Library Service further avoids the influence of members of the Local Library Authority in day-to-day management of libraries. Mysore Act has created a special state library service and it ensures proper administration and economy through State Library Service. But KPLA gives to KSLC and Local Library Authorities that is DLC and TLU the powers to appoint and control required officers and servants.

FINANCE

For the growth and development of a public library system in a State, there must be a specific provision in the Act for required financial support. Since education is an essential responsibility of a welfare State, public library system should obviously be established and maintained at the expense of the State.

The Model Act of Ranganathan, the suitable sources for this purpose are:

- Library cess,
- Grants from the State Governments, and
- Grants from Central Government.

In the provisions related to finance; KPLA accepts all the generally accepted principles. The Act provides that the KSLC shall levy a library cess in the form of surcharge on building tax or property tax collected by local bodies at the rate of five paise for whole rupee. The cess shall be paid to the KSLC by local bodies. The government may also make every year a grant to the KSLC of a sum which shall not exceed one per cent of the budget for education. This amount of grant is insufficient.

Ranganathan's Library Development Plan, the documents on National Policy on Library and Information Science and Indian Library Association suggests that six per cent of the Education budget of the State should be set apart for libraries. The Act also provides for a State Library Fund from which all expenses of KSLC, DLC and TLU shall be met. Grants of State and Central Governments to KSLC, contributions by persons, bodies or authorities etc. to KSLC and other funds transferred to it shall be credited to State Library Fund. KSLC shall distribute from State Library Fund such amounts as required for each DLC and TLD. Against creating such Library funds as suggested by Model Act and some State Acts at State and local levels; these provisions of KPLA related to finance providing a centralized fund are truly a notable improvement.

LIBRARY SERVICES

The libraries have transformed drastically from store-houses for books and journals to the powerhouses of knowledge and information since the middle of the 20th century. The information and communication technology is responsible for this revolution. The very existences of libraries are dependable on users' satisfaction. Users are getting satisfied when the library is able to rise to his or her expectation or meet the actual needs. A quality service is said to be one, which satisfy the users' expectation resulting a good experience.

Throughout the history, libraries were mainly concerned with collection development and processing. The library profe-ssionals gave less concern to quality in product and services, never checked whether the users were satisfied or not. Gradually the social and economic changes have prompted the libraries to develop services. The staff has a vital role in the satisfaction of users. The library being a service organization, its prime objective is to provide the right documents, infor-mation and services to its users. Only the users' satisfaction survey will facilitate the assessment of their satisfaction with products and services offered. There are various methods, tools and techniques to measure, control and improve the quality of library services. Quality measurement and evaluation assumes great importance in modern libraries, as it brings immense benefits to the library as well as user community. Different methods such as collection of data for measuring the performance and quality of libraries; The SERVQUAL method, a multiple item scale to measure service quality; The LibQUAL, a tool developed on SERVQUAL for measuring the quality of library products and services.

WHAT IS QUALITY

The word 'quality' has several definitions. The conven-tional definition is " One that wears well, is well constructed will last for long time" and the strategic definition is "meeting customers' requirements."

- According to Juuran 'The quality is fitness for purpose'.

- According to Robinson, "Quality is meeting the requirements of customer-now and in the future."
- According to Sarkar "Quality of a product or service is the ability of the product or service to meet the customers' requirements.

QUALITY CONCEPT IN LIBRARY SERVICES

The library is an organization to offer reference and information services to its users. Library service is the combination of the services-process and its delivery. In a library, the service offered from acquisition section, technical section, maintenance section etc. are the processes carried out there and thereafter delivered to the users. The quality should start from the acquisition section, which should be carried uniformly to circulation section. A user who had an unpleasant experience from the library will tell it to many people, but a good experience will be told to very few. Therefore it is very necessary for librarian to understand the users, what they want, how they want, and when they want the documents and information.

HOW TO IMPROVE THE QUALITY IN LIBRARY SERVICES

In this information age it is very easy to make a quality based library if the parent body or concerned authority assist financially as well as collectively. It is very necessary for the librarian and its parent body to look forward for the present and future generation to cope up with international phenomena. A user must be educated with proper technology to use the library effectively.

He or she should have knowledge of what facilities and services are available in the library and information centre and how to access those efficiently and effectively. To improve the service quality the user satisfaction survey is a tool that provides both quantitative and qualitative data. It is an important part of libraries for process and performance measurement.

Main steps to measure users' satisfaction are:

- Conducting sample survey.
- Data collection.
- Process and analysis of data.
- Interpret and present the data.
- Finding out result.

With the help of the result the librarian can take new steps for development of library. The regular survey will enable the library to understand the changes in users satisfaction and to plan the services accordingly.

The Users' Satisfaction is based on Many Factors Like

- A source of up-to-date information, knowledge, accessing facilities and assistance.

- The library should organize its facilities visible to the users; otherwise they may not have it and get dissatisfied.
- *Accessibility:* The library resources and services should be easily accessible. Books should be arranged in shelves in proper classified order, so that the users can locate books quickly. In case of electronic library the electronic database like OPAC will help the users to find out the books in stacks.
- *Tangibles:* The tangibles of libraries, namely the building, furniture and other physical facilities, collection, staff, machines etc. should be sufficient and appropriate and useful for the users.
- *Courtesy/Friendliness:* The library staff should be very courteous and friendly with the users.
- *Physical Appearance/Atmosphere/Cleanliness/Comfort:* The appearance of library, its facilities, collection, staff and services should be attractive and pleasant. A Welcoming atmosphere should be must. Furniture, floor, racks, documents etc. should be neat and clean.
- *Process-Reliability/Communications:* The processing part of the library should be dependable and efficient that suffices the expectations of the users. The way of communication, assistance and guidance also greatly affect the satisfaction of the users.
- *Some Useful Criteria to Measure Users' Experience in a Library are:*
  - Speed of services delivery (Access time, location, processing, etc.);
  - Value added services such as Xerox service, CAS, SDI etc.; and
  - Technology used.

It is observed that if something goes wrong that can be very easily learned from the users, so the users' complaints can be taken as good measure of user satisfaction.

Steps for Staff to Meet the Users' Needs

- Being responsible for the total service quality to the users both the Technical staff and frontline staff in the library should serve the users.
- Services must be provided to the users in a most effective way.
- Providing maximum benefits to the users form collection and facilities.
- Stay close to users: Library can not understand users' needs, tastes, interests etc. without listening to them, and services without users' interest will be a mere wastage.
- Users must be treated well, informed well and acknowledged well about the services to the users.

IMPACT OF RANGANATHAN'S FIVE LAWS IN QUALITY SERVICE

The five laws of Ranganathan help in quality improve-ment of service as those are concentrated to the users very seriously. The laws directly advocate towards libraries' collection development, speedy processing, maintenance and quick retrieval of information by users.

The First Law

"Books are for Use" is a direction for measuring the quality of a library; quality in terms of contents, accessibility and availability as and when needed.

The Second Law

"Every reader his/her books" implies needs of users. In order to meet this law the library has to index all micro and macro documents so that every reader can find out his or her requirements.

The Third Law

"Every Book/Information its reader" implies the importance of book/information selection in a library. The law advocates scientific document selection, subject based organization, advanced and in depth indexing, efficient and effective searching and locating tools, Staff assistance, open access, extension services, publicity programs etc.

The Fourth Law

"Save the time of Reader" indicates the importance of fast and efficient services to the users with the advanced technologies, method, techniques and tools.

Open access, digital services, classified arrangement of documents in shelves, location and directing guides, excellent searching tools, and techniques *i.e.* Online public Access Catalogue (OPAC) in an automated library, Xerox facility, Online Information services, qualified and experienced staff will ensure fast service to the users.

The Fifth Law

"The Library is a growing organism" implies collection development, changing of all components of a library.

Everyday the world of documents and information is changing tremendously. Now the information is recorded not in papers alone, to many media, the latest being the electronic and digital form. So in today's world the library may called as information and knowledge house of world as a whole if it is supported by advanced information and communication technologies.

MEASURING QUALITIES OF LIBRARY SERVICES

The important measuring tools and techniques are:

- TQM (Total Quality Management).
- SERVQUAL.
- LibQUAL.

The TQM is one of the techniques used for the improvement and maintenance of quality or performance of the library. It is to provide the right information to the right users at the right place and time and also at the right cost.

The most important components of TQM in a library are:

- Benchmarking.
- Performance Measuring and Monitoring.
- Qualification and experience of staff.

Benchmarking is a process of comparing the operations, products and services of a library with a library doing quality processes and offering quality products and services to the users. Performance measurement is necessary to identify the problems, if any and find out new ways for improving the products or services. It requires both qualitative and quan-titative data.

The major performance indicators of the library functions are:

- *Acquisition:* Efficiency, effectiveness, cost productivity.
- *Classification:* Accuracy, Time factor, cost.
- *Cataloguing:* Efficiency, Time effectiveness.
- *Technical Processing:* Efficiency, effectiveness, cost productivity.
- *Collection Management:* Efficiency, ease, accessibility, effectiveness.

Quality of service depends on quality and experience of staff. The TQM supports user education, sufficient and convenient technical infrastructures. SERVQUAL is the most popular assessment tool of service quality. It is designed by the marketing research team of Berry, Parasuraman, and Zeithaml. SERVQUAL evolve a set of five dimensions to assess the service quality-

- *Tangibles:* Appearance of physical facilities, equip-ments, personnel, and communication materials.
- *Reliability:* Ability to perform the promised service dependably and accurately; giving correct infor-mation asked.
- *Responsiveness:* Willingness to help users and provide prompt service making new information available.
- *Assurance and Empathy:* Knowledge and courtesy of employees and their ability to convey confidence to users. It involves politeness, friendliness, skill to provide information.
- *Access:* It means there are adequate staff and equipments as well as hours of operation. Location of library is central and convenient.

- *Communications:* It involves understanding the users' needs precisely, provision of user education, teaching library skills to users, the use of language understandable to different categories of users.
- *Security:* It involves physical safety within the library, and keeping library dealings secured.

LibQUAL + is a library service quality measurement tool based on the SERVQUAL models of assessing service quality. It is standard survey instrument used in many libraries.It is a tool measuring users' perception of service quality and identifies gaps between desired, perceived and minimum expectation of services. LibQUAL +TM 2002 is the latest version to listening the users

USERS' EXPECTATIONS: QUALITY OF SERVICES

- Modern building and furniture are required for a good library.
- A good library provides excellent facilities and services.
- Required books and journals in adequate number will be available with attractively displayed in a good library.
- In a good library, the staff will assist the users for locating a document.
- Accurate information and proper records will always be available in a good library.
- The staff of a good library will have sufficient knowledge to answer user's questions.
- Easy accessing and convenient working hour should have in a good library.

USERS' PERCEPTION: QUALITY OF SERVICES

- My library has modern building and furniture.
- My library provides me excellent facilities and services.
- Necessary books and journals in adequate number are available displayed attractively in my library.
- My library assists the users for locating the documents needed.
- Accurate information and proper records are always kept in my library.
- The staff of my library has proper knowledge to answer my question.
- My library is easily accessible with convenient working hours.

FACILITIES IN A QUALITY BASED LIBRARY

Physical Facilities:

- Good library is easily accessible.
- Good layout for a good library.
- Sufficient Space, lighting and ventilation.
- Clean, tidy and hygienic.

- Cozy and comfortable furniture.

Library Collection:

- Good collection of textbooks, journals, reference books, online journals, ebooks, etc. is needed in a good library.
- Good library displays new arrival of books in separate shelves.
- Good library offers open access to the collection.

Library Staff:

- Staff in a good library should be experienced with knowledge of modern technology.
- Staff should help the users to locate the documents needed and do their works in time.
- Sufficient staff to run the library.

Technical Processing:

- Good library acquire new documents in time.
- Shelf arrangement and rectification is a never ending process in a good library.
- Good library has proper catalogue or database for collection (OPAC etc.).
- Good library has prompt processing, charging and discharging system.

SERVICES IN CENTRAL LIBRARY, IIT GUWAHATI

The Central Library, one of the important central facilities of the Institute, currently has about 85,000 volumes, including textbooks, reference books, conference proceedings, back volumes, standards, and non-book material such as CD-ROMs, audio tapes, video tapes, slides. The Library also subscribes to about 484 current periodicals.

All operations of the Library are automated with the help of an integrated library software package (LIBSYS). The database for the entire collection has been created and available through On-Line Public Access Catalogue (OPAC) to the users via campus network. Now this facility is also available through Institute's Intranet as a Web enabled OPAC.

The Library is a member of INDEST consortium (Indian National Digital Library in Science and Technology Consor-tium), under the aegis of the MHRD, provides online access to few important science and engineering abstracting database services, such as COMPENDEX and INSPEC, MathSciNet, SciFinder Scholar, Web of Science etc and several full-text journals and Indian Standards. The Central Library Intranet Page provides the IP based online accesses to these resources.

Opening hours is from Morning 8 a.m. to 11 p.m. Average number of users in library is 200 per day.

LIBRARY AND INFORMATION SCIENCE EDUCATION IN INDIA

THE STRUCTURE AND LEVELS OF LIS EDUCATION

Professional higher education in library and information science (LIS) in India, now nine decades old, is centred in universities. Exceptions are two national institutes, namely, the Documentation Research and Training Centre (DRTC) in Bangalore, and the education section of the Indian National Scientific Documentation Centre (INSDOC) in New Delhi. These two institutes concentrate on the training of professi-onals for special and industrial libraries and information centres. Their course contents are biased towards information science and technology.

These two institutes are a class apart from other progra-mmes in their environment and products. There are some regional library associations conducting certificate courses of a few months duration and women polytechnics offering post-masters twoyear diplomas in library science to train paraprofessionals.

At the university level, the Master's degree in library and information science is earned in two yearlong (or, in some places, four semesters) courses after 10+2+3 years of education in any faculty. Of late there are two streams: the majority of the universities conduct two separate courses for the Bachelor's degree followed by the Master of Library and Information Science of one year (or two semesters) duration each. In recent years, some institutions have offered two years of integrated courses in four semesters. This integrated approach affords space for a cohesive and non-repetitive syllabus. Indeed syllabi in such schools are quite modernised. Students have the advantage that they do not have to reseek and compete for admission to master degree courses. In some of the places admission to the Master's degree course could be a competitive ordeal.

CURRICULUM

The University Grants Commission (UGC), a statutory body to plan, co-ordinate, audit and partially finance (non-technical) higher education in India, has from time to time recommended the broader outlines of courses to be taught. The latest effort has been through a UGC Curriculum Development Committee. Every university being autonomous is free to frame its own course of studies. Debate has been going on whether we should go in for a uniform syllabus at least at regional levels. But there seems no obvious advantage to this drab uniformity. In fact there is no co-ordinating body to do this.

Verbal pleas and repeated seminar resolutions to have some national level accrediting body (as the American Library Association in USA) have not borne fruit. The classes taught at the bachelor level are the library in society;

cataloguing and classification (theory and practice); reference service and sources; library operations and management; and introduction to information systems and retrieval techniques. There are more variations at the Master's level.

The basic set of courses includes universe of knowledge and research methodology; sources of information and bibliography in social/natural sciences/ humanities, etc.; information retrieval systems and techniques; library systems in public/academic/special libraries; computer applications in libraries; and a small research project to be completed before the commencement of examination.

In principle there are many optional classes available to the students. But due to the shortage of teachers most students have to opt for a topic for which a teacher is available. Syllabi are not very relevant and no worthwhile effort has been done at the national level to do research on the relevance of the curricula. There is an urgent need to widen the scope of studies available and to respond to the market forces.

INTAKE AND TEACHING METHODS

There is always a rush for admission. The number of admission seekers is more than the seats available. This is despite the opening of many distance education programmes that rarely disappoint the admission seekers. But the intake of students is generally of poor quality.

Library science courses are never the first option of the majority of students. Most of the students turn to library science after having failed to secure admission to other prestigious courses of study. Thus, it is a career of the mediocre at best.

Teaching is predominantly by the lecture method. In some central states, Hindi is also allowed as a medium of examination as a general policy of the state government.

Only a few schools have apprenticeship programmes for the students–otherwise classroom teaching with blackboard and chalk is the norm. Dictation of notes and their cramming by students are still popular. Neither class discussion nor questioning by students is encouraged. New methods of teaching are not tried. Use of educational technology in teaching is rather rare.

It can be easily inferred from one of the recommendations of the 15th IATLIS Seminar (1997):

- It is observed that majority of LIS schools are lacking adequate infrastructure facilities to teach/train LIS students in IT. Hence it is recommended that the UGC should provide special financial assistance to develop adequate need-based IT infrastructural facilities in LIS schools.

INFRASTRUCTURE

About a dozen universities have introduced the M.Phil. Degree, predominantly an intermediate research degree. During the last decade there has been a mushrooming of LIS courses available through correspondence courses or by the more respectable nomenclature of distance education. Except for one, most of such open schools are ill equipped for LIS education, though they have proved money minting machines for the parent universities due to higher enrolment. Some such schools do not have even full-time or regular teachers–good libraries or workshops are not even considered. There is always a cry for improvement or for closing of such courses–but they go on thriving.

PROLIFERATION OF LIBRARY EDUCATION

At present about 107 institutions, mostly university colleges and polytechnics, have library science education courses. Of these, the M.Lib.I.Sc. course is being offered by 67 universities; 11 universities offer the M.Phil. though this degree has no value in the job market. Today 32 Universities have Ph.D. research facilities.

One University recently awarded a D.Litt. that it claimed to be the first such degree in library science all over the world. It may not be an odious comparison that up to 1986 only 38 universities had master programmes; and 18 universities provided doctoral research facilities though not all these 18 universities had master programmes then. The words of the eminent librarian, former President of the Indian Library Association, and former President of the *Indian Association of Teachers of Library and Information Science* (IATLIS), P.N. Kaula, starkly hold true today.

A decade ago, Kaula said:

> "It has been observed that more and more institutions and libraries are opening library science courses without having even the minimum facilities for teaching. Even with poor libraries and funds they have started M.L.I.Sc. Programmes. In some universities there are not full time teachers to teach B.L.I.Sc. courses and yet some of them have also started M.L.I.Sc. programme. Open universities have also started [M/]B.Lib. Sc. programmes. Some private colleges have been conducting large number of C Lib. Sc. programmes with little or practically no facilities for books and libraries. This uncontrolled growth has bought down the standard of the courses. Library associations have also been having large intake of students without accessing the employment opportunities of the products.

Another problem with library schools has been a lack of public relations and marketing of their images and products.

The late C. G. Vishwanathan, a veteran librarian, aptly wrote:

"At present library schools and professional training centres in India are yet to receive a kind word from any section of the public... Even the academic world still does not believe that there can be anything like education for librarianship and curriculum of studies for library science. But at the same time everyone wants library service to be first rate.

THE BEGINNING OF RESEARCH IN LIBRARY AND INFORMATION SCIENCE

The roots of research in our profession are not very deep. Research in library science is a twentieth century occurrence ushered in by the library school of the University of Chicago in mid-1920s. The visionary efforts of the Chicago School bore abundant fruit and offered leadership to the world in library science research.

The pace of library research is picking up everywhere today due to social pressure as well as inspiration. In justifying the Ph.D. programme in our profession, it has been urged that "if librarianship aspires to become a profession, it should depend upon research to develop its knowledge base and its theoretical framework".

THE INDIAN CONTEXT

In India following British tradition and American precedent as established by Asa Don Dickinson, Librarian, Panjab University, Lahore, 1915-1916, library schools for advanced professional education have remained attached to universities. The growth of universities in Independent India ensured their constant growth. In a university, apart from teaching, a teacher is expected to do and guide research. The third function of a university, namely service and consultation, has always remained weak in India despite many newly established universityindustry linkage programmes.

RANGANATHAN'S WORK

The credit for the formal institution of the doctoral degree programme in library science in India goes undeniably to Dr. S.R. Ranganathan. In 1951, he started one at the University of Delhi surmounting many difficulties and facing personal ridicule. The University of Delhi awarded the first de jure degree in library science in 1957 to D.B. Krishan Rao who worked on a faceted classification for agriculture. Doctoral research remained in the wilderness when Ranganathan shook the Delhi soil off his feet in 1955. The *Documentation Research and Training Centre* (DRTC) in Bangalore, founded by Ranganathan in 1962, is technically not empowered to award the Ph.D.

Therefore, for the rest of his life, from 1962 to 1972, Ranga-nathan only advocated solo and team research with stress on quality, relevance and basics.

No big research projects were taken up at DRTC though individual teachers and students maintained both the quality and the tempo of research. Since the death of Ranganathan almost the entire DRTC faculty has earned Ph.D.s from other Indian universities on topics of research relevant to DRTC. Now the DRTC teachers are approved Ph.D. guides in many Indian universities, and they have already produced many Ph.D.

GROWTH OF DOCTORAL RESEARCH IN INDIA

Elsewhere in India other individual librarians and library science teachers eager to earn doctorates were hampered by the non-existence of programmes. In the 1960s and 1970s some doctorates on library-related topics were earned by library professionals from some other faculties such as sociology, history, law, economics, management, and the like.

The mantle of reviving and furthering doctoral research facilities was assumed by J. S. Sharma, then the university librarian and head of the library science department of the Panjab University, Chandigarh. Under his guidance the second *de jure* Ph.D. in library science was awarded in 1977 after a gap of full two decades. Thereafter, there was no looking back. Many universities followed with mostly individual efforts and enthusiasm. Doctoral research got a fillip in the 1980s. India maintained its Third World leadership in library research as well as in library education and literature. Ph.D. programmes have rather mushroomed even despite the lack of facilities or adherence to standards.

FACILITIES FOR RESEARCH

A conscientious university teacher is always in a dilemma over how to divide the time between teaching and research. Teaching is a primary compulsive and urgent duty to be performed. Students expect their teachers to give them time and personal attention. There may be appreciation in good teaching but the rewards lie in research. The university expects its teachers to do research for its prestige and fame lie therein. But when it comes to supporting of research many universities in India are neither generous nor unambivalent.

Ordinarily piecemeal research, especially in social sciences, is not supported financially. Internal support for research trickles through a tedious and off-putting bureaucracy and political manoeuvring. Colleagues are unsupportive. They are unappreciative, intolerant and jealous. Library facilities are poor. Thus most of the teachers are driven to the passivity of guiding doctoral research instead of doing postdoctoral work.

THE DETERIORATION OF STANDARDS

The University Grants Commission (UGC) preconditions for faculty employment and promotions have prompted many library professionals to acquire Ph.D. degrees, though many may not have the aptitude and the intrinsic ability to do research. Standards have not only been diluted but have been kept at abeyance. Supervisors and the examiners have become obligingly compromising. The cut-off date of December, 1992 for obtaining the Ph.D. degree to get an exemption from the national level test for teaching jobs in universities/colleges has done incalculable damage to research standards.

An eminent academician has corroborated the ill effects of this policy:

> "They were required to submit their theses before the deadline regardless of the date of registration. Some of the candidates on whom Ph.D.'s were conferred were not fully acquainted with the contents of their dissertations. In some cases even the supervisors were innocent of any knowledge of what the theses were about. The incitement came from the UGC".

Programmes for Ph.D. research have been introduced and expanded mindlessly. As a result, there has been a bit of doctoral boom – a spectacular rise in Ph.D. awarding universities and awardees – though many institutions lack utterly the resources of people or material or both. A 1987 bibliography listed 41 Ph.D. theses written from 1957 to 1985. In a recently published bibliography of doctoral dissertations in India from 1950 to March 1997 about 340 titles have been listed. This record of 340 dissertations, though not wholly authentic, is reliable by and large. In productivity the Panjab University, Chandigarh, led up to the mid-1980s. Thereafter, it lost the number game to the universities of the south.

The universities that have so far awarded up to ten degrees are ranked below:

- Karnatak University, Dharwad 44
- Jiwaji University, Gwalior 27
- University of Rajasthan, Jaipur 26
- Andhra University, Visakhapatnam 25
- University of Delhi 17
- University of Pune 16
- Gulbarga University 15
- Utkal University, Bhubaneswar 11
- University of Burdwan 10

The universities in Bangalore, Banaras Hindu University in Varanasi, and Nagpur University are picking up in research.

RELEVANCE OF RESEARCH

In a developing country like India, there could not be a dearth of research problems to be investigated. But there seems a lack of perception to visualise and identify valid problems for research. A cursory glance of the topics worked on will at once reveal that the topics chosen do not have a problem or hypothesis but merely survey the state of the art or the existing conditions. The popular areas for research have been, in order of popularity: university libraries, bibliometrics, library use and user studies, information seeking behaviour, information systems, classification and indexing, special libraries, library history, reference service and sources, and library science education.

Document selection and procurement, cataloguing, and experimental designs in library management are the least popular topics — though these seem practical and relevant to present day needs. That basic research is the most neglected area is endorsed by other surveys of doctoral research. Library automation, library software, networking and information technology are just emerging. There is need to revive research in classification especially in context of OPACs, information networks and the electronic information environment in general. The Curriculum Development Committee (CDC) on Library and Information Science of the University Grants Commission rehashed the importance of research, though it did not dwell at length on this aspect in its report.

The blue document listed some areas for research, which are no less broad than the current courses being taught at the Master's level:

- Structure and development of knowledge.
- Classification, cataloguing and indexing.
- Infometric studies.
- Computer applications.
- Historical studies.
- Social and economic aspects of librarianship.
- Library and Information management and systems analysis.
- Applications of techniques of library and information science to evaluate other disciplines.

The list could have been more specific. Though not much revered, the report rightly lays emphasis on standards in research. It uncompromisingly asks for a clear declaration from Ph.D. candidates that the "work is based on the discovery of new facts by the candidate or the new relations of facts . . . and how the work tends to the general advancement of know-ledge". While it is normally expected of every completed piece of research, yet it rarely happens. The evaluation process, however formal, is easily manipulated without qualms. Examiners are obliging on a reciprocal basis.

In a small profession like ours this interplay of mutual usability comes in easily. It is often said jocularly that the degree is recommended more for the supervisor than for the candidate. We must admit that the library profession has failed to lure the best brains and even more to retain them. Mediocrity thrives; hypocrisy reigns. But this is not to overlook the genuine research and researchers. Apart from not so relevant topics, theses have contributed little towards pushing the frontiers of knowledge; few are models of methodology. Indian library research seems to have no moorings in the prevailing realities.

Topics are ideal, superficial and bookish. Even experi-enced librarians keen on earning the Ph.D. degree rarely come with an important problem for research. The supervisor who shies from controversial topics usually suggests the topic. Criticising individuals in formal black-and-white mode or exposing harmful tendencies of a class are not for them. Even a mild and healthy criticism is not tolerated in India. Feudal norms still lie deep in the Indian social ethos.

In addition, there is a dire paucity of data archives and reference works. Collecting data and information is considered a satisfactory end to the job — the goal of the research exercise. It is very difficult to collect data by questionnaire in a vast country like India. Each researcher has a bag full of woeful tales to tell. Library associations at all levels seem to have washed their hands of the research responsibility. These do not even collect and compile statistics of the professional activities pertaining to their areas. Their libraries are poor. They have no research budget. For quite a time professionals have been talking, writing and conferencing about library education and research in India.

Every year the Indian Association of Teachers of Library and Information Science (IATLIS) holds a seminar on topics of library education and research. That it is the most popular topic with the teachers and librarians can be gauged from the fact that the FID/ET seminar was the largest of all the 49th FID pre-conference seminars held in India. The literature on library education and research is enormous, though repetitive and inflated. We have given lip service to the change of curricula and the raising of standards of research. But the needed change has not come through. The blame is wholly put on the lack of infrastructure and unavailability of funds. That is not the entire reason. The lack of effective collective efforts to safeguard the standards seems no less major cause.

THE CONTRIBUTIONS MADE BY RESEARCH

Contrary to expectations, dissertations are not fountain heads of the rest of the literature to grow and mature. These primary sources of information are distanced from relevance. The National Social Science Documentation Centre systema-tically procures one copy of each research dissertation in social sciences to preserve and make them available to researchers for consultation within the premises of its library. Retro-spective bibliographies of LIS dissertations in India are available.

The latest information on theses awarded, Ph.D. degrees and Ph.D. research in progress is available in the featured column of the weekly University News of the Association of Indian Universities, New Delhi. It is a major source to keep track of the dissertations awarded Ph.D. degrees by Indian universities in all disciplines. In spite of availability, other researchers do not adequately use these dissertations; nor are these works cited or quoted by teachers or textbook writers.

Working librarians rarely use research results to solve their professional problems. There is no precedent of a library inviting a library school to do research on a problem confron-ting them. At the risk of calling attention to a red herring, it is worthwhile to have this idea corroborated from a veteran library leader.

Professor P.N. Kaula candidly observed:

- That LIS departments have little or no understanding and cooperation with the central library . . . The problem is more psychological than academic . . . Much harm has been done to the teaching of library science by the disharmony....

Librarians go in for local, *ad hoc* and *pro-tem* solutions for their practical problems. Researchers consult a teacher or a fellow researcher for a topic of research rather than a practitioner. It is not only true in India but elsewhere too. Thus research has become divorced from reality–a theoretical exercise at best. This seems a universal phenomenon in our profession. Carl Keren doubting the value of research in information science daringly suggests that "It would be worthwhile to find out how much of it has really contributed to our body of knowledge and to the methods used by practitioners." He himself understands that "As suggested, probably be rather disappointed".

American teacher Margaret Steig endorses this notion:

- Research done by library and information science educators seems to receive little respect from professionals, and if they do not find it of value one has to wonder who will.

6

Online Learner's Role in Governance

The ability and potential of online learning to enhance access to education, particularly higher education, is largely determined by the potential learner's circumstances, which in many ways define the learning environment. Not surprisingly, online learning's evolutionary predecessor, distance learning, has been applied to two situations in which access to education is problematic. The first occurs when a very large population has access to a limited number of "seats" in conventional educational institutions. This situation gives rise to what Daniel refers to as "megauniversities"— distance teaching universities with 100,000 students or more.

Indira Gandhi National Open University (IGNOU), with an estimated 500,000 students, is one example, and the Open University of Hong Kong (OUHK), with over 400,000 students, is another. The second situation is one of sparse population—one in which the community of learners is spread over a wide geographical area. The fledgling University of the Arctic is an example of a response to this situation. In both of these cases, the learner's physical environment presented a need that online learning could address. A third situation is emerging.

Learners who wish to use technology to structure their learning environment are seeking out the means by which they can do so. In a sense, their preferred learning environment presents the access issue that online learning can address.

In all three situations, the challenge is to provide access to higher learning, determining what the learner brings to the environment, and what they need in terms of support. These factors can vary— after all, the first two situations are artifacts of geography, whereas the third has more to do with personal learning preference.

That is why designing learner supports requires an understanding of the learners' circumstances. This chapter discusses the importance of setting up a supportive learning environment for online learners, and provides some practical advice. Underlying this advice is a philosophy that encourages an environment that aims to develop the learner's independence, while ensuring that supports are readily available when needed. Student supports that are flexible, clear, and continuously available are described, and best practices outlined.

KNOWING THE LEARNER

It is a good idea to remind ourselves that the learning enterprise is not about us as educators: the focus should be placed on the learning, not the teaching. Similarly, in providing learner supports, we should focus on what the learner needs, not on what we want to or are able to supply, but it is surprising how easily this emphasis can be lost in our wish to help. We identify real needs best if we know our learners. Therefore, we must ask questions about the learner's readiness for online learning, access to and familiarity with the technology required, proficiency in the language of instruction, individual learning style, and educational goals, as well as about how aspects of the individual's culture can affect learning.

These are some of the things that we need to understand about the learners; they are also things that the learners need to know about themselves in order to benefit from the learning experience. Once the institution has this information, it must determine what supports are most critical for learners, and must establish priorities to ensure that resources, which are always limited, are directed to the most useful supports. In doing so, the institution must keep in mind that some learners will require more support than others, and that any learner may need more help at one point in their educational career than at others. So the institution must find a balance between "just-in-case resources" and "just-in-time resources" that recognises that an online learner is often an adult with responsibilities other than their educational goals.

Flexible, continuously available, easily accessible learner support systems are required, but such systems must be genuinely useful. Learners have been clear that they need to see the value added by a resource, or they will not use it; they have also let us know that supports should be available but not intrusive.

LEARNER READINESS FOR ONLINE LEARNING

The learner brings a set of skills, experiences, and expectations to the learning environment. This section outlines the resources necessary, first, to assist potential online learners to make informed decisions about their readiness for this form of learning experience, and then, to provide advice for making specific programme decisions.

To encourage independence in the learner, the focus should be on self-assessment, although counseling backup should be available when needed. The list below presents a series of questions that learners who are thinking about post-secondary study online should ask themselves, and identifies the kinds of assessment tools that are available to answer them.

- Am I ready for university?—This type of online resource provides the opportunity for the prospective learner to determine their readiness from academic, financial, family support, and time perspectives. Such a self-assessment, which is Web-based and easily completed by the student, serves to highlight areas that might need special attention. It guides the learner through a series of questions in which they examine their own expectations and readiness. Once the assessment is complete, follow-up e-mail counseling complements the process.
- Am I ready for studies in the English language (or other language of instruction)?—This type of online resource assists the learner to decide if their command of the language is sufficient to allow for success, and places the learner in specific language course levels. The learner may be directed to online remedial resources, and should always have the option of contacting an advisor.
- Am I ready for online learning? This type of online resource assists potential learners to determine if they have the necessary hardware and networking capabilities, and should help them to explore whether this learning environment is comfortable. Short sample experiences should be available to assist with the process.
- What is my preferred learning style?—As does any form of learning, online learning makes demands on the learner. The institution can make many resources available in a variety of formats, to suit different learning styles and preferences. However, a learner may not have identified the format they find most useful, and it can be helpful if the institution assists the learner to examine their own learning style. Interactive tools are available on the Web to help the learner to do so; however, these tools vary in quality, and the institution can assist by providing an annotated evaluation of these resources.
- Am I ready for university-level mathematics?—Proficiency in mathematics, as well as in language of instruction, has proven to be a significant success factor, particularly for adult learners returning to the educational environment after some time away. However, mathematics can also be a significant stressor. Assisting the prospective learner to identify their strengths and weaknesses in mathematics, and making remediation available, can reduce this stress. An online self-assessment can be designed to help the learner to determine their readiness for particular mathematics courses, to recommend a mathematics course appropriate to the learner's level, and to identify remediation resources.
- Do I have the skills to be successful in my chosen programme?—This type of online resource outlines what skills are needed for

particular areas of study. The resource should be programspecific and should refer the student to online tutorials if needed.

MATCHING EDUCATIONAL PROGRAMMES TO CAREER INTERESTS

Often, potential learners will seek out online learning opportunities to create or enhance career goals. As educators, we may want to view the educational experience outside the context of career development, the learning experience is not about us.

The fact is that learners bring that context to their educational decisions, and we need to understand that they do so. Online resources designed to assist learners to determine their own interests and skills, and then provide a career map aligned with educational programmes, is a reasonable expectation. After all, most of these learners will experience several career changes—some of them quite significant—throughout their working lives.

The United Kingdom's Open University focuses on the learner's need to contemplate the future in making educational choices. "Mapping Your Future" on the Athabasca University Services to Students Web site provides the learner with a means of exploring career clusters and the credentials required to pursue them. After an initial exploration, the learner may wish to communicate online with a counselor to refine their career goals. Once this is achieved, electronic "programme plans" are designed by an advisor, taking the career goals as well as prior learning into account. It is important to have the learner explore first, and then have counselors provide assistance as needed.

SUPPORTING THE LEARNER

Well-designed course materials and strong academic and tutorial support are necessary in all educational enterprises, and the special considerations in the case of online learning are the subject of a separate chapter. This chapter deals with non-academic supports for the learner. Having assisted the potential learner to make an informed decision to pursue online learning, we have enhanced their chances for success, but quite different support is now required.

Once again, the balance between being available and being intrusive is important. Learners require support in different areas, and as providers, we must anticipate the array of needs, and then work with individual learners to clarify what is needed at a given time. Learners need to know exactly what they can expect in support, how to interact with the institution, what is expected of them, and how to determine when they need assistance.

EXPECTATIONS

Learners need to know both what is expected of them, and what services they can expect to receive from the institution. Online learning may be a new experience for the learner, and it is important that service standards be clear and easily available: How long should it take to receive confirmation of my registration?

How much time does it take to receive my examination grade? How quickly should I expect a response to e-mail? Who should I contact for library assistance? These standards should be published for all students to see, and can serve as benchmarks for service units within the institution.

INFORMATION AND ADMINISTRATIVE SUPPORT

Daniel points out that a key component of supported open learning is "effective administration and logistics." Institutions engaged in distance and online education know that smooth administrative processes can be as much a factor in learner success as the design of learning resources.

The learners themselves report that flexibility of access and smooth administrative support are important to the learning environment. One would expect that learners who have chosen an online learning environment prefer to perform administrative functions (such as registration) online as well, and this is proving to be the case. Institutions that provide online learning report that students express a preference for having the control that online administrative processes afford.

Providing online administrative access is not without challenges, and improved technology, carefully designed Web pages and helpdesk support are crucial.

Constant monitoring and updating of procedures is required, to find smoother interactions and to tease out administrative frustrations. Designing Web pages and then forgetting them is simply not acceptable.

The following list outlines a process for the continuous improvement required:

- Design the administrative Web page;
- Test the technology and revise as necessary;
- Observe the learners using the Web page and ask for feedback, then revise;
- Monitor the use of the Web page regularly;
- Look for enhancements and improvements, and incorporate them; and
- Always have helpdesk attendants available to troubleshoot.

At the institutional level, regular learner satisfaction surveys can ensure that administrative interactions are not barriers to learning. Portals designed to individualise and personalise interactions enhance the learner's experience. Portal software is growing in popularity as more institutions become involved in online learning.

TECHNOLOGICAL SUPPORT

The learner must know what technology is needed for the online environment, before they decide to register. A person engaged in online learning requires technological support that is clear and readily available. Drawing the line between technological support on the one hand and academic support on the other is often a challenge, and these types of support must be coordinated carefully. There are three common support formats: an information center provides institutional and programme information; computing helpdesks troubleshoot technological issues; and call centers are frequently used to support a particular programme area. All three must work together to support the whole learning process.

Successful information centers, helpdesks, and call centers have the following characteristics:

- Reliable networks;
- Asynchronous access "24/7";
- Synchronous access at clearly identified times;
- Quick response, with acknowledgment and follow-up;
- Follow-through to resolution of the issue;
- Simple, clear instructions;
- Access by attendants to all critical databases and expertise; and
- The ability to identify problems with policies, procedures, or systems, and to suggest change.

STUDY SKILLS ASSISTANCE

The online learner may be returning to learning after some time away, may be new to post-secondary study itself, or may not have experienced online learning before. Assisting the learner to identify particular needs in the area of study skills can reduce stress and enhance the experience. For example, it is critical to understand that "life happens" and the learning experience may be just one of the demands that the learner faces. This is particularly true for adult learners. Some resources that may help online learners who was facing challenges to their study skills include

- Web pages designed to assist in the development of time management and study schedules;
- Resources to help students learn to balance educational pursuits with other life demands;
- Tools for facilitating "study buddy" connections for peer assistance;
- Online strategies and exercises to reduce "exam anxiety";
- Resources to assist in reading for comprehension;
- Assistance in annotating online resources such as e-books;

- Resources to assist in writing papers;
- Clarification of rules for citation and avoiding plagiarism;
- Assistance in searching library resources on line; and
- Assistance in making critical analyses of information from online resources.

ONLINE EDUCATIONAL COUNSELING

Well-prepared Web resources can be provided online, but asynchronous counseling assistance is required as well, particularly for learners who are experiencing difficulty. The online environment is one in which learners can "fall through the cracks" if assistance is not readily available. From time to time a learner may need someone to assist in keeping a positive outlook and determining if an intervention is needed. Learners need to know that help is there if they need it.

The institution should provide this resource and all institutional staff should be trained to identify when a learner might benefit from a session with a counselor. It is important to remember, however, that while referrals can be made, the decision to pursue them belongs to the learner. The work of the counselor in an online learning environment has three aspects. The first is to work with Web designers to develop online resources to help learners to identify and address barriers to reaching their educational goals. The second is to interact with the learners when an intervention is required. The third is to work with other institutional staff to ensure that processes and procedures enhance learning. Educational and career counseling are well suited to the online environment, but personal counseling is less so. Personal counseling should be limited to immediate crisis resolution and referral. Counseling units need information about community resources to which they can refer clients.

ONGOING PROGRAMME ADVISING

Distance and online learners are often adults and they frequently spread their learning over a number of years. They report that they need programme planning that will help them achieve educational goals in an expeditious manner. Moreover, learners often transfer between institutions and jurisdictions, increasingly so in a global learning environment. Learners need to plan their coursework based on particular programmes, while remaining aware of course transferability.

The role of advisors is to assist learners to understand programme requirements, match courses they may be transferring into a programme, and then plan the remainder of their programme accordingly. Since, the adult learner may change career and educational goals at any time during the process of completing a programme, advisors need to be readily available and to have access to all programme and transfer information. Software products are available to allow advisor and learner to navigate this process. Academics, counselors, and others within the institution need to know when to refer learners to an advisor.

THE DIGITAL LIBRARY

In the early years of distance education, providing library support to learners was a challenge. Courses were developed in print format, and comprehensive course packages were sent to each learner. The library typically developed a collection that was made available, by mail or fax, to the learner on request. Distance educators worried that learners were not gaining the library search experience that would enhance their studies and their research skills.

Online sources of information have transformed libraries in distance education: where in the past libraries focused on holdings, they can now focus on access; where they used to be information repositories, they can now be gateways to information. This transformation has allowed the library experience to be more profound for the learner and more integrated within the learning process.

From a learner support perspective, a welldesigned online library

- Is easily found among other institutional Web pages;
- Provides an up-front tutorial for the new learner;
- Is integrated with the institution's online courses;
- Provides tools to assist with online searches; and
- Provides access to personal assistance, if needed.

The transformation of libraries in distance education has posed some interesting fiscal issues for institutions. In the past, acquisitions budgets provided for purchasing holdings that became part of the collection, part of the assets of the institution. Annual funding was provided for collection development and updating. Even subscriptions to periodicals, an annual expense, resulted in a "holding." Subscriptions to online resources are another matter entirely. As libraries move towards becoming gateways rather than repositories, a new way of viewing funding is needed.

ACCESS FOR STUDENTS WITH DISABILITIES

Online learning can enhance access for people with disabilities. New assistive technologies can allow access to learning opportunities previously denied to this population. Increasingly, the legal requirements to provide accommodations that allow access are being defined by the courts, and institutions are required to ensure that necessary accommodations are provided, without compromising academic rigour. In an online environment, the following services are expected:

- Administrative accommodation with respect to timed assignments and examinations;
- Alternative formats for learning materials;
- Advocacy within the institution;
- Advice about assistive technologies;
- Advice about funding sources;
- Referral for specific needs; and
- "Reasonable accommodation" as outlined in law.

STUDENT RIGHTS AND ACCESS TO OMBUDS SERVICES

Online learners have as much need of clearly articulated rights as do learners in traditional educational settings. An advocacy process designed for online learners is one in which the learner is made aware of student rights and responsibilities. An institution can fulfill its basic legal responsibility by making a student code of conduct available on the Web and in print on request. However, a prudent institution will go well beyond this demonstration of due diligence. Web sites that clearly outline intellectual honesty expectations should be readily available on the Web and should be referred to frequently. Reminders just prior to assignment preparation reduce the chance that the learner will fail to provide proper scholarly acknowledgment.

Traditions regarding what constitutes intellectual property and what is generally accepted common knowledge are not universal concepts, nor are they always understood. Cultural views about ownership of knowledge vary, and if the rules that are to apply within the institution are to be understood, then the institution must ensure that they are properly explained. For example, although many educators do not accept the idea, the reality is that students do not always understand the concept of plagiarism, much less how to avoid it.

To address this problem, the University of Puget Sound has designed an excellent Web page that provides learners with exercises to enhance their understanding of the concept of plagiarism and to assist them in avoiding it. All efforts to provide smooth interactions between the learner and the institution notwithstanding, there will be situations in which the learner becomes ensnared and does not know where to turn. A highly visible ombuds office should be available. Moreover, from the institutional perspective, the ombuds office can assist in identifying policy and procedure problems that require attention within the institution.

THE ONLINE LEARNER'S ROLE IN GOVERNANCE

Online learners have valuable contributions to make to an educational institution. Institutions that specialise in distance and online learning can provide opportunities for students to participate in institutional governance. Student government is possible in such an institution as well, but administration must make special arrangements to facilitate the process. In many ways, the student union has the same issues in keeping in touch with its constituency as does the institution itself. Both are vying for the attention of a learner who may be juggling learning with other life demands. It is in the institution's best interests to have a healthy student union and to work with that union to meet the needs of the learners.

Some means by which to achieve these goals include

- Making networks available to the student union;
- Providing one main institutional contact with whom student union representatives can interact;
- Assisting in collecting student union fees;
- Making information available, within the confi-dentiality guidelines;
- Having student representatives on all decision-making bodies;
- Having decision-making bodies meet through electronic means (video-conference, online conference, etc.) to maximize participation;
- Keeping the student representatives and the student union apprised of significant events, initiatives, etc. (*e.g.,* strategic planning, budgeting, tuition fee increases);
- Engaging in shared initiatives with the student union (include them in convocation, copublish newsletters, etc.);
- Seeking advice from the student union on important issues; and
- Demonstrating appreciation for the work of the student union.

LEARNER SATISFACTION MONITORING AND ENVIRONMENTAL SCANNING

Regular monitoring of the learners' satisfaction levels and scanning of the student services environment assist the institution to make continuous improvements. Year-over-year comparisons are possible if the survey instruments are carefully designed. In this way, trends and areas in need of attention will become apparent. Focus groups are being successfully conducted online by institutions that are at a distance from their constituents. Such groups can be used, for example, to test out the efficacy of a new course, programme, or service.

UNIVERSITY OF THE ARCTIC— STRETCHING THE LIMITS

University of the Arctic is a virtual university in the real sense of the word. It is a consortium of universities and colleges from the northern countries known as the "Arctic Eight" (Canada, Finland, Greenland, Iceland, Norway, Russia, Sweden, and the United States). It was formed because there was a sense that these northern countries represented a community that transcended national boundaries by virtue of their "circumpolarity." There was also a sense that the northerly parts of these nations shared cultural, environmental, and learning issues with one another that the more southerly parts did not necessarily experience. The founding principles were based on notions of development "in the north, by the north, for the north." This university would develop an issues-based curriculum culminating in a Bachelor of Circumpolar Studies. At the time of writing, five courses have been developed.

The first, *Introduction to the Circumpolar World,* has been pilot tested in classroom format in one location, and as a Web-based offering involving learners from institutions from four of the Arctic Eight countries. The Web-based offering stretched the limits of online learning, and serves as an example of the potential of online learning to acknowledge a community of learning based, not simply on geography, but on shared realities.

SOME EARLY DECISIONS

Language of instruction was one of the first decisions taken. It was decided to develop the courses in English and translate them at a later date. Subject matter experts from Russia, Greenland, Finland, Canada, Norway, and the United States wrote the curriculum in English, and the material was edited into fourteen modules. Another early decision was that the online delivery would take place within a portal environment that would foster a community of learning.

WebCT was used for delivery, largely because this platform was well recognised throughout the circumpolar world. The portal was designed to provide a supportive learning environment, and at the same time, an uncomplicated technical environment. The realities of the variability of technical resources across the Arctic became apparent, and the motto became "as inclusive as we must be, striving to become as innovative as we can be." It was important that no group be excluded from the project. Reliability of networks was seen to be important, as was the need for a "Plan B." The course was housed on the server of the institution that was thought to have the most reliable server arrangement. In addition, learners were provided with print materials should any technological mishaps occur. The pilot of the introductory course began in mid-February 2002, and lasted for fourteen weeks. Learners from Russia, Greenland, Finland, and Canada all worked with their local university or college. There was a site coordinator at each location, and the instructor was located in Canada.

THE COMMUNITY OF LEARNING

Largely because of the instructor's skill, but also because the learners shared so many issues, a community of learning soon developed. Asynchronous discussions formed the basis for exchange, with informal study groups (often conducted in the local language) arranged by on-site coordinators. Because of the time zone issues, chat rooms were not initially designed into the portal, but the students asked that this utility be added. This was done, and a few hardy souls spent the wee hours of the morning communicating with colleagues across the North Pole. Learners shared resources via the Web, and each institution was expected to provide library and other student support resources.

LESSONS LEARNED

The decision to keep the technology simple was a wise one. The simple portal and WebCT worked quite well, but a more comprehensive orientation to WebCT and online learning will be designed for the next offering. The best approach to the orientation is to have a training session with the site coordinators first, and have them, in turn, conduct an orientation with the learners.

This strategy allows first-language assistance with the technology. Because of the variation in institutional resources, subsequent online offerings will include computing helpdesk access, which will be provided by the institution that is most experienced in online delivery of services. Although it was expected that the up-front preparation by the curriculum developers, Web designers, and the instructor would be substantial, the workload for the instructor was excessive. This was partly because the volume of the learner postings was larger than expected. In addition, more of the learner activities could have been built into the course materials themselves.

A surprising outcome was the extent to which learners for whom English was not the first language felt quite comfortable participating. The concern that the sessions would be dominated by learners for whom English was a first language, was not borne out. The participating institutions had ensured that the learners had a sufficient command of the English language before registering them. Attempts to incorporate traditional knowledge into the course materials were a challenge because of the large number of Aboriginal groups around the circumpolar world. In the end, this issue was best addressed by having students share information with colleagues.

The result was somewhat serendipitous, but this strategy may be preferable to something more structured. Attempts to ensure that all of the students had broad access to online library resources across all institutions were not successful, largely because of the language issue. It may be that in cases where such geographically and linguistically diverse groups are brought together, the provision of learner support in areas such as library, counseling, and so forth are best left to the "home" institution. This suggestion assumes that learners will inevitably be tied to an institutional setting. More investigation is required as these kinds of initiatives develop.

CONCLUSION

As the learning environment becomes a global community of learning, the cognitive sciences are merging with computing and telecommunications technologies to form what distance educators refer to as "knowledge media". The Organisation of Economic Cooperation and Development (OECD) recognises that these trends can provide more equitable access to higher education, and hence, more social equity, as campus-bound and distance-education paradigms merge and complement each other. There is an ongoing discussion about new terminology that should replace "distance education," but at the same time be more inclusive than "online education." Terms such as "distributed learning," "technology mediated learning," and "telematics" are often used in North America. Elsewhere, other terms are being used, such as "resource based learning" and "flexible learning". This discussion exemplifies the role that technology can play in placing the focus on making resources available for the individual learner. Whatever we call it, however, online learning only enhances a focus on the learner as an individual within a community of learning if individual differences are acknowledged and addressed in the design of learner support services.

7

Library Management System Using Association Rule Mining

INTRODUCTION

Data Mining, also popularly known as *Knowledge Discovery in Databases* (KDD), refers to the nontrivial extraction of implicit, previously unknown and potentially useful information from data in databases. While data mining and are frequently treated as synonyms, data mining is actually part of the knowledge discovery process.

Data Mining software is one of a number of analytical tools for analysing data. It allows users to analyse data from many different dimensions or angles, categorize it, and summarize the relationships identified. Technically, Data Mining is the process of finding correlations or patterns among dozens of fields in large relational databases.

The data mining is actually a step in a larger KDD process. The KDD process employs data mining methods or algorithms to extract or identify knowledge according to some criteria or measure of interestingness, but it also includes steps that prepare the data, such as preprocessing, sub-sampling, and transformations of the database.

Fig. shows data mining as a step in an iterative knowledge discovery process.

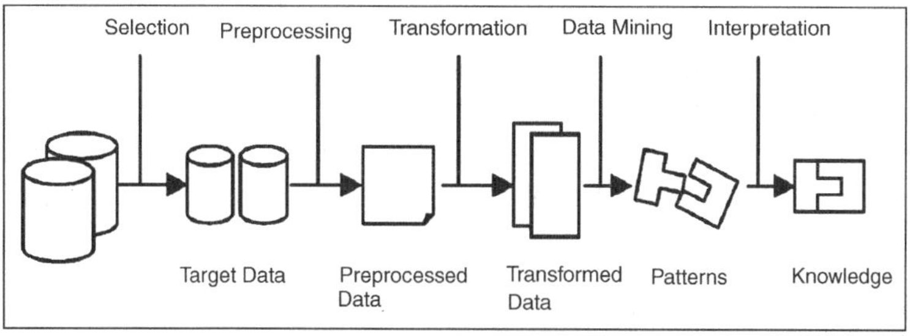

Fig. Data Mining is the Core of Knowledge Discovery Process

The first step in the KDD process is to select data to be analysed from the set of all available data. In many cases, the data is stored in transaction databases. These databases are quite large and extremely dynamic. Therefore a subset of the data must be selected from those databases, since it is unnecessary in the early stages to attempt to analyse all data. The KDD is an iterative process. Once the discovered knowledge is presented to the user, the evaluation measures can be enhanced, the mining can be further refined, new data can be selected or further transformed, or new data sources can be integrated, in order to get different, more appropriate results.

EXISTING WORK

STATISTICAL TECHNIQUE

Statistical techniques were being used long before the term data mining was coined. However, statistical techniques are driven by the data and are used to discover patterns and build predictive models. Today people have to deal with up to terabytes of data and have to make sense of it and glean the important patterns from it. In statistics, prediction is usually synonymous with regression of some form. There are a variety of different types of regression in statistics but the basic idea is that a model is created that maps values from predictors in such a way that the lowest error occurs in making a prediction. The simplest form of regression is Simple Linear Regression that just contains one predictor and a prediction.

The relationship between the two can be mapped on a two dimensional space and the records plotted for the prediction values along the Y axis and the predictor values along the X axis. The simple linear regression model then could be viewed as the line that minimized the error rate between the actual prediction value and the point on the line. Adding more predictors to the linear equation can produce more complicated lines that take more information into account and hence make a better prediction, and it is called multiple linear regressions.

The Disadvantages of Statistical Technique

Certainly statistics can do more than answer questions about the data but for most people today these are the questions that statistics cannot help answer. Consider that a large part of data the statistics is concerned with summarizing data, and more often than not, the problem that the summarization has to do with counting. Statistical Techniques cannot be useful without certain assumptions about data.

CLUSTERING TECHNIQUE

Clustering is concerned with grouping together objects that are similar to each other and dissimilar to the objects belonging to other clusters. Clustering techniques is used by the end user to tag the customers in their database. Once this is done the business user can get a quick high level view of what is happening within the cluster. Clustering can be used for discovery or prediction. There are two main types of clustering techniques, those that create a hierarchy of clusters and those that do not. Those techniques are: *Hierarchical Clustering Techniques and Partitional Clustering Techniques*.

The Disadvantages of Clustering Technique

The interpretation of how interesting a clustering is will inevitably be application-dependent and subjective to some degree. Clustering techniques suffer from the fact that once a merge or a split is committed, it cannot be undone or refined. Sometimes clustering is performed not so much to keep records together as to make it easier to see when one record sticks out from the rest.

PROPOSED WORK

ASSOCIATION RULE

An association rule tells us about the association between two or more items. For example, If we are given a set of items where items can be referred as books and a large collection of transactions which are subsets of these items/ books.

The task is to find relationship between the presence of various items within these baskets. In order for the rules to be useful there are two pieces of information that must be supplied as well as the actual rule: *Support* is how often does the rule apply? and *Confidence* is How often is the rule is correct. In fact association rule mining is a two-step process: Find all frequent itemsets/ booksets - by definition, each of these itemsets will occur at least as frequently as a predetermined minimum support count, and then generate strong association rules from the frequent itemsets – by definition, these rules must satisfy minimum support and minimum confidence.

Advantages of Association Rule Technique

Association rule algorithms can be formulated to look for sequential patterns. The methods of data acquisition and integration, and integrity checks are the most relevant to association rules.

MODULES

The following modules in this project are:

- Administrator
- Librarian
- User

Administrator

Administrator has the full authority to modify the library database like creating an account for a new user, deleting the account, adding a new book and deleting the book. Administrator monitors the library database updations (Figure. 8.2).

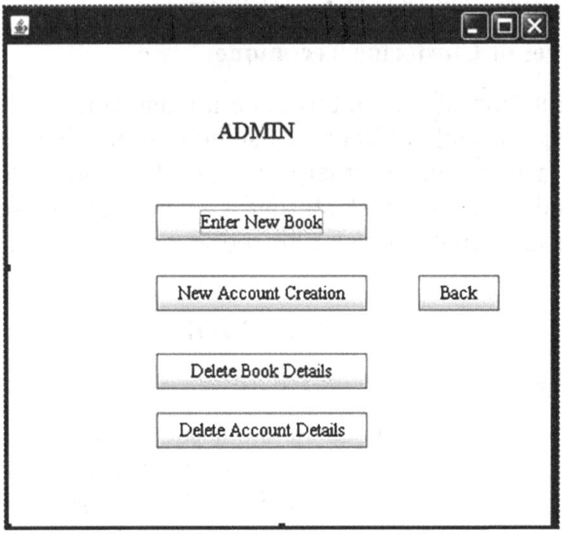

Enter New Book Details

The book id is a automatically generated whenever a new book is entered in the library. The various entries should be entered such as the book name, ISBN, author name, cost, and date.

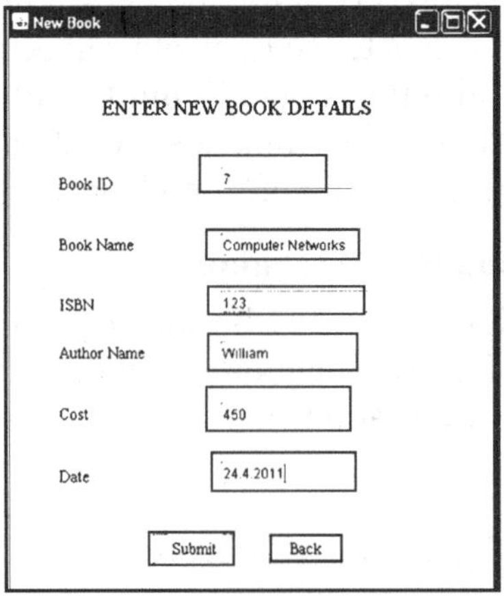

New Account Creation

The user is classified into two types.

Fig. Other user

Fig. Staff user

Delete Book Details

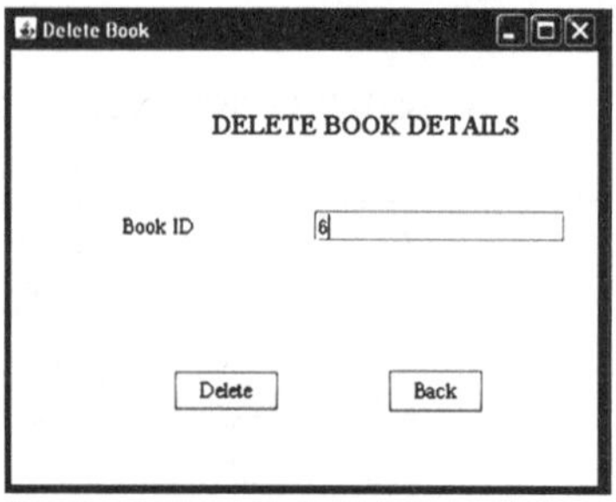

Delete Account

Librarian Module

Librarian handles the library action like to issue the book and return back the book. Librarian collects the daily report and submits it to the administrator.

8

Technology Laws

INTRODUCTION

Libraries across India, as in other parts of the world, are facing sweeping changes on account of the media in which information is generated, transmitted, disseminated and archived due to the increasing presence of electronic formats. There is no doubt that information in electronic form is a potential asset, and that it can be vigourously applied in any environment. The advent and spread of electronic formats has made a major difference in the information processing and service environments in libraries, especially after the emergence of the Internet and Web as the dominant pathway and repository of electronic information resources.

In an increasingly networked world, it is possible that universities may be able to take back control of scholarly information, and libraries may risk being cut out of the author-publisher-dissemination loop. Libraries act as facilitators to provide the right information to the right user at the right time. Users visit libraries to borrow identified documents, or to take photocopies/printouts of those documents from reference collections or journals not issued out normally.

The advent of Web-enabled information resources, such as e-journals, e-books and e-reference sources, and their access through networks has taken the library to the users and a significant amount of information access is now taking place beyond the four walls of the library. In many cases users want a 'pinpointed precision' in the information search process whereas the library attempts for an 'exhaustive recall' to comply with the various ways in which an information source is approached and to satisfy each user's diverse interests. This information overload may cause doubts in the users regarding the relevance of information services as perceived from a professional angle. Along with quantifying use, it is equally important to assess the qualitative attributes of implicit and explicit use and examine the difficulties of users in properly framing their requests for information.

The limitation on the part of library professionals to perceive and represent what is demanded by users in information systems, and the dilemmas of information organization and retrieval to handle these demands must be effectively addressed. Libraries and professionals are equally concerned about the emergence of Internet as an information repository beyond the library's walls, as amply demonstrated by enhanced citations of Web resources. As library acquisitions are falling, information sources are increasing, and a single site library satisfying the user's needs is a doubtful proposition; users are forced to look beyond the library for their information needs. Thus the only option for the libraries is to enter into collaborations, networking and consortia and to reorient their roles as information services and access centres from their previous roles as information warehouses.

At the same time, the technical advances resulting from enhanced research in science and technology have made it possible to reduce drastically the time involved in information collection and identification. Also the extra time required in adapting printed information to client service through cumbersome manual routines of classification and cataloguing is considerably reduced by the availability of electronic information, leaving the professionals to concentrate more on tasks to support the extensive teaching and intensive research environment.

ACADEMIC AND RESEARCH LIBRARIES

The application of computing to library work in India has a history of at least three decades because since the time the computer entered premier academic institutions and selected R & D facilities, it has been explored for improving information processing and management routines. *Information technology* (IT) enriched library services arrived initially for *science and technology* (S&T) information handling and for the special libraries attached to *research and development* (R&D) centres and academic libraries in higher education institutions.

In comparison to other libraries, academic and research libraries have better infrastructure and skilled manpower in greater numbers, making them able to offer information services comparable to advanced countries. Like qualified teaching and research personnel and well-equipped laboratories, the right information service is another vital element in the trinity which completes a fruitful academic or research environment.

MARKET-DRIVEN COLLABORATION

Academic and research libraries, especially in developing countries, are passing through a very challenging phase in their existence due to unfriendly trends in the emerging information market. On the one hand, these libraries are still left with many of the old problems such as poor budgetary support and weak infrastructure, as well as staff in fewer numbers and often with less expertise. But the new information marketing techniques, like the possibilities of delivering and accessing electronic information in diverse channels, force these libraries to be very vigilant and cautious in their approach towards information acquisition and services. Libraries and professionals in India were quick to understand the emerging information environment was forcing their users to depend largely on those resources, which are becoming more expensive day by day due to the rise in production costs, fall in subscriptions and inflationary trends of Indian currency.

When individual libraries found that alone they are not in a position to satisfy the information requirements of their clients, they formulated various collaborative arrangements with other libraries such as,

- *Interlibrary loan* (ILL) services,
- *Document delivery services* (DDS),
- Resource-sharing, and
- Consortia-based subscriptions.

PRESENT PRACTICES AND EMERGING GOALS

The special libraries attached to research and higher education were lucky enough to garner resources to automate their in-house routine operations and for hosting online public access catalogues (OPACs); some of them also set up facilities to search electronic databases. A few of them evolved the desired infrastructure for Internet surfing, for hosting of full-text database access, and for setting up digital libraries. The major advantage of the progress in computerization is a considerable increase in the amount of information available online. We have experienced that at the start of computer applications only the surrogates (metadata) existed online, but some full-text content has been made accessible online in recent years.

These libraries are experiencing the virtues of electronic information in different forms such as e-journals, e-books, bibliographic/full-text electronic databases on CD-ROMs and through Web access. Due to publishers' 'electronic plus' policies, libraries are able to access electronic versions of printed sources such as journals either for free or by paying an additional fee. However the goal these libraries in specialized research and academic centres should have set for themselves is to enhance their information facilities to fully functional digital libraries, comparable with similar facilities in the developed countries.

CULTURES AND CONFLICTS FACED BY LIBRARIES

The fixed roles suggested by Levy for researchers, publishers and libraries are either overlapping or changing in the electronic scene. There are cases where an author or a library is acting as electronic publisher, and there are publishers providing a wide variety of information packages beyond the contents of printed journals.

The real question is: has the library really lost ground in the emerging information scene? Even the critics will not say so. The concerns expressed are only to revitalize the professional skills of librarians, rejuvenate the style of working and reorient the library towards its rightful place in effective dissemination of information. Maybe the common feeling that the library is a central place in the institution visited everyday by large numbers of users, like any public utility, has lost some ground in the electronic scene. Nonetheless, apart the continuing provision of information services for print sources, the electronic revolution has reaffirmed the library more as an information service and access centre than as an information storehouse.

TECHNOLOGY-ENHANCED LIBRARY SERVICES

TECHNOLOGY ADVANCES

The major technology breakthroughs in the context of libraries include:

- Advent of printing press and mass production of printed documents enabled democratization of information. Libraries had a major role in the print era, as no one can own a large number of books on a particular subject whereas libraries by their very purpose concentrated on doing so.
- Microforms helped to preserve less used information in a compact space and as a smoother delivery option for voluminous sources. Libraries had their unchallenged role even in the microform era as the special purpose readers for microfilms and microfiche were costly and exclusively housed in the library.
- The economical and affordable copying technology revolutionized the concept of information use as it spearheaded the trend of owning copies of relevant portions of library resources. The copying technology freed the user from sitting in the library for long duration for reading, since one can simply get a copy quickly and leave.
- Computing is the biggest technology revolution so far, as it is a major enabler in the information dissemination chain; also it is not a stand-alone technology unlike earlier technologies and can be networked and integrated with a whole lot of other devices and technologies. It not only revolutionized the production of books and microforms but also brought the arrival of online and CD-ROM databases, electronic information resources, Internet and the digital revolution.

PRODUCTS AND SERVICES

Adapting IT for library applications is an ongoing process, right from procuring or developing IT enabled information products through computer aided processing and management to delivering IT-enriched services. Library professionals in India are already exposed to the different offshoots of IT for library organization and information services.

LIBRARY AUTOMATION PACKAGES

The availability of a wide variety of library automation software to suit the varied needs of libraries themselves is a reflection of the progress libraries have made in automating the operations of procuring, processing and providing information sources. Procurement is the end of the story for many other software/databases used in a library, whereas library automation systems will open a floodgate of issues. What the vendor provides is a structure to build information concerning the collection and users, to conduct various aspects of organizing the collection and offering information services.

Thus software needs to be evaluated for its suitability for the target library before purchase. This may include case studies from other libraries using the software, evaluation of hardware and operating system required, computer awareness among staff and users, network as well as computer infrastructure in the institution, and above all estimation of cost and charges for after-sales support. Using suitable software for library automation will significantly reduce manual operations and enable professionals to dedicate more time for professional jobs.

CD-ROM AND ELECTRONIC DATABASES

Due to the poor communication infrastructure prevalent in India and to the immense costs involved, online database services were used only by few institutions. The distribution of the same content of online data repositories subsequently in CD-ROMs made it affordable to a larger number of institutions. While the library automation package gave search-and access facility to information sources present in the local collection, CD-ROM databases attempted consolidated access irrespective of holdings to the bibliographic data of publications in a discipline. CD-ROM databases have also freed library professionals from conducting searches and allowed the end user to conduct the searches. CD-ROM is so common nowadays that a library holds a good number of them not only for bibliographic, numeric and full-text databases, but also those received along with printed books and other reference sources. Managing and serving these high capacity discs was a problem earlier due to the stand-alone software required, whereas the onset of networking and hard-disk cached solutions provides an effective and functional way to enable access to them through the intranet.

WEB

Since the 1990s, the Internet has changed the dissemination of information, such as electronic copies of traditional paper-based journals and conference proceedings, free electronic-only refereed journals, haphazard copies of all kinds of material on home pages and a handful of electronic preprints archives. Most libraries in India now have a website and they use the site to present the basic strengths of the library and to host services such as the OPAC and Web access to electronic information.

The 'size of the catalogue card' and the field lengths of primitive database technology are surpassed in the Web era. Types of information resources on the Web also vary from authentic primary information about the latest research results to ephemeral product catalogues. Issues worth consideration are often the content of the sites that are deleted, modified or changed to new machines without proper redirection and the extraction mechanism through search engines, when a flood of sources is retrieved against a query, of which few are relevant. The Internet and Web demonstrate that a large amount of electronic information can be hosted in a decentralized fashion in a cost-effective manner. The Web has also freed the user's dependence on library resources for finding information related to address and contact details of a person/institution, contents pages of books, journals, etc.

As far as possible, especially for reference and information services, looking at the Web has become an innovative trend in the reference service to complement dated print sources. Many publishers visibly feel the benefits and reach of the Web, and have considered it as an alternate medium for delivering information sources; some publishers even permit unrestricted access of tables of contents and abstracts of their primary journals. As a result of these initiatives, the 'print and distribute' paradigm is challenged by 'distribute and print' paradigm.

CONSORTIAL LICENSES

The term 'consortial licenses' designates library groupings to negotiate access rights to electronic information with publishers and vendors aiming at enhanced access to more resources at better pricing. "Consortia can be a means to introduce products to a previously untapped market" for vendors and "consortia provide shared expertise, access to new electronic and print resources, professional development, new sources of funds, and safety in numbers" for libraries. In contrast to earlier library collaborative arrangements such as ILL and resource sharing, the publisher and trade community are parties in the consortial agreements.

In resource-sharing, libraries concentrate on collaborative subscriptions by avoiding duplication, where as in consortial licenses, the emphasis is to strike the 'best deals' even if the library suffers some duplication. The publisher community experience is that increased subscription costs lead to a reduction in the total number of subscriptions, further raising the subscription cost every year. Publishers also found it difficult to enforce ownership rights with electronic sources, even after adopting the latest technology tools and forcing libraries to sign the toughest of the legal clauses.

The good marketing wisdom of the publisher and trade community prevailed to open up information access rights through consortial licenses for a large part of the product spectrum to at least those libraries or groups of libraries which procure products beyond a certain threshold value. The *Indian National Digital Library in Engineering Science and Technology* (INDEST) is the first and the major consortium in India. It is under the aegis of the *Ministry of Human Resource Development* (MHRD). Before the creation of the consortium, access to electronic journals in these institutions remained at 60% of subscribed titles, but the number of online journals has increased 10 times after the establishment of the consortium.

The rates for access offered to the consortium are lower by 50% to 90% depending upon the category of institution and the consortium paid only 11% of the list price to access these resources. Info net, another consortium, floated by the *University Grants Commission* (UGC) for Universities, is also gaining strength. Similar consortia are also operational for research institutions under the Council of Scientific and Industrial Research (CSIR) and the Department of Atomic Energy (DAE).

DIGITAL LIBRARIES

Libraries in India are engaged in the development of prototypes of digital information resources, as influenced by developments in other countries. There are certain types of content which lie inaccessible or less used in their present physical forms that can be put to more visible and enhanced use through digitization. Also heavily used content presently available in limited numbers of copies can be identified for conversion to electronic format. The linear text in many of the print sources presents difficulties for providing a hypertext approach or a multimedia feeling, for simulating learning by doing; sustaining attention and interest for long duration calls for using electronic technologies to enable content to be more functional.

The static content in printed sources fails to attract users who are increasingly exposed to the widely appealing features of broadcasting and IT-intensive presentation tools. Multimedia-enabled digital information will be useful to a large percentage of illiterate and older population also. There are cases such as papers in journals and conferences in print form that never get their deserved visibility and often end up with out reaching the target population. The digital dissemination of this content may lead to very effective teaching and more focused research in most areas.

To demonstrate the efficacy of digital libraries and collections, libraries must be able to identify materials in the public domain, sources generated in-house, and similar materials to overcome the constraints of copyright. Digital library (DL) development needs a two pronged strategy to digitize local content as well as to devise options for providing access to external resources obtained as free or as part of existing subscriptions or access licenses.

The typical academic or research library in-house digital library on an Intranet must include the following components:

- Consortial access to electronic journals and electronic databases;
- Free/paid Web access to journals subscribed in print format;
- Subject gateways and virtual libraries;
- Free/paid e-books from publishers and portals;
- Intranet access to bibliographic and full-text databases, and CD-ROM publications;
- Local archiving of free and paid e-books;
- LAN serving of e-supplements of purchased books;
- In-house digitization of copyright-owned and copyright- free printed books in the collection;
- Born-digital in-house publications such as research reports, annual reports, convocation reports, teaching materials, theses and dissertations, in-house journals, proceedings of conferences, seminars, workshops, etc., conducted by the institution;
- Preprints and post-prints of research papers sent for publication to journals, conferences, and books, especially with respect to the Open Archives Initiative gaining ground to provide further access to research published in toll journals and to make the results of publicly funded research available to those who need them;
- Publications in the public domain, such as government publications, publications from non-profit institutions, etc.

But many libraries are unable to provide these components due to lack of awareness or due to the hurdles invariably faced by libraries in India. The lack of interest on the part of parent institutions and the absence of action plans or priorities is the major hindrance. Though computer and communication infrastructure is improving, their availability for information work is not appreciated in many organizations. Paschoud commented how several of the speakers and many of the delegates at the International Conference on Digital Libraries (ICDL) 2004 conference in New Delhi focussed on addressing what most European libraries would consider very basic issues such as network/ Internet connectivity and management.

Even in places where infrastructure is available, there is an acute shortage of competent labour to take up the task of digitizing local content and evolving digital information repositories. The students, faculty, curriculum and training methodology at the disposal of library schools have to be improved visibly to meet this challenge. Coupled with this is the need for continuing education for retraining the working professionals. Institutions, individuals, or private publishers have rights over content, and motivating them to ease these rights when they are not inclined towards digitization is not a simple task. Levying charges for access is a distant proposition; instead sponsorships from institutions, government bodies and library suppliers can be explored.

Even when hosted as a free facility, enough security mechanisms must be evolved to prevent any trespassing by hackers. Selecting useful content requires careful review and evaluation by subject experts, as digitization will only help to preserve the record, and not its enhanced and continued access. Internet bandwidth in India has to be sufficiently augmented to allow faster access to Web content as more content is being hosted on the Web. The different funding agencies, research councils and institutions are not currently offering monetary support to the desired extent for digital library development.

CULTURE AND CONFLICTS FACED BY USERS

MANUAL AND ELECTRONIC SEARCH

Searching for manual sources required scanning catalogue cards or indexing and abstracting sources. As cross-references often increase the number of cards or pages, there was a difficulty in being very exhaustive. Conducting selective dissemination of information (SDI) services had been extremely difficult as the document profiles must be matched with user profiles with the aid of semi mechanical systems. Most of these limitations are easily eliminated in the electronic environment due to the very nature of information processing and organization in electronic form.

The inherent advantages of indexing electronic information help the user to search for any or all the fields in a timesaving manner. Since document profiles are already stored in the database and search software supports creation of user profiles, current awareness services (CAS) and SDI services are achieved more easily. The concern for end-user searching was dominant right from the beginning of early CD-ROM database systems since the time spent for searching does not involve communication costs as is the case with online searching. Also with the universe of knowledge getting increasingly complex as a result of continuing advances in research in intra and inter-disciplinary areas, vitiating the search conducted by a generalist like a librarian may not be effective in amassing the user's information requirements completely or not achieving the desired results expected by the user.

The convoluted information requirements of present day researchers require sufficient knowledge of their disciplines and since the users are increasingly exposed to the computerized work environment, they feel very confident to conduct information searching on electronic systems. The professional ethos and egos also plays a part as users find more satisfactory results from electronic systems than manual systems, and in a relatively easy and convenient way. The librarians should recognize the confidence and maturity of users to conduct searches on their own as they have better knowledge of their disciplines, more exposure to the different keywords and their relationships and because of the inherent advantages of locating related sources serendipitously while scanning the retrieved results.

There should be closer interaction and effective communication between library professionals and users to understand each other's views about information needs and use. Library user meetings, orientation sessions for new users, special help for research scholars, training programmes about usage of print and electronic resources, a help desk at reference counter, holdings locator services, interacting with users through phone and e-mail, encouraging users to approach the librarian, ask a librarian, and user friendly websites are some options practiced in libraries in India.

INFORMATION USE

Information services provided by a library are primarily based on subjective input from users and hence justify users commenting about misses or noise in electronic information service outputs. An information need is what an individual *ought* to have; an information want is what an individual *would* like to have; an information demand is what an individual *asks* for; an information use is what an individual actually *uses*; and an information requirement denotes what is *needed*, what is *wanted* or what is *demanded*. Information needs are affected by a variety of factors such as the range of sources available, the uses to which information will be put, individual characteristics of the user, social, political and economic systems surrounding the user, and the consequences of information use.

Accessibility of information resources is usually assumed to depend on a range of cognitive, social, and physical factors, such as whether a person is aware of a resource, has the knowledge and skills needed to access it, and has the resource close at hand. Scientists spend 50–60% of their time communicating. The computerised environment has increased the quantum of information available nearby, but it has not enhanced a person's information consumption skills. There is a burden of effort in information storage and retrieval that may be shifted from author to indexer to index language designer to searcher to user. Though the user is exposed to more microfilms, Xerox copies, and electronic information on desktop/ Intranet/Web, ready to display at the touch of a button, the more time one spends in searching and collecting information, the less time s/he gets to use the information. Scholarly articles are identified for reading in five basic ways: browsing, automated searches, citations found in the literature, mentions by other people, and current-awareness tools.

How much information one requires to work on a particular problem is also subjective as human beings observe the 'principle of least effort'. Perhaps one may easily deal with an information crisis by identifying a part of the total references and by using few of what is identified.

USER BYPASSING

Though libraries in India are progressing well on the automation and information access front, there is a definite case of fewer users present in the library due to different reasons. The real question is whether electronic services of libraries have in any way affected the user interests or have the users found more confidence in an information superhighway beyond the library. The same proportions of scientists still browse to identify scholarly articles to read, but more are using online searches and the proportion of readings identified through online searches appears to be increasing. Library acquisitions suffered a serious setback in recent years unable to withstand the price rise and these budgetary constraints forced users to look beyond the library for their varied information requirements.

Hence research publications in some disciplines now cite more Web resources. Librarians are not yet acting as true consumers and hence cannot blame predatory publishers for taking advantage of the situation. Another issue involves the very large and rapidly increasing number of articles obtained through photocopying, interlibrary loan, document delivery, preprints, and reprints. The right step in assessing whether there is a depleted user interest in libraries is to study use patterns over the years and, in a populous country like India, just going by the numbers will not address the qualitative aspects. There has not been much reduction in book issues in an academic library, but are the new acquisitions being used to the same extent? But what is seen is the fall in library attendance, as observed and reported by many library managers.

It is evident that fewer users actually visit the library, and very few still spend more time, a lot of others use the library through lending, photocopies, electronic access through networks, etc. It becomes difficult to quantify use as the library has statistics only about explicit use, but there are also implicit uses through browsing or reading inside the library, which are difficult to quantify. There are also vital questions about whether mere issuing a book or taking a photocopy of a journal article attribute to use and hence comes the need for a qualitative assessment of use. Perhaps professionals are afraid to look at these issues as the results of such assessment may force the authorities to examine critically the investments in a service institution like the library. Like Reenen's comment about false consumers, it seems that librarians fear self-assessment of library usage or to undergo a performance audit.

THE LIBRARIAN'S IDENTITY CRISIS

EDUCATION AND TRAINING

As stated previously, the students, faculty, curriculum and training methodology at the library schools have to be visibly improved to meet the challenges posed by electronic information and impatient, highly demanding users. There are also problems of infrastructure and a directionless attitude in the teaching and research sector often forgetting the interdisciplinary aspect of the subject. Working librarians have good exposure to new databases, their acquisition and use, pragmatic implementation of various routines etc., which are not accessible to library schools.

Thus apart from teaching faculty, expert practitioners in the discipline would also be involved in education programmes to bridge the gap between preaching and practice. The existing courses must always look at the sweeping changes in the library workplace and adapt well to enable the students to face the challenges with confidence, giving ample opportunities for improving reasoning, communication skills, general awareness, and other characteristics identified for a multi-tasking service organization. The age-old teacher-centric teaching has to be circumvented by student oriented and professional (job)-centric teaching.

JOB OPPORTUNITIES

Though the major employer, the government is not recruiting many, more and more universities/institutions are offering library courses in the regular and distance modes. And this upheaval in quantity does not contribute in any way to the quality of these courses. For a prospective student/parent, the job advertisements provide an impression of plenty of jobs in the field, as library jobs at different levels in different institutions do not follow standard designations. But only when one finishes the course and looks for job openings, does the actual state of affairs come to light. Actually the increase in library-related jobs is merely additive, and not multiplicative, like computers, management or engineering, and should not show an exponential rise at any point of time.

CONTINUING EDUCATION

Since the mode and rate at which information is generated, organized and used is witnessing sweeping changes in the perfectly wired information age, a continuously evolving discipline like LIS is meant to tackle the intricacies of information for societal development; thus it shall not be learned effectively and practiced perfectly by exposing students to a framed curriculum in formal education only.

The discipline has changed drastically from being based totally on print sources; aware of the increasing richness of information in electronic forms and available over networks thus is leading to embracing vigourously other disciplines like computers, management, and information and communication technology. It is imperative for the information practitioners to continuously monitor and augment their professional skills through continuing education (CE) to discharge their duties to users, employer and profession. The present initiatives on CE are generally being made by national institutions and suffer limitations such as: they are of short duration, generally infrequent, claiming comparatively high fees, working professionals finding it difficult to get sponsorship from their institutions, involve travelling to far off destinations hampering their regular work, etc.

CULTURES AND CONFLICTS FACED BY LIBRARIANS

Gone are the days of close-minded librarians and the quality of candidates entering the profession is continuously improving. As technology-intensive librarianship is gaining ground in the country, working librarians are getting much exposure to new technology tools for providing better information products and improved information services. Working librarians in at least the major academic and research institutions have better computer infrastructure and possess better expertise on the latest information products and services.

It is quite natural in the emerging print plus electronic hybrid library scenario that a library professional right from first job is expected to be conversant with the electronic apart from the manual means of information collection, processing, management and servicing. But there are also apprehensions about the level of technology appropriate to conducting well in the challenging and demanding academic and research setup. A library professional must be distinct from a computer professional due to the very nature of their profession and the expected deliverables. But the acute emphasis on technology has created a situation that a professional can hide many of his/her professional ignorance by a little computer knowledge which is not going to be good either for the profession or for the libraries. Google cannot and will not be replacing libraries because both can co-exist with their diverse functionalities catching the attention of users at different occasions.

The professional nature of the librarian's job always motivates him or her to help the users unlike administrative staff in the institution who are always rule-based; sometimes this may lead to not so proper upkeep of administrative procedures and records, and in some cases cause unnecessary rivalry with the administrative staff. There are also personnel problems as the librarians fail to command a leadership role in many institutions thereby eclipsing their role in strategic planning. Institutions attach prime importance to libraries but are they doing the same towards the personnel in their libraries? It is a strange case of all the virtues are of the system and the problems are due to the staff. Largely a service wing in many institutions, not enjoying the power, visibility, service conditions, and career prospects of the research and teaching staff, the status of library professionals in many of these institutions is not a morale booster, leaving many of them underperforming.

It is not uncommon to see non-professionals heading many libraries, maybe just because they are senior teachers or good administrators or researchers and not because they are good as librarians. There are also problems of the lack of a peer group in the profession resisting such attacks on the profession as many senior professionals have become self-centred, and professional associations compete for minor issues. The professional staff members working in many libraries in developing countries are totally engrossed in administrative and routine jobs related to library operation and administration. Many institutions do not demand their library professionals to pursue an offensive role. The users always need quick services and they never respond to any of the reasonable operational or managerial delays.

The real situation is that the libraries have very little control over their suppliers whereas their consumers have too much control over them. Users are not patient enough to interact constantly with the library staff to tune their profiles to improve the relevance of information services, maybe due to time constraints on their parts. Again by a rough assessment, it seems that less than 10% of the users usually respond to SDI results and the remaining are either using it as it is or rejecting it straightaway. Out of those responding, only a few show their willingness to give feedback to modify their keywords to improve the utility of such services. Users may sometimes get so arrogant with the helpful nature of library staff and doubt it as their weakness.

IMPLICATIONS OF MONUMENTAL CONSTRUCTION

In 2001, when the new public library in Alexandria opened, the designers and developers of the project declared that they planned to establish one of the largest libraries in the world and thereby revitalize the idea of the antique library of Alexandria. Similarly, the builders of the library in Shanghai, who call it the "palace of knowledge," include its large dimensions among its unique characteristics.

The size of the building housing Library 21, in Stuttgart, Germany, described by its manager as the city's "meteor," is said to reflect the library's tremendous significance. Indeed, since the 1990s we have witnessed a wave of construction of large, even monumental, libraries around the world, construction of the type that characterized the ancient world.

This phenomenon occurs in an age of advanced information technologies; an age which is characterized by developments in computerization, in general, and the development of telecommunications and the Internet, in particular, which enable easy access to information. It is characterized as well by the development of user friendly search engines which provide access to sources from any place at any time; and in addition by the rapid development of advanced technologies for non-paper storage and preservation of information which saves space. The purpose of the present study is to examine the implications of the current wave of large, even monumental, library buildings for the functioning and status of public libraries.

FUNCTIONS OF PUBLIC LIBRARIES OVER TIME

In the library in Nineveh, all collections were gathered: documents, certificates, correspondence, religious writings and historical descriptions, as well as works in various scientific fields. Hessel claims that these collections effectively declare the purpose of establishment of the library, to serve the state, to glorify the eternal memory of its founder and also for science. Since those distant days, libraries have assumed a variety of forms but their primary, "classical" function as guardians of the collective memory of human culture has remained unchanged from their earliest development until today. Over the years, another central function has been added: not only do libraries collect and preserve information, but also they now routinely process and disseminate new information.

This change occurred gradually, beginning with the introduction of paper and the invention of the printing press and climaxed in the 20th century. This development occurred simultaneously with the continued strengthening of libraries' position as public institutions with a social-education function of the utmost importance. Throughout the 150 years of its existence, the modern public library has undergone changes in its goals and functions, and as a result in the services it offers the public.

During each period, it attempted to meet the demands of the times. Since the latter half of the 19th century, libraries have become a part of the public sector and are funded by public monies. Therefore, they not only protect and preserve the knowledge that belongs to the community, but also have added services intended for the general public, in order to make education available not only to elites and academics. Initially, the library was an auxiliary institution in the field of education, a continuation of, and supplement to, the public schools that were established during the same period. As an adaptive institution, its functions have changed with the times. Therefore, in the late 19th century, the public library moved into the field of leisure and began offering popular books for pleasure reading or folklore evenings, following the waves of immigration at the time.

Furthermore, in the 1950s and 1960s, the library began to serve as an information centre for the general public and fulfilling a supplementary role by providing information services to public and economic institutions, both governmental and voluntary. In the 1960s and 1970s, libraries began to participate in social projects and reach out to various groups of non-users.

IFLA clearly states that other functions have been added to the library's traditional role as a supplier of books, because the library has become a cultural and social centre in the community. As such, the library offers the community lectures, clubs, exhibitions, concerts, films, a venue for performances, the possibility of integrating a museum into the library and even a meeting place for different groups, including the elderly. It is almost superfluous to note that in recent years, libraries have been required to go beyond their traditional services and adapt themselves to the information revolution by supplying their clients with new services using advanced technologies.

However, the IFLA Core Programme repeatedly emphasizes and reaffirms the value of library collections and archives as vital for both the survival and development of culture and scholarship. It seems that among those working on the portrait of the current and future library, the voices that tend towards greater emphasis on social-cultural aspects are increasing.

VISION OF THE VIRTUAL LIBRARY VERSUS THE REALITY OF THE MONUMENTAL LIBRARY

Many people would claim that the future has already arrived. Not only have the needs of information consumers changed significantly, but most importantly, the variety of means and possibilities for obtaining information have changed. It is hard to imagine the library's clients continuing waiting for a busy librarian to supply traditional service when they have not only telephone, facsimile and e-mail at their disposal, but also a home computer or laptop which can be used to connect directly to the Internet. Young people tend to position the library as a marginal institution in future society and expect that it will become sort of a museum for "antique" materials. Awareness of the possibility that libraries might disappear is evident in almost every treatment of the issue.

For example, in their book *The Incredible Vanishing Library*, Gross and Borgman describe the importance of the library both as a social institution and as an organization that supplies information from various sources. However, they claim that decision makers do not sufficiently understand and acknowledge the great importance of the library in fulfilling these roles and, therefore, they are gradually becoming an invisible institution. Hage believes that the basic tools used by libraries will remain unchanged despite the advanced technology. A similar line of argument is taken by Schement, who believes that even in the digital age, the role of librarians as skilled mediators between information and the public should be maintained since most people lack the skills to navigate between the many sources of information.

Despite this, Schement does consider the possibility of the vanishing library realistic and believes that librarians should also provide "remote" information services outside of the library building. As early as 1972, almost 20 years before the trend towards building new, large libraries began, Rohlf claimed that public libraries would not only continue to exist and expand the variety of services they offer, but also grow in size. Architects, Rohlf claimed, are currently required to plan libraries with a long-term vision and create buildings that are capable of adapting to developments and changes, house large quantities of electronic gadgetry, while at the same time being filled with light, space and having a layout that gives people a feeling of belonging and humanity.

In the face of all of the predictions of a world without books and without libraries, Naisbitt and Aburdene claim, "In every place where the information economy has spread... the need for arts, new museums, cultural and literary renewal has experienced unprecedented growth." The authors even present data showing that more new titles and new editions of books are published in the United States every year. A similar spirit of wonder, it appears, rests on most representatives of the large libraries that were constructed or expanded in the late 20th Century. Beyond the superlatives used to describe the buildings themselves, most of the library directors refer to the close connection between the rejuvenation of the library's visual aspect and its content and popularity level. For example, the directors of the new public library in Rotterdam, the new library in Stuttgart, Germany, the new Queens Borough Public Library, New York and the new library of San Antonio, Texas all describe the impressive building as one of the city's outstanding landmarks and note an increase in the number of visitors and users of library services. Do these changes in the character and image of the public library help strengthen and preserve its original goals and will they, in the future, position it as an institution with a central role in society? The purpose of this study is to attempt to clarify these issues.

METHODOLOGY

RESEARCH QUESTIONS

- Does the change in a library building have implications for its popularity? In other words, is there a significant increase in the number of visitors and users to monumental library buildings?
- Is the change in the form of library buildings indeed being accompanied by a change in content? In other words, in the new public library, is it possible to identify a change in direction, transforming it from an institution that focuses on "traditional" services into a significant cultural centre in the community and society?

RESEARCH POPULATION

The research population included:

- Directors of 24 libraries in Israel and other Western countries, whose libraries meet two criteria:

- The library was built and opened to the public after 1990.
- The library could be included in the category of monumental structures. To meet these criteria, the study included libraries in Israel with a constructed area of more than 2,000 square meters and libraries in other countries that are five or more stories tall or cover an area of 10,000 meters square or more.

Most of the large libraries in the study were opened to the public between 1995 and 2001. Out of the 24 libraries included in the study, 79.2% are in new buildings and 28.8% are libraries that continue to function in an old building that has been expanded.

- In addition, we interviewed 42 people from five relevant professions: nine futurists, seven sociologists, ten architects, seven urban planners and nine experts from the fields of information and library science.

RESEARCH TOOLS

- A questionnaire was completed by the directors of the 24 selected libraries. The purpose of the 15-question questionnaire was to examine the characteristics of the people who use the library services and to see whether there had been a quantitative increase, in addition to examining the functioning of the public library through the lens of the services that it offers in the new building and the different ways it is used, as compared to how it functioned in its previous building.
- Structured interviews with 42 experts and a questionnaire each interviewee was asked to complete at the end of the interview. Analysis of the interviews was done according to a qualitative research approach, while the accompanying questionnaire was analysed quantitatively.

The interviews lasted between 30 and 90 minutes. All of the interviews were recorded, with the consent of the interviewees, transcribed and processed with a long process of summarization and adaptation of the statements to categories relevant to the research questions.

FINDINGS

LARGE BUILDINGS– MORE USERS

Can a Public Library in a Magnificent Building Serve as a Centre of Attraction

One of the questions asked of the experts in various professions was whether, in their opinion, a magnificent, respectable public library building would encourage more people to visit the library. Table presents the division of answers given by the interviewees who answered the question positively, according to professional groups. The data in table indicate that most of the interviewees, including all of the architects and most of the information and library scientists and futurists and more than half of the others, indeed believe that a large, respectable public library building will encourage more people to visit the library.

Table. Does a Magnificent New Public Library Building Encourage More People to Visit the Library? Comparison between Groups of Interviewees (by Percentage)

Profession	Architects	Information and Library Scientists	Futurists	Urban Planners	Sociologists	Total
Percentage of positive answers	100.0	88.9	77.8	57.1	50.0	77.5

Did the Number of Visitors to the Library Increase

From the research data we received, it emerges that after the construction of a new library building, there is a dramatic increase (in percentage) in the number of library visitors. Of the library directors, 96% answered that there had been an increase in the number of visitors. Most responded there was a 100% increase in the number of people visiting the library, meaning that the number doubled. Two directors reported an even higher increase.

Was there an Increase in the Number of Regular Clients

Most of the libraries that participated in the study (68.4%) reported that one-fifth of the city's residents are registered subscribers. Four libraries reported that over half of the residents are registered as regular users. These numbers represented the number of subscribers *registered* as regular library clients. To these numbers, we must add the other, unregistered residents, who the library, as a public institution, serves with a variety of services that do not require registration. All of the libraries, except one, reported a significant increase in the number of registered clients.

From the data that we received, it emerges that the average increase in the number of registered subscribers at the new large libraries was 95.8%. This means that the number of regular clients increased by the same amount as the number of visitors to the library. From these findings, it clearly appears that the construction of a large library building increases the number of people who use the library whether they come to visit, surf the Internet or even just to be with people. Furthermore, it increases the percentage of regular customers who take advantage of the services offered by the public library.

FUNCTIONS OF THE PUBLIC LIBRARY IN THE VIRTUAL AGE

The Library as a Centre of Social-cultural Life in the City

Experts in various professions were asked to express their position regarding the library as a social- cultural centre. Figure presents the percentage of respondents who believe the library is a centre for social-cultural activity in city. It shows that 90% of the architects would locate the library in the centre of a city's social and cultural life.

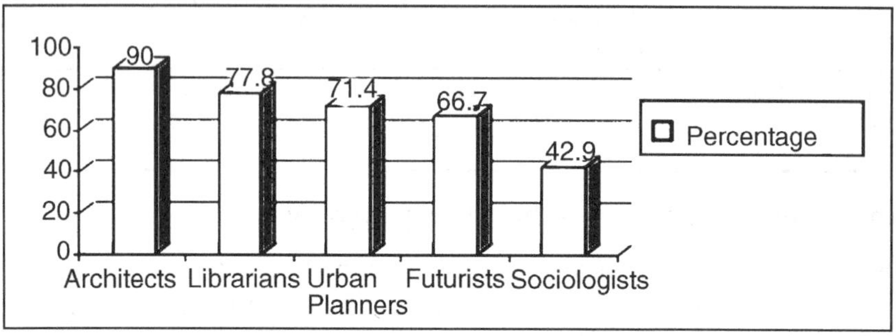

Fig. Division, by Professional Group, of Answers Regarding the Library Placement in the City's Social_Cultural Center

They are followed by the information and library scientists and urban planners. Only 42.9% of the sociologists believe that a library needs to be in the centre of social or cultural life in the city. Most of the interviewees (71.4%) believed that libraries should be in the social-cultural centre of the city.

Roles of the Public Library in the 21st Century – Analysis of the Interviews

After we learned about the interviewees' opinions regarding the public library and its location in the centre of the city's social and cultural activity, we continued by asking what, in the interviewees opinions, should be the library's role in future society.

Information and Library Scientists

After analysing the statements by the interviewees from the field of information and library science regarding this question, it emerges that all members of this group agreed on one function: the library is a place for holding cultural activities and a meeting place for spending leisure time. "We are a society that is built on personal meetings ... some of the readers have a limited need for the collection ... they come in order to meet ... therefore the place is lively ... (V.B.).

"The library of the 21st century is a social meeting place ... beyond this, the library needs to allow for clubs and generally be a cultural centre" (B.L.). Regarding other library functions, approximately one-half of the interviewees from this group said that the library should be a place to learn and acquire skills, in addition to locating the necessary information. "The library is a place to sit and do homework, a place to study..." (S.H.).

"The library has a very important role in acquiring the skills for locating and processing knowledge and information... it has a role in developing taste in reading and encouraging reading" (M.R.). There are those who connect the public library's instructional function with its democratic function: providing equal opportunity for every one to access information. "In the 21st century it is important that the library instruction teach the use of computer and Internet – to reduce the digital gap" (S.B.). Only two of the information and library scientists interviewed mentioned the traditional functions of the public library – preserving knowledge and lending books. Perhaps these things seem to be self-evident.

Architects

The function of the public library all of the architects agreed upon and mentioned was social meeting. "Library is like a house of prayer – these are buildings where large numbers of people gather" (Y.G.). The library has a role in preserving books and also in bringing together resources in all existing media. Most of the architects agreed on this point. "Practically speaking, a library is 'a museum of knowledge,' a warehouse of information for coming generations ... on paper and on electronics" (M.K.).

Urban Planners

This group had many doubts and there was not even a single function mentioned by all members of this group. Despite this, most of the urban planners interviewed noted that in the future the library would be a place for preservation or storage, but with the possibility of accessing this preserved material. "First of all, preservation for future generations is necessary ... but also presentation, to make all of the literature accessible and visual ..." (A.L.).

Sociologists

In this group, too, there was no agreement regarding the main purpose of the library. However, most of the sociologists interviewed think that the library must make information broadly available on a full range of media. "First of all, a centre of knowledge, a centre that facilitates access to knowledge ..." (S.N.).

There were those who made a connection between libraries' offerings and equality in society. "This is in the context of people who do not have the means to purchase all of the books ... to provide information at no cost" (S.K.). Of the sociologists, three noted that libraries should continue their traditional functions of "lending, reading, guidance and reference" (Z.Z.).

Futurists

Most of the futurists interviewed do not consider the public library an essential institution, because of the technological changes that have already occurred and which are continuing to occur. However, when we asked what, despite this, roles of a library would have in the future society, several of the interviewees mention the role of the library as a meeting place and also the necessity of a place that will gather and organize information and be responsible for preserving the culture.

Several of the people interviewed referred to the role of the library in providing professional instruction and assisting the educational system:

- The public library will not remain a source of information – that's over, but it will have other functions such as meetings with books, meeting to exchange information... people need the social interaction and everyone looks for an appropriate place. People are looking for a reason to meet. Some meet in a restaurant, others in a movie theatre, others in their living room and yet others in a library. (A.A.)

Functions of the Public Library in the Opinion of All Groups (Analysis of Questionnaires)

Functions of the Public Library in the Opinion of All Respondents

Table presents rankings of the public library functions according to the opinions of all participants in the study.

Table. Functions of the Library – Comparison between Professional Groups (in percentages)

	Library Function	Futurists*	Sociologists	Architects	Urban Planners	Information and Library Science	Library Directors	Total
1	Reading	44.4	100.0	100.0	71.4	88.9	95.8	81.0
2	Reference	44.4	100.0	100.0	85.7	100.0	91.7	85.7
3	Study place	77.8	100.0	90.0	85.7	88.9	95.8	88.1
4	Newspapers	44.4	85.7	90.0	57.1	100.0	91.7	76.2
5	Educational video	55.6	85.7	100.0	71.4	100.0	82.3	82.3
6	Entertainment video	44.4	85.7	90.0	57.1	77.8	87.5	71.4
7	Information center	66.7	85.7	80.0	28.6	88.9	75.0	71.4
8	Communications center	33.3	71.4	100.0	42.9	66.7	70.8	64.3
9	Cultural center	44.4	100.0	90.0	85.7	88.9	95.8	81.0
10	Public clubs	44.4	57.1	90.0	57.1	77.8	87.5	66.7
11	Leisure activities	55.6	85.7	80.0	71.4	100.0	100.0	70.6
12	Meeting of distinctive groups	33.3	71.4	60.0	42.9	88.9	66.7	59.5
13	Attraction for visitors	22.2	57.1	50.0	28.6	55.6	66.7	42.9
14	Cultural preservation	66.7	100.0	90.0	100.0	77.8	70.8	85.7
15	Archive	66.7	85.7	70.0	85.7	33.3	54.2	66.7

Note: *Approximately one-quarter of the futurists refused to answer the question regarding functions, claiming that the library has no future.

We found that a majority of the participants think that a public library should be a place for study and research. Other functions noted were, in descending order, provision of reference services, cultural preservation, providing educational videos and reading books and being a cultural centre. Furthermore, it should be noted that only three-quarters of the futurists assigned any function to libraries in the future, consistently claiming that there will be no need for the public libraries and they will have no function in the future society.

Functions of the Public Library – Comparison of the Interview Groups

Examination of table reveals that differences exist between the perceptions that members of different professions have regarding public libraries. All (100%) of the sociologists and architects think that the libraries' traditional functions, providing books for reading and reference, are most important, compared to only 44.4% of the futurists who indicated that these would be among the public library functions in the future. The sociologists added that the library also functions to preserve the culture and serve as a cultural centre that offers lecturers, cultural events, etc.

People interviewed from the field of information and library science responded that the most important functions are to supply reference materials as well as being a place for recreation and leisure. In contrast, the urban planners gave greater weight to the role of cultural preservation, while the futurists apparently considered the public library's functions less important for future societies.

To determine if there are significant differences between the different professional groups on the question of public library functions, c2 analysis was done. This analysis found that there were significant differences regarding several functions: Regarding the library's function as a provider of reading books, it was found that all of the sociologists, architects and interviewees from the field of information and library science thought that this is an important function, in comparison to the futurists who thought otherwise: $c^2 = 12.56$, $p < .05$. Regarding the function of the library as a supplier of reference books and encyclopaedias, we found that all of the people interviewed from the field of information and library science, architects and sociologist thought that this function is important, unlike the futurists: $c^2 = 16.85$, $p < .01$.

Regarding the library's function as a place to read newspapers and magazines, we found that all of the people interviewed from the field of information and library science and most of the architects think that this is an important function, unlike the futurists: $c^2 = 10.61$, $p < .05$. Regarding the provision of video and audio recordings and recorded music for purposes of study and education, there was a significant difference between the people interviewed in the field of information and library science and the architects, in comparison to the futurists: $c^2 = 9.54$, $p < .05$. Regarding the role of the public library as a communications and Internet centre, we found a significant difference between the architects and the futurists and urban planners: $c^2 = 10.89$, $p < .05$. On this question, we did not find a significant difference between the people interviewed from the field of information and library science and the sociologists. Regarding the function of the public library as a centre for culture and leisure, performances, etc., a significant difference was found between the sociologists, architects, urban planners and interviewees from the field of information and library science, in comparison to the futurists: $c^2 = 10.43$, $p < .05$.

Functions of the Public Library in the Opinion of Library Directors

From the data in table it is possible to see that all of the library directors who participated in this study included serving as a place for leisure time activities in the library functions. Three additional functions: providing reading books, a place for study and research and serving as a cultural centre were also noted by 95.9% of the library directors. Over 90% of library directors included the provision of local and international newspapers and reference books in their list of library functions. The library directors expressed less support for several of the functions, including serving as a place for unique groups to meet, an attractive place for tourists, the functioning to preserve the culture and being a centre for Internet communications. When comparing the responses of library directors in Israel to those from abroad, we did not find any significant differences for any of the functions presented. It should be noted that there were library directors who added functions that were not included among the options presented on the questionnaire. In particular, they emphasized instructional functions. In their opinion, the public library plays an active role in education, instruction and nurturing reading.

PUBLIC LIBRARY FUNCTIONS: OR HAS THE EXTERNAL CHANGE BEEN ACCOMPANIED BY A CHANGE OF CONTENT

After we examined the functions of the library, in the opinion of all interview groups, as well as the library directors, we attempted to learn what was actually happening inside the libraries, which services they are providing in the new buildings that were opened in the last decade and which of these services were not provided previously, in the old building.

THE PUBLIC LIBRARY AND ITS SERVICES TO THE PUBLIC: THE DESIRABLE VERSUS ACTUAL (ANALYSIS OF THE QUESTIONNAIRE FOR LIBRARY DIRECTORS)

From the library directors, we attempted to learn what is actually happening within the libraries, what services they provide in comparison to the services that are, in their opinion, desirable. Table presents the desired functions compared to the actual functions, those that are actually being provided by the libraries.

Table. Library Functions (Desirable) Compared to Services Actually Provided (Actual)

Library Function	Desirable %	Actual %	Wilcoxon
Place for leisure activity	100.0	78.2	0.02*
Reading books	95.8	95.8	1.00
Plays for study or research	95.8	71.7	0.16
Cultural center	95.8	79.2	0.04*
Reference books	91.7	91.7	1.00
Local and international newspapers	91.7	79.2	0.18
Video and audio – for pleasure	87.5	79.2	0.32
Public clubs	87.5	75.0	0.08*
Video and audio – educational	83.3	75.0	0.41
Public information center	75.0	62.5	0.18
Public communication center – Internet	70.8	75.0	0.56
Cultural preservation	70.8	66.7	0.32
Meeting place for distinctive groups	66.7	58.3	0.32
Attractive place for visitors	66.7	62.5	0.56
Archive for storing existing collections	54.2	45.8	0.32

Note: * p<.05

The Services that are Actually being Provided

From the table, it emerges that two of the services were indicated by most of the library directors, more than 90%, are traditional library services: providing books for reading and reference books. Slightly less than 80% of the library directors indicated that their libraries supply local and international newspapers, video and audio recordings for pleasure and that their library is a cultural centre for lectures, exhibitions, etc. or serves as a locale for leisure activities. Fewer than half of the libraries included in the study also serve as an archive.

It should be noted that most of the libraries claimed that the library is egalitarian and democratic, yet the table shows that only 58.3% of the libraries provide services for distinctive groups with special needs in their community. Again, there were librarians that chose to add services which, in their opinion, are important, but were not included in the possibilities listed on the questionnaire: virtual library services, the ability to access library databases without necessarily being present in the library but rather over the Internet, developing early childhood reading, purchasing and maintaining a large collection including antique books and museums, access to electronic data for the business community, special services for adolescents, and renting library rooms/halls. Table shows a sweeping difference between desirable and the actual.

The library directors think that the library ought to fill many important functions but in actual practice, the libraries offer the public fewer services than their directors believe would be desirable. Regarding traditional library functions – the provision of reading books for lending and serving as a reference room – there is a correlation between the services that libraries are supposed to provide the public and what they actually provide.

For all of the other possible library functions included on the list, except providing Internet, more library directors indicated that the possibility was part of a library's desirable functions than actually provide that service to the public in their library.

All of the library directors (100%) believe that one of the library's functions is to serve as a cultural centre for leisure time activities, yet only 78.2% open their doors for leisure time activities. Similarly, 95.8% think that the library building should serve as a home for cultural events such as lectures, exhibitions, performances, thereby serving as a municipal culture centre, but only 79.2% allow this type of activity. Likewise, 87.5% of the library directors indicated it would be desirable for the library to serve as a place for holding club meetings for the general public, yet only 75% of the libraries actually offer clubs.

The Differences between the Desirable and the Actual

To highlight the discrepancy between the desirable library functions and the actual services provided by the libraries a nonparametric, Wilcoxon analysis was conducted.

This analysis reveals significant differences for three library functions, as follows: the library as a cultural centre, holding club meetings in the library and the public library as the place for leisure time activities. These three functions express the social need for meetings in a cultural locale, such as the public library. All three of these functions are desired more than they are actually provided.

New Services in the New Building

Having examined the opinions of library directors, the functions of public libraries and the services provided by the libraries, we examined whether new library services, which were not provided in the previous building, are being provided in the new building. In other words, has the public library changed only its external appearance or also its contents? Does a new, larger building make it possible to provide services that were not offered in the old the building? The library directors were asked to indicate which of the services, currently provided by their library, were not offered by their library in its old building. Of the 24 library directors who participated in the study, only 19 answered this question.

Table. New Services in the New Building (Percentages)

New Services the Library Offers the Public	Percentage
Cultural Centre	47.4
Local and international newspapers	42.1
Video and audio recordings – for pleasure	42.1
Public communication centre – Internet	42.1
Attractive place for visitors	36.8
Video and audio recordings – educational	31.6
Public clubs 31.6 Place for leisure activity	31.6
Place for study or research	26.3
Public information centre	26.3
Meeting place for distinctive groups	21.1
Cultural preservation	21.0
Archive for storing existing collections	15.8
Reading books	0
Reference books	0

The following table presents the distribution of the library director answers regarding *new* services in their library, in descending order (by percentage). A new library building makes it possible to offer several new services that were not available in the library's old building. Approximately one-half of the libraries reported that the library now serves as a cultural centre for lectures, art exhibits, performances, meetings with authors, and other events. Approximately 40% report that they now have a place for reading local and international newspapers and magazines, that they can provide video and audio recordings for pleasure and that they can serve as an Internet communications centre.

Approximately one-third of the respondents indicated additional new services: an attractive place for visitors, video and audio recordings for educational purposes, public clubs and a place for leisure activity while slightly more than 20% noted that the new library they manage serves as a meeting place for unique groups, and a similar percentage said that cultural preservation is one of their library's new functions, which was not possible in the old building. Only 15% reported that the library now serves as an archive for existing collection.

In this section, too, some library directors noted additional, new functions that were not included on the list of possible library functions: virtual services and expanded programmes for children.

It should be noted that there was no difference in the responses of library directors in Israel and abroad on this subject. The responses from the library directors received clearly indicate that a new, more spacious library building does allow the library to offer more services, not necessarily traditional library services, but rather leisure activities: clubs, exhibitions (rare book displays), performances, theatre, space to read newspapers and magazines.

DISCUSSION

LARGE BUILDINGS–ARE THERE MORE USERS

The first research question asked whether the change in library buildings has implications for their popularity. The research findings clearly show that all of the new, large, magnificent buildings that have been built as public libraries receive at least twice as many visitors as their predecessors and there has also been a very significant increase in the percentage of library users and regular clients. Research conducted among public libraries in Israel found a direct connection between the image of the library and its use, both in terms of the number of users and the number of books borrowed.

The present study shows that these new buildings have apparently improved the reputation of the library and thereby increased use. This finding is very important because many libraries around the world report a general decrease in the number of readers, the number of books borrowed and the number of regular clients. By contrast, it is worth noting the research conducted by Westin and Finger, which claims that the number of users increases in every place where a new library was built, regardless of size. Their claim is that any change in the library influences the library's environment and usage. Therefore, they recommend constant revitalization of the library's image. Yet another perspective is presented by McCabe who claims that the number of users increases because a wider variety of services are offered and it is the larger building that makes the services possible.

LIBRARY FUNCTIONS IN A VIRTUAL AGE

Most interviewees considered it important for the library to be at the centre of the social and cultural life of the city. Another function mentioned by most of the interviewees, in most of the groups, was the function of gathering, organizing and storing information, as well as making it accessible. All of the people interviewed from the fields of information and library science emphasized the role of the library in the field of cultural activity and in facilitating social meetings. All of the architects consider the library a place for leisure time entertainment. Most of the members of this group referred to the library as a democratic, egalitarian place where social gaps, especially the digital divide, can be narrowed.

They also noted the role of the library in preserving culture, whether through books or other media. Most of the urban planners emphasized the role of the library in preserving existing collections and culture. Sociologists and futurists did not place special emphasis on any one function. The literature deals with the concept of the public library as "the people's university," but in this study only seven of the 42 people interviewed mentioned this function. Furthermore, when we presented the library as a place for unique populations in society, this function was given a low ranking. Sannwald claims that libraries are becoming a place of social interaction, and research conducted in the United States found that the most important function of the library is to provide access to technology for people of modest means. Westin and Finger stress that the public library should live up to its name: public and free and therefore, by its very nature, serve as a bridge between knowledge and all strata of the population. The library's traditional services were mentioned by the experts in information and library science and the architects. The latter also added the library's function as a communications centre that provides access to the Internet All of the library directors positioned serving as a place for leisure time entertainment as the most important library function, followed by serving as a place for study, circulation and a cultural centre.

SERVICES OFFERED BY PUBLIC LIBRARIES: OR HAS THE EXTERNAL CHANGE BEEN ACCOMPANIED BY A CHANGE OF CONTENT

The second research question examined whether the external change was accompanied by a change of content. Did the large buildings allow changes in or additions to the services provided by the library? If so, is it possible to identify a change that transformed the library from an institution focuses on providing traditional library services into a significant cultural centre for society and the community, as emerges from the opinions of the interviewees? As noted in the literature review, public libraries have shown, throughout their history, the ability to adjust and adapt to the needs of the environment. Although they began as a municipal service to intellectuals by providing reference materials, they quickly opened their doors to the general public, lending books and offering guidance, to make knowledge accessible to all. Over the years, collections have become more varied and services have been added or changed. Knowledge is now available both on paper and on digital media, and the library attempts to provide a response in both the cultural and social realms.

This service actually began in the late 19th century, when the public library entered the field of leisure by offering popular reading books and folklore evenings. The leisure field expanded and libraries also began to offer lectures, clubs, exhibitions and meeting places for different groups. It is interesting to note that the 1972 UNESCO Manifesto states, "The public library is a natural cultural centre for the community, bringing together as it does people ... Space and equipment are therefore necessary for exhibitions, discussions, lectures, musical performances and films ..." yet the next UNESCO Manifesto, published in 1994, does not mention the library's cultural and social function. The current study clearly shows that the emphasis in library functions and services to the public is shifting to the cultural and social realms. All of the library directors believe the public library should serve as a place for leisure entertainment and almost all (95.8%) believe the library building should serve as a municipal cultural centre.

On this issue, all of the architects and a majority of the other interviewees repeated that the library had to serve as "a meeting place with a cultural experience." Most of the people interviewed thought that the public library should be "a cultural shopping mall" that serves as a source of knowledge offered to the general public. Sociologists and architects emphasized the guidance and instructional services for finding the necessary materials, while it was actually the futurists who placed heavier emphasis on cultural preservation. From library directors' responses, it emerges that the most widely accepted services provided by libraries are traditional services, such as providing reading and reference materials. We also found that in almost all cases the desirable functions exceeded the actual services available. In three cases there were significant differences between the desirable than the actual: the library as a cultural centre, the library as a place for leisure activities and the library as a place that allows public clubs. These differences reflect the changes in library services in the society of the future.

All of the library directors believe that the most important function of the library is to be a place of leisure-time activity, and approximately 96% believe the library should serve as a cultural centre. Indeed, most of the libraries do provide this service. Approximately one-half of the library directors report that the library as a "cultural centre" is a new service that was not provided previously in their old library and that the move to a new building has made this possible. This finding confirms the second research assumption that where monumental library buildings are built, the library becomes a social and cultural centre.

Additional services that have been added after the move to a new building include supplying local and international newspapers, Internet communications centre, collections of local and international newspapers and viewing and borrowing movies for pleasure.

9

The Karnataka Public Libraries Act, 1965

STATEMENTS OF OBJECTS AND REASONS

ACT 10 OF 1965

The Madras Public Libraries Act, 1948, is in force in the Madras Areas and in Bellary District. The Hyderabad Public Libraries Act, is in force in the Hyderabad Area. There are no corresponding enactments in the other areas in the State. Government in their order No. ED 52 TEL 61, dated the 11 the September 1961 constituted a committee for drafting a Bill on public libraries with Dr. S.R. Ranganathan as Chairman. The Committee submitted its Report on 16th February 1963. The present Bill is based on the draft bill prepared by the Committee. This Bill is intended to bring about uniformity in the law relating to public libraries and enable the establishment and maintenance of a system of public libraries, and for the comprehensive development and organisation of city, rural, and other classes of library service in the State. The Bill provides, among the other things, for the following, namely.-

1. Constitution of the Mysore State Library Authority;
2. Establishment of a Department of Public Libraries;
3. Constitution of local library authorities in the Cities and in the Districts;
4. Levy of Library cess;
5. Creation of a State Central Library by vesting the Bangalore Public Library in the State Central Library Authority. Hence this Bill.

(Published in the Karnataka Gazette (Extraordinary) Part IV - 2A No. 135 dated 9-6-1964 at page 33.)

AMENDING ACT 45 OF 1976

At present the Minister incharge of Education will be the Ex-Officio President of the State Library Authority, it may so happen that the Minister for Education may not be incharge of Public Libraries. It is therefore considered necessary to make the Minister incharge of Public Libraries the Ex-Officio President of the State Library Authority.

The Library cess is collected by the local authorities. It is proposed to give ten per cent of the cess collected to the local authorities concerned towards costs of collection.

Opportunity has been taken to incorporate the new designation of the District Educational Officer and to omit the reference to Bangalore District (Rural) and Bangalore District (Urban) which are no longer in existance.

(Obtained from L.A. Bill No. 6 of 1976)

AMENDING ACT 30 OF 1984

In the State of Karnataka the Head of the Department of Libraries is designated as "State Librarian". It is considered necessary to redesignate the said post, as Director of Public Libraries. In the neighbouring States of Andhra Pradesh, Tamil Nadu and Maharashtra, also the Head of the Department of Libraries is called as Director of Public Libraries. The Karnataka Public Libraries Act, 1965 (Karnataka Act No. 10 of 1965), is proposed to be amended for the above mentioned purpose.

(Obtained from L.A. Bill No. 2 of 1984. File No. LAW 28 LGN 1983.)

AMENDING ACT 31 OF 1998

The State Government grants annualy to every District Library Authority an amount equal to 3% of the Land Revenue Collection of the district. To improve infrastructure of the libraries in the district, Government has decided to grant annualy 6% instead of 3%. Therefore, it is considered necessary to amend the Karnataka Public Libraries Act.

As the matter was urgent and the Karnataka Legislative Council was not in session the Karnataka Public Libraries (Amendment) Ordinance, 1998 (Karnataka Ordinance 7 of 1998) was promulgated.

Hence this Bill.

(Obtained from L.C. Bill No. 6 of 1998.)

THE [KARNATAKA] PUBLIC LIBRARIES ACT, 1965

(Received the assent of the President on the Twenty-second day of April, 1965).

(As Amended by Acts 45 of 1976, 30 of 1984 and 31 of 1998)

An Act to provide for the establishment and maintenance of public libraries and the organisation of a comprehensive rural and urban library service in the [State of Karnataka] WHEREAS it is expedient to provide for the establishment and maintenance of public libraries and the organisation of a comprehensive rural and urban library service in the [State of Karnataka] and for matters connected therewith;

BE it enacted by the [Karnataka State] Legislature in the Sixteenth Year of the Republic of India as follows:-

1. Adapted by the Karnataka Adaptations of Laws Order 1973 w.e.f. 1.11.1973

CHAPTER I . PRELIMINARY

- Short title, extent and commencement.
  - This Act may be called the [Karnataka] Public Libraries Act, 1965.
- Adapted by the karnataka Adaptations of Laws Order 1973 w.e.f. 1.11.1973
  - It extends to the whole of the [State of Karnataka]
- Adapted by the karnataka Adaptations of Laws Order 1973 w.e.f. 1.11.1973
  - It shall come into force on such [date] as the State Government may, by notification, appoint.
- Act came into force w.e.f. 1.4.1966 vide Notification No. ED 23 SLS 66 dt. 28.3.1966
- Definitions: In this Act, unless the context otherwise requires,-

1. 'Academic library' means a library maintained by a university, college, school or research institution;
2. 'Aided library' means a library declared by the [Director of Public Libraries] to be eligible for aid from the Government in accordance with the rules made under this Act;
   - Substituted by Act 30 of 1984 w.e.f. 22.5.1984
3. 'Book' includes,-
   (i) Every volume,part or division of a volume, and pamphlet, in any language;
   (ii) Every sheet of music, map, chart or plan separately printed or lithographed:
   (iii) Newspapers, periodicals and other such materials;
4. 'Chief Librarian' means the Librarian appointed to be in charge of a City Central Library or a District Central Library and other Libraries and the library service under the control of a City Library Authority or a District Library Authority, as the case may be;
5. 'City Library Authority' means a Library Authority constituted for a city or other urban area under sections 16 and 17;
6. 'State-owned Library' means a library maintained by a Department

of the State Government, the State Legislature, the High Court or any other court or any authority of the State;

7. 'District' means a revenue district;
8. 'District Library Authority' means a Library Authority constituted for a district under sections 16 and 18;
9. 'Library cess' means a cess levied under section 30;
10. 'Local Library Authority' means a City Library Authority or a District Library Authority;
11. 'Notification' means a notification published in the official Gazette;
12. 'Outlier library' means any library other than a public library;

13 'Prescribed' means prescribed by rules made under this Act;

14 'Public library' means:

   (a) A library established or maintained by a Local Library Authority, including the branches and delivery stations of such library;
   (b) A library established or maintained by the State Government and declared open to the public;
   (c) A library established or maintained by any local authority and declared open to the public;
   (d) A library declared to be eligible for aid and receiving aid from the State Government; and includes, any other library notified by the State Government as a public library for the purposes of this Act;

15. 'State Central Library' means the library declared to be the State Central Library under Chapter VI;
16. [Director of Public Libraries] means the [Director of Public Libraries] appointed under this Act;
    – Substituted by Act 30 of 1984 w.e.f. 22.5.1984
17. 'State Library Authority' means the Authority constituted under section 3;
18. 'Year' means the financial year.

CHAPTER II . THE [KARNATAKA STATE LIBRARY AUTHORITY]

1. Adapted by the Karnataka Adaptations of Laws Order 1973 w.e.f. 1.11.1973

3. Constitution and composition of the State Library Authority.- (1) As soon as may be after the commencement of this Act, the State Government shall, by notification, constitute for the purposes of this Act, an authority to be called the State Library Authority. Such authority shall be a body corporate having perpetual succession and a common seal with power, subject to the provisions of this Act, to

acquire, hold and dispose of property, and to contract, and may by the same name sue and be sued.

(2) The State Library Authority shall consist of,-

(a) [The Minister in charge of Public Libraries] who shall ex-officio be the President of the Authority;

1. Substituted by the Act 45 of 1976 w.e.f. 5.6.1976

(b) Four persons elected by the [Karnataka Legislative Assembly] from among its members;

(c) Two persons elected by the [Karnataka Legislative Council] from among its members;

(d) One person elected by the Syndicate of each of the Universities in the State from among the members of the Syndicate;

1. Adaptation of the Karnataka Laws Order 1973 w.e.f. 1.11.1973

Explanation.- For purposes of this clause, in respect of the University of Agricultural Sciences, "Syndicate" means the Board of Regents.

(e) One person elected by the Executive Committee of the [Karnataka Library Association] from among the members of the Association;

1. Adaptation of the Karnataka Laws Order 1973 w.e.f. 1.11.1973

(f) One person elected by the City Library Authority of the City of Bangalore from among its members;

(g) One person elected by the City Library Authority of one of the cities in the State other than the City of Bangalore for which a City Library Authority is established, from among the members of such Authority, subject to the condition that such election shall be made by each City Library Authority for one term in such order or rotation as the State Government may by order determine;

(h) One person elected by the District Library Authority of one of the Districts in each Revenue Division of the State from among the members of such Authority, subject to the condition that such election shall be made by each District Library Authority in every Revenue Division for one term in such order of rotation as the State Government may by order determine;

(i) The Secretary to the Government, Education Department;

(j) The [Director of Public Instruction in Karnataka] ;

(k) Three persons nominated by the State Government who in the opinion of the State Government are experts in library science:

1. Adaptation of the Karnataka Laws Order 1973 w.e.f. 1.11.1973

Provided that at the first constitution of the Authority for purposes of clauses (f), (g) and (h), six persons ordinarily resident in the cities and districts of the Revenue Divisions for which the Library Authorities may be established, shall be nominated by the State Government.

(3) The [Director of Public Libraries] shall ex-officio be the Secretary of the State Library Authority.

1. Substituted by Act 30 of 1984 w.e.f. 22.5.1984

4. Functions of the State Library Authority.- The State Library Authority shall advise the State Government on all matters connected with the administration of this Act, shall be the managing authority for the State Central Library, and shall exercise and perform such powers and duties conferred and entrusted to the said Authority by this Act, and such other powers and duties as may be prescribed.

5. Nomination of members in default of election.- If any of the bodies referred to in sub-section (2) of section 3 does not, by such period as may be prescribed, elect a person to be a member of the State Library Authority, the State Government shall, by notification, nominate to the vacancy a person qualified for election thereto; and the person so nominated shall be deemed to be a member of the Authority as if he had been duly elected by the said body.

6. Term of office:

   (1) Save as otherwise provided in this Act, the term of office of members of the State Library Authority, other than ex-officio members, shall be for a period of three years commencing from the date on which the first meeting of the Authority is held after the election or nomination of the members under section 3.

   (2) An outgoing member shall continue in office until the election or nomination of his successor.

   (3) An outgoing member shall be eligible for re-election or re-nomination.

7. Vacancies.- In the event of a vacancy arising out of death, resignation, disability or otherwise, previous to the expiry of the term of office of any member of the State Library Authority, the vacancy shall be filled by election or nomination, as the case may be, of another person in the manner provided in sub-section (2) of section 3, and any person elected or nominated to fill the vacancy shall hold office only so long as the member in whose place he is elected or nominated would have held office if the vacancy had not occurred.

8. Disabilities for continuing as member.- If any member other than an ex-officio member of the State Library Authority, during the period for which he has been nominated or elected,-

   (a) absents himself without excuse sufficient in the opinion of the

Authority, from three consecutive meetings of the Authority; or

(b) in the case of a member elected by any body referred to in sub-section (2) of section 3, ceases to be a member of the body concerned, his office in the Authority shall become vacant.

9. Disqualifications.- A person shall be disqualified for being chosen as, and for being, a member of the State Library Authority,-

(a) If he has been sentenced by a criminal court for an offence involving moral turpitude and punishable with imprisonment for a term exceeding three months, such sentence not having been subsequently reversed, quashed or remitted, unless he has, by order, which the State Government is hereby empowered to make in this behalf, been relieved from the disqualification arising on account of such sentence;

(b) If he is an undischarged insolvent;

(c) If he is of unsound mind and stands so declared by a competent court.

10. Meetings of the State Library Authority:

(1) The State Library Authority shall meet at least twice a year on dates to be fixed by the President. One of such meetings shall be the annual meetings.

(2) The President may also, whenever he thinks fit, convene a special meetings of the Authority for the transaction of urgent business.

(3) Subject to prescribed conditions special meetings shall be convened by the President to discuss matters of urgent importance upon a requisition by the members of the Authority.

(4) Two-fifths of the total number of members of the Authority, shall be the quorum for a meeting of the State Library Authority.

(5) The President, if present, shall preside at every meeting of the Authority. In the absence of the President, the members present at the meeting shall choose one from among themselves to preside.

11. Procedure of State Library Authority.- The State Library Authority shall transact business in such manner and in accordance with such procedure as may be prescribed.

CHAPTER III . DEPARTMENT OF PUBLIC LIBRARIES

12. Department of Public Libraries.- For the purposes of this Act, a Department of Public Libraries shall be constituted with a [Director of Public Libraries] as its head and such other officers and servants as the Government may by order specify.

1. Substituted by Act 30 of 1984 w.e.f. 22.5.1984

13. Functions of the Department:

(1) Subject to the control of the State Government, the Department of Pubic Libraries shall be responsible for the administration of this Act.

(2) In particular and without prejudice to the generality of the foregoing power, the Department shall,-

(a) Superintend and direct all matters relating to all public libraries;

(b) Promote the establishment of public library service so as to achieve the purposes of this Act;

(c) Supervise and direct all matters relating to libraries receiving aid from the State Government;

(d) Maintain State Registers of Libraries and of Librarians;

(e) Superintend, direct, and deal with the exercise of powers and the performance of duties by Local Library Authorities under this Act;

(f) Ensure the proper utilisation of the Library Funds and library man-power of the State;

(g) Perform such other functions as may be entrusted to the Department by or under the provisions of this Act.

14. [Director of Public Libraries]:

(1) A whole-time officer having the prescribed qualifications to practise the library profession shall be appointed by the State Government as the [Director of Public Libraries] .

1. Substituted by Act 30 of 1984 w.e.f. 22.5.1984

(2) The [Director of Public Libraries] shall,-

(a) Function as the Librarian of the State Central Library;

(b) Superintendent, direct, and deal with all matters relating to the Press and Registration of Books Act, 1867 (Central Act 25 of 1867) and to the maintenance and service of the books sent under the said Act;

(c) Control the appointments, postings, and transfers of officers and servants in the State Library Service;

(d) Generally assist the State Library Authority in performing its functions;

(e) Exercise such other powers and performs such other duties as may be conferred or imposed on him by or under this Act.

1. Substituted by Act 30 of 1984 w.e.f. 22.5.1984

15. State Library Service:

(1) Notwithstanding anything contained in any other law, all posts

in the Department of Pubic Libraries, the State Central Library and every Local Library Authority shall be filled by appointment of persons belonging to the [Karnataka State Library Service] .

1. Adapted by the karnataka Adaptations of Laws Order 1973 w.e.f. 1.11.1973

(2) The [Karnataka State Library Service] shall consist of the [Director of Public Libraries] , Chief Librarians of Cities and Districts, Librarians and such other classes and categories of posts as the State Government may from time to time determine. All members of the said service shall be Government servants, and their recruitment and conditions of service shall, subject to the provisions of Article 309 of the Constitution, be regulated by such rules as may be prescribed.

1. Adapted by the karnataka Adaptations of Laws Order 1973 w.e.f. 1.11.1973

2. Substituted by Act 30 of 1984 w.e.f. 22.5.1984

(3) The salary, allowances, gratuity, pension and other benefits of the members of the [Karnataka State Library Service] shall be met from the Consolidated Fund of the State.

1. Adapted by the Karnataka Adaptations of Laws Order 1973 w.e.f. 1.11.1973

CHAPTER IV. LOCAL LIBRARY AUTHORITIES

16. Constitution of Local Library Authorities:

(1) For the purpose of organising and administering Public Libraries in the State, there shall be constituted Local Library Authorities,-

(a) For the Cities of Bangalore, Hubli-Dharwar, Mangalore, Mysore and Belgaum, and for such other urban area having a population of more than one lakh, as the State Government may by notification specify, called the City Library Authority; and

(b) For each revenue district, excluding the area for which a City Library Authority is constituted, called the District Library Authority;

[Proviso x x x]

1. Omitted by Act 45 of 1976 w.e.f. 5.6.1976

(2) Every Local Library Authority shall by the name of the area for which it is constituted, be a body corporate having perpetual succession and a common seal with power, subject to the provisions of this Act, to acquire, hold and dispose of property, and to contract, and may by the same name sue and be sued.

17. Composition of City Library Authorities:

(1) Every City Library Authority shall consist of,-

(a) The Mayor of the municipal corporation or the President of the municipal council or other municipal body of the City who shall ex-officio be the Chairman of the Authority;

(b) A principal of a First Grade College in the city nominated ex-officio by the State Government, who shall be the Vice-Chairman of the Authority;

(c) Two persons elected by the municipal corporation, municipal council or other municipal body of the city from among its members;

(d) One person nominated by the State Government from among the members of governing bodies of aided libraries in the city;

(e) A Headmaster of a High School in the city nominated ex-officio by the State Government;

(f) One person nominated by the council of the city branch, if any, of the [Karnataka Library Association] ;

1. Adapted by the Karnataka Adaptations of Laws Order 1973 w.e.f. 1.11.1973

(g) An officer of the Department of Public Instruction having jurisdiction over the city, nominated ex-officio by the State Government.

(h) Two persons nominated by the State Government from among persons ordinarily resident in the city.

(2) The Chief Librarian of the city shall ex-officio be the Secretary of the City Library Authority and of the Committees of the said Authority.

18. Composition of District Library Authorities:

(1) Every District Library Authority shall consist of,-

(a) The Deputy Commissioner of the district who shall ex-officio be the Chairman of the Authority;

[(b) the Deputy Director of Public Instructions incharge of the district;]

1. Substituted by Act 45 of 1976 w.e.f. 5.6.1976

(c) Two persons elected from among its members by the District Development Council;

(d) One person elected from among its members by each municipal council or other municipal body in the district with jurisdiction over a municipal area other than an area for which a City Library Authority is established having a population of not less than fifty thousand;

(e) Two persons nominated by the State Government from among the members of municipal councils or other municipal bodies in the district with jurisdiction over a municipal area having a population of less than fifty thousand;

(f) One person nominated by the council of the District Branch, if any, of the [Karnataka Library Association] ;

1. Adapted by the Karnataka Adaptations of Laws Order 1973 w.e.f. 1.11.1973

(g) One person nominated by the State Government from among the members of the Taluk Development Boards in the district;

(h) Two persons nominated by the State Government from among the members of the village panchayats and town panchayats in the district;

(i) Two persons nominated by the State Government from among the members of the governing bodies of aided libraries in the district;

(j) A Principal of a First Grade College in the district nominated ex-officio by the State Government ;

(k) A Headmaster of a High School in the district nominated ex-officio by the State Government ;

(l) An officer of the Department of Public Instruction having jurisdiction over the district or a part thereof nominated ex-officio by the State Government;

(m) Three persons nominated by the State Government from among persons ordinarily resident in the district;

(2) The Vice-Chairman of the District Library Authority shall be elected by the members from among themselves.

(3) The Chief Librarian of the district shall ex-officio be the Secretary of the District Library Authority and of the Committees of the said Authority;

19. Nomination of members in default of election.- If any of the bodies referred to in section 17 or 18 does not by such period as may be prescribed elect or nominate a person to be a member of the City Library Authority or the District Library Authority, as the case may be, the State Government shall, by notification, nominate to the vacancy, a person qualified for election thereto; and the person so nominated shall be deemed to be a member of the Authority as if he had been duly elected by the said body.

20. Term of office:

(1) Save as otherwise provided in this Act, the term of office of members of a Local Library Authority, other than ex-officio members, shall be for a period of three years commencing from the date on which the first meeting of the Authority is held after the election or nomination of the members under sections 17, 18 and 19.

(2) An outgoing member shall continue in office until the election or nomination of his successor.

(3) An outgoing member shall be eligible for re-election or re-nomination.

21. Vacancies.- In the event of a vacancy arising out of death, resignation, disability or otherwise, before the expiry of the term of office of any member of a Local Library Authority, the vacancy shall be filled by election or nomination, as the case may be, of another person in the manner provided in section 17 or section 18, as the case may be, and any person elected or nominated to fill the vacancy shall hold office only so long as the member in whose place he is elected or nominated would have held office if the vacancy had not occurred.

22. Disabilities for continuing as member.- If any member other than an ex-officio member of a Local Library Authority, during the period for which he has been nominated or elected,-

(a) Absents himself without excuse sufficient in the opinion of the Authority, from three consecutive meetings of the Authority; or

(b) In the case of a member elected by any body referred to in section 17 or section 18 ceases to be member of the body concerned, his office in the Authority shall become vacant.

23. Disqualifications.- A person shall be disqualified for being chosen as, and for being, a member of the Local Library Authority,-

(a) If he has been sentenced by a criminal court for an offence involving moral turpitude and punishable with imprisonment for a term exceeding three months, such sentence not having been subsequently reversed, quashed or remitted, unless he has, by order, which the State Government is hereby empowered to make in this behalf, been relieved from the disqualification arising on account of such sentence;

(b) If he is an undischarged insolvent;

(c) If he is of unsound mind and stands so declared by a competent court.

24. Meetings of Local Library Authorities:

(1) Every Local Library Authority shall meet at least twice a year on dates to be fixed by the Chairman. One of such meetings shall be the annual meeting.

(2) The Chairman may also, whenever he thinks fit, convene a special meeting of the Authority for the transaction of urgent business.

(3) Subject to prescribed conditions, special meetings shall be convened by the Chairman to discuss matters of urgent importance upon a requisition by the members of the Authority.

(4) A Local Library Authority shall transact business in such manner and in accordance with such procedure as may be prescribed.

25. Powers and duties of Chairman and Vice-Chairman:

(1) The Chairman of a Local Library Authority shall,-

(a) Preside at the meetings of the Authority;

(b) Watch over the financial and executive administration of the Authority and exercise general supervision and control.

(2) The Vice-Chairman of a Local Library Authority shall,-

(a) In the absence of the Chairman, preside at the meetings of the Authority;

(b) Exercise such powers and perform such duties of the Chairman as the Chairman may, from time to time, delegate to him.

26. Powers and functions of Local Library Authorities (1) It shall be the duty of every City Library Authority and every District Library Authority to provide library service to the persons residing in the area within its jurisdiction. The Library Authority shall in every City establish a City Central Library and Branch Libraries and in every district establish a District Central Library and branch libraries.

(2) For purposes of sub-section (1), a Local Library Authority may,-

(a) Provide suitable lands and buildings for public libraries, and the furniture, fittings, equipment and other conveniences necessary for the purpose;

(b) Provide such libraries with books, periodicals, newspapers, maps, gramophone records, manuscripts, works and specimens of art and science, lantern slides, films, cinema projectors, recorders and the like;

(c) With the previous sanction of the Government shift or close any public library;

(d) Accept any endowment or gift for any purpose connected with its activities; Provided that no gift or endowment of an immovable property shall be accepted without the previous sanction of the State Government;

(e) Provide for lectures and conduct other activities as may be conducive to the carrying out of the purposes of this Act;

(f) With the consent of the management and the previous sanction of the State Government acquire any library on such conditions as may be approved by the State Government ;

(g) With the sanction of the State Government do any other thing that may be conducive to the furtherance of the purposes of this Act;

(h) Exercise such other powers and perform such other duties as may be conferred or imposed by or under this Act.

27. Library Development Plan:

(1) Subject to the general or special orders of the State Government , as soon as possible after a Local Library Authority is constituted and thereafter as often as may be required by the [Director of Public Libraries] every Local Library Authority shall, and whenever it considers it necessary so to do, a Local Library Authority may, prepare a plan (hereinafter referred to as the 'Local Library Development Plan') for establishing libraries and spreading library service within the jurisdiction of such Authority in such form and manner and containing such particulars as may be prescribed.

1. Subsituted by Act 30 of 1984 w.e.f. 22.5.1984

(2) The salient features of every Local Library Development Plan prepared under sub-section (1) shall be published in such manner as may be prescribed along with a notice inviting objections and suggestions from all persons interested in the Plan within such period as may be specified in the notice. Any objection or suggestion which may be received from any person with respect to the Local Library Development Plan shall be considered by the Local Library Authority and such modifications in the Plan shall be made as the Authority deems fit.

(3) The Local Library Development Plan shall thereafter be sent to the [Director of Public Libraries] along with a copy of the objections and suggestions received under sub-section (2). The 1[Director of Public Libraries] shall with his comments on the Local Library Development Plan submit it to the State Government for sanction.

1. Subsituted by Act 30 of 1984 w.e.f. 22.5.1984

(4) The State Government may if it deems fit after ascertaining the views of the State Library Authority sanction the Local Library Development Plan with such alterations as it considers necessary. The State Government may on application by the Local Library Authority concerned, modify any Local Library Development Plan sanctioned under this sub-section.

(5) (a) As soon as may be after the State Government sanctions a Local Library Development Plan under sub-section (4), the [Director of Public Libraries] shall in conformity with the provisions of the said Plan make an order called the Local Library Order for the area, specifying the Central Library and the Branch Libraries including branches, to be located in educational institutions, prisons and hospitals and the service stations, which shall be established and maintained by the Local Library Authority, the measures to be taken by the Local Library Authority for providing adequate library service to the people in the area and the stages in which such measures shall be taken.

1. Subsituted by Act 30 of 1984 w.e.f. 22.5.1984

(b) A Local Library Order made under clause (a) may be amended in consultation with the Local Library Authority, whenever the [Director of Public Libraries] considers it expedient to do so.

1. Subsituted by Act 30 of 1984 w.e.f. 22.5.1984

(6) Every Local Library Authority shall give effect to the Local Library Development Plan as sanctioned by the State Government and the Local Library Order made under sub-section (5).

28. Local Library Authority to appoint committees:

(1) Every Local Library Authority shall constitute the following committees by election from among its members, namely:-

(i) The Executive Committee; and

(ii) The Finance Committee.

(2) A Local Library Authority may constitute committees for such other purposes as it deems fit.

(3) The Chairman of the Local Library Authority shall ex-officio be a member and Chairman of the Executive Committee, and the Finance Committee.

(4) (a) The Executive Committee shall be responsible for the executive functions of the Local Library Authority.

(b) The Finance Committee shall scrutinise proposals for increase of revenue, examine the receipts and expenditure statements, consider all new propositions affecting finance and shall generally supervise the revenue and expenditure of the Local Library Authority.

29. Advisory Library Committees:

(1) For the purpose of advising on local requirements relating to library service of each branch library and each service station in a village served by travelling library service, Advisory Committees shall be constituted in accordance with the provisions of this section.

(2) Every Branch Library Committee shall consist of,-

(a) The Branch Librarian who shall ex-officio be the Chairman and convener of the Committee;

(b) One person representing the area which the Branch Library serves, on the municipal council or other municipal body or the panchayat having jurisdiction over that area, elected by the body concerned;

(c) Three teachers of educational institutions in the area in which the branch library is located, nominated by the Chief Librarian of the City or the Chief Librarian of the district, as the case may be;

(d) Three persons from among the registered borrowers of the branch library nominated by the Chief Librarian of the City or the Chief Librarian of the district, as the case may be.

(3) Every Village Service Library Committee shall consist of,-

(a) The Travelling Librarian visiting the service station in the village who shall ex-officio be the Chairman and convener of the Committee;

(b) Two teachers of educational institutions in the area served by the service station, nominated by the Chief Librarian of the District;

(c) Two persons from among the registered borrowers in the area served by the service station, nominated by the Chief Librarian of the district.

(4) The nominated members of the Branch Library Committee and the Village Service Library Committee shall hold office for a period of three years or until their successors are nominated.

CHAPTER V . FINANCE AND ACCOUNTS

30. Library Cess:

(1) With effect from the date of commencement of this Act,-

(a) A library cess in the form of a surcharge on,-

(i) tax on lands and buildings;

(ii) tax on entry of goods into the local area for consumption, use or sale therein;

(iii) tax on vehicles;

(iv) tax on professions, trades, calling and employments; shall be levied in the area within the jurisdiction of every City Library Authority under the relevant laws relating to local authorities providing for the levy of such taxes, at the rate of three paise for every rupee of the taxes so levied;

(b) A library cess in the form of a surcharge on tax on lands and buildings shall be levied in the area within the jurisdiction of every District Library Authority, under the relevant laws relating to local authorities providing for the levy of such tax at the rate of three paise for every rupee of the tax so levied.

(2) A City Library Authority or District Library Authority may, with the previous sanction of the State Government , by notification, increase the rate of library cess levied on any item of tax specified in clause (a) or (b) of sub-section (1), subject to the condition that the rate shall not exceed six paise for every rupee of the tax levied.

(3) The cess levied under clause (a) or clause (b) of sub-section (1) or increased under sub-section (2) shall be collected by the municipal corporation, municipal council or other municipal body, or the village panchayat or other local authority having jurisdiction over the area as if the cess were a tax referred

to in the said clause payable under the relevant laws for the time being in force in the area, and all the provisions of the said laws relating to the levy and collection of the said tax shall apply subject to such modifications as may be prescribed.

(4) Out of the cess collected by it under sub-section (3) every local authority shall be entitled to retain ten per cent of the amount collected towards the cost of collection and the balance shall be paid to the City Library Authority or the District Library Authority, as the case may be.]

1. Substitued by Act 45 of 1976 w.e.f. 1.4.1969

31. Government grant to District Library Authority of a portion of land revenue:

(1) The State Government shall make annually a grant to every District Library Authority of an amount equal to [six per cent] of the land revenue collection of the district.

1.Substituted by Act 31 of 1998 w.e.f. 24.11.1998

(2) The amount granted to a District Library Authority under sub-section (1) shall be credited to the District Library Fund at such times and in such manner as may be prescribed.

(3) Land Revenue collection of a district for the purposes of sub-section (1) shall mean,-

(a) Until the revision settlement of land revenue under Chapter X of the [Karnataka] Land Revenue Act, 1964, the land revenue determined on the basis of the average land revenue collection of the district for a period of three years preceding the date of such determination;

1. Adapted by the Karnataka Adaptations of Laws Order 1973 w.e.f. 1.11.1973

(b) After the determination of land revenue on the basis of the aforesaid revision settlement, the land revenue collected during the year preceding the year for which the grant is made.

32. City and District Library Fund:

(1) Every City Library Authority and District Library Authority shall maintain a Fund called the City Library Fund and the District Library Fund, as the case may be, from which all its payments under this Act shall be met.

(2) There shall be credited to the City Library Fund and the District Library Fund, as the case may be, the following sums, namely :- [(a) the amount of cess paid by the local authority under sub-section (4) of section 30;]

1. Substituted by Act 45 of 1976 w.e.f. 1.4.1969

(b) The grant under section 31;

(c) Contributions, gifts, and income from endowments, made to the Library Authority for the benefits of public libraries;

(d) Grant which the Central Government or the State Government may make;

(e) Funds and other amounts collected by the Local Library Authority under rules or bye-laws made under this Act.

33. State Library Fund:

(1) The State Library Authority shall maintain a Fund called the State Library Fund from which all its payments under this Act shall be met.

(2) There shall be credited to the State Library Fund the following sums, namely :-

(a) The grants made by the State Government to the State Library Authority to perform the duties entrusted to it;

(b) Grants which the Central Government may make;

(c) Contributions and gifts made to the State Library Authority;

(d) Funds and other amounts collected by the State Library Authority under the rules or bye-laws made under this Act.

34. Accounts:

(1) An account shall be kept of the receipts and expenses of the State Library Authority and of each City Library Authority and District Library Authority.

(2) The accounts shall be open to inspection, and shall be subject to audit, disallowance and surcharge and shall be dealt with in all other respects in such manner as may be prescribed.

CHAPTER VI . STATE CENTRAL LIBRARY

35. Vesting of Bangalore Public Library in the State Library Authority:

(1) With effect from such date as the State Government may, by notification appoint (hereinafter referred to in this Chapter as the appointed day), the entire management and control of the Public Library, Bangalore, now vested in the Committee of Management of the Public Library, Bangalore, shall be vested in the State Library Authority.

(2) As from the appointed day, the Committee of Management of the Public Library, Bangalore, a society registered under the Mysore Societies Registration Act, 1904, now deemed to be registered under the [Karnataka] Societies Registration Act, 1960, shall stand dissolved and all property, movable and immovable, and all rights, powers and privileges of the said society which immediately before the appointed day belonged to or vested in the said society shall vest in the State Library Authority and shall be applied for the purposes specified in this Act and such other purposes as may be prescribed.

1. Adapted by the Karnataka Adaptations of Laws Order 1973 w.e.f. 1.11.1973

(3) As from the appointed day, all debts and liabilities of the said society shall stand transferred to and vest in the State Library Authority.

(4) Every employee of the said society shall, as from the appointed day, become an employee of the State Government and shall hold his office under the State Government as a member of the [Karnataka State Library Service] on the same tenure, at the same remuneration, and upon the same terms and conditions, and with the same rights and privileges as to provident fund, gratuity and other matters, as he would have held the same, as an employee of the said society, and shall continue to do so unless and until his remuneration, terms and conditions are duly altered by the State Government.

1. Adapted by the Karnataka Adaptations of Laws Order 1973 w.e.f. 1.11.1973

36. [Karnataka State Central Library] :

(1) As from the appointed day, the Public Library, Bangalore, shall be the [Karnataka State Central Library] .

1. Adapted by the Karnataka Adaptations of Laws Order 1973 w.e.f. 1.11.1973

(2) (a) The [Karnataka State Central Library] shall be maintained as a reservoir of books and other materials for the proper functioning of the State Library system.

1. Adapted by the Karnataka Adaptations of Laws Order 1973 w.e.f. 1.11.1973

(b) In addition to a general library, the State Central Library shall consist of the following sections namely.-

(i) A State Bureau of Copyright Collections;

(ii) A State Library for the Blind;

(iii) A State Bureau of inter-library loans;

(iv) A State Bibliographical Bureau;

(v) A State Bureau of Technical Service;

(vi) such other sections as may be prescribed.

37. Sections of State Central Library:

(1) (a) One copy of each book received under the Press and Registration of Books Act, 1867 (Central Act 25 of 1867) shall be kept in the State Central Library as a Bureau of Copyright.

(b) Copies of books in the Bureau of Copyright shall not be issued by way of loan of any kind but may be made available for reference in the library premises.

(2) (a) The production and storage of books, sound records of books and kindred materials for the blind and the issue of such books and materials for

the use of the blind shall be dealt with in the section relating to the State Library for the Blind.

(b) The State Central Library may collaborate with other Libraries for the Blind in India and undertake such work as may be necessary for purposes of such collaboration.

(3) (a) The State Bureau of inter-library loan shall implement such schemes of inter-library loans among the public libraries, academic libraries, State-owned libraries, aided libraries and the outlier libraries in the State as may be prescribed.

(b) The State Central Library may with the approval of the State Government, collaborate in any scheme of inter-State library loans.

(4) (a) The State Bibliographical Bureau shall undertake such bibliographical work as may be prescribed and may for this purpose collaborate with Departments of Government and educational and other bodies in the State.

(b) The State Central Library may, with the approval of the State Government, collaborate with Bibliographical Bureaux or agencies in India and undertake such bibliographical work as may be necessary for purposes of such collaboration.

(5) (a) The State Bureau of Technical Service shall be maintained for centralised technical services, such as, acquisition, classification and cataloguing of books for public libraries, academic libraries, State owned libraries, aided libraries and outlier libraries, in accordance with such schemes as may be prescribed.

(b) The State Central Library may, with the approval of the State Government, collaborate with other similar Bureaux of Technical Service in India and undertake such technical work as may be necessary for purposes of such collaboration:

Provided that no scheme under sub-section (3) or sub-section (5) shall be implemented in respect of any library other than a library owned or controlled by the State, except with the concurrence of the authority which owns or controls such library.

CHAPTER VII . REPORTS, RETURNS AND INSPECTION

38. Reports and returns.- Every Local Library Authority and every person in charge of a public library shall submit such reports and returns and furnish such information to the [Director of Public Libraries] or any person authorised by him in this behalf as the said librarian or authorised person may, from time to time, require.

1. Substituted by Act 30 of 1984 w.e.f. 22.5.1984

39. Inspection of libraries.- The [Director of Public Libraries] or any person authorised by him in this behalf may inspect any public library or any institution

attached thereto for the purpose of satisfying himself that the provisions of this Act and the rules and bye-laws made thereunder are duly carried out.

1. Substituted by Act 30 of 1984 w.e.f. 22.5.1984

40. Annual Report.- (1) The [Director of Public Libraries] shall, in respect of each financial year, prepare an annual report of the progress made by the Local Library Authorities during the year along with such information and particulars as may be prescribed and submit such report to the State Government before such date as the State Government may by order specify.

1. Substituted by Act 30 of 1984 w.e.f. 22.5.1984

(2) The [Director of Public Libraries] shall, in respect of each financial year prepare an annual report of the activities of the State Library Authority during the year along with such information and particulars as may be prescribed and submit such report to the State Government before such date as the State Government may by order specify.

1. Substituted by Act 30 of 1984 w.e.f. 22.5.1984

CHAPTER VIII . MISCELLANEOUS

41. Power to make rules:

(1) The State Government may, after previous publication, by notification, make rules to carry out the purposes of this Act.

(2) In particular and without prejudice to the generality of the foregoing power, such rules may provide for,-

(a) The method of election or nomination of members to the State Library Authority, the Local Library Authorities, the Branch Library Committees and the Village Service Library Committees;

(b) The maintenance of a State Library Fund and the City and District Library Funds;

(c) The administration, inspection and management of the State Central Library;

(d) The maintenance of accounts by the State Library Authority and the Local Library Authorities and the publication of audited statement of accounts and the reports of auditors;

(e) the grants-in-aid to aided libraries and the standards to be maintained by such libraries;

(f) The maintenance of State Registers of Libraries, and of Librarians;

(g) The constitution of committees by the State Library Authority and the Local Library Authorities;

(h) The restrictions and conditions subject to which the State Library Authority or a Local Library Authority may enter into contracts, or acquire, hold or dispose of property.

(3) Every rule made under this Act shall, as soon as may be after it is made, be laid before each House of the State Legislature while it is in session for a total period of thirty days which may be comprised in one session or in two or more successive sessions and if before the expiry of the session in which it is so laid or the sessions immediately following, both Houses agree in making any modification in the rule or both Houses agree that the rule should not be made, the rule shall thereafter have effect only in such modified form or be of no effect, as the case may be, so however, that any such modification or annulment shall be without prejudice to the validity of anything previously done under that rule.

42. Power of State Library Authority and Local Library Authorities to make bye-laws:

(1) The State Library Authority and every Local Library Authority may, subject to the provisions of this Act and the rules made thereunder and with the previous sanction of the State Government, by notification, make bye-laws generally to carry out the purposes of this Act.

(2) In particular and without prejudice to the generality of the foregoing power, such bye-laws may provide for all or any of the following matters, namely:-

(a) The admission of the public to the public libraries under the control of the State Library Authority or the Local Library Authority subject to such conditions as may be specified in such bye-laws:

Provided that no fees shall be charged for such admission;

(b) The guarantee or security to be furnished by persons desiring to use such libraries, against injury to, or misuse, destruction or loss of the property of such libraries;

(c) The manner in which the property of such libraries may be used and the protection of such property from injury, misuse, destruction or loss;

(d) The authority to be exercised by the officers and servants of the State Library Authority or the Local Library Authority for the purpose of exclusion or removal from any such library of any person who contravenes or does not comply with any provisions of this Act or any rule or bye-law made thereunder;

(3) Every bye-law made under this section shall be subject to the condition of previous publication for a period of not less than thirty days, and such publication shall be in the official Gazette and in such other manner as may be prescribed.

(4) The State Government may by notification modify or cancel any bye-law made by State Library Authority or a Local Library Authority under this section:

Provided that before modifying or cancelling any bye-law, the State Government shall give the State Library Authority or the Local Library Authority concerned a reasonable opportunity to make its representations in the matter.

43. Offences and penalties.- Whoever,-

(a) In a public library or other institution maintained under this Act acts in any manner likely to cause annoyance or disturbance to any person using such library or institution, or behaves in a disorderly manner or uses violent or abusive language in any such library or institution; or

(b) After due warning persists in remaining therein beyond the hours fixed for closing, shall be liable to be removed from such library or institution and shall also be punishable with fine which may extend to rupees ten and for a second or subsequent offence with fine which may extend to rupees fifty.

44. Control of Local Library Authorities by Government:

(1) If, at any time, it appears to the State Government that a Local Library Authority has failed to perform its functions or has exceeded or abused any of the powers conferred upon it by or under this Act, the State Government may communicate the particulars thereof to the Local Library Authority, and if the Local Library Authority omits to remedy such failure, excess or abuse or to give an explanation which in the opinion of the State Government is satisfactory within such time as the State Government may fix in this behalf, the State Government may supersede the Local Library Authority for such period as the State Government may direct.

(2) If a Local Library Authority is superseded,-

(a) All the powers and duties of the Authority shall, during the period of supersession, be exercised and performed by such person or persons as the State Government may from time to time appoint in this behalf;

(b) All property vested in the Local Library Authority shall during the period of supersession, vest in the State Government; and

(c) On the expiry of the period of supersession, the Local Library Authority shall be reconstituted in the manner provided in this Act.

45. Liability of members for loss, waste or misapplication:

(1) Every member of a Local Library Authority shall be personally liable for the loss, waste or misapplication of any money or other property of the Authority to which he has been a party, or which has been caused or facilitated by his misconduct or neglect of his duty as a member.

(2) If after giving the member or members concerned a reasonable opportunity for showing cause to the contrary the [Director of Public Libraries] is satisfied that the loss, waste or misapplication of any money or other property

of the Local Library Authority is a direct consequence of misconduct or neglect on his or their part, the [Director of Public Libraries] shall by order in writing direct such member or members to pay to the Local Library Authority before a specified date, the amount required to reimburse it for such loss, waste or misapplication.

1. Substituted by Act 30 of 1984 w.e.f. 22.5.1984

(3) If the amount is not so paid, it shall be recoverable as an arrear of land revenue.

(4) An appeal shall lie from the decision of the [Director of Public Libraries] to the [Karnataka Revenue Appellate Tribunal] within such period as may be prescribed, and the decision of the [Karnataka Revenue Appellate Tribunal] on such appeal shall be final.

1. Adapted by the Karnataka Adaptations of laws Order 1973 w.e.f. 1.11.1973

46. Members and employees of Library Authorities to be public servants.- Every member of the State Library Authority or a Local Library Authority and every officer and servant employed under such authority shall be deemed to be a public servant within the meaning of section 21 of the Indian Penal Code.

47. Savings of validity of acts and proceedings.- No act done, or proceedings taken under this Act shall be questioned merely on the ground,-

(a) Of any vacancy or defect in the constitution of any Authority or any committee thereof; or

(b) Of any defect or irregularity in such act or proceedings not affecting the merits of the case.

48. Provisions relating to suits, etc:

(1) No suit or other legal proceeding shall be instituted against the State Library Authority or a Local Library Authority or any of its officers or any person acting under its direction until the expiration of two months next after notice in writing shall have been delivered or left at the office of the Authority or at the place of abode of such officer or person; such notice shall state the cause of action, the relief sought, the amount of compensation, if any, claimed, and the name and place of abode of the intending plaintiff.

(2) No suit or other legal proceeding shall lie against the State Government, the [Director of Public Libraries] , the State Library Authority or a Local Library Authority, or any member, officer, servant or agent of such Authority acting under its direction, in respect of anything done or intended to have been done lawfully and in good faith under this Act or any rule, bye-law or order made thereunder.

1. Substituted by Act 30 of 1984 w.e.f. 22.5.1984

49. Power to remove difficulties.- If any difficulty arises in giving effect to the provisions of this Act, the State Government may, by order, make such provisions as appear to it to be necessary or expedient for removing the difficulty.

50. Transfer of certain libraries.- (1) (a) With effect from such date as the State Government may by notification appoint (hereinafter referred to in this sub-section as the appointed day), the entire management and control of the Public Library, Mysore, now vested in the Committee of Management of the Public Library, Mysore, shall be vested in the Mysore City Library Authority.

(b) As from the appointed day, the Committee of Management of the Public Library, Mysore, a society registered under the Mysore Societies Registration Act, 1904, now deemed to be registered under the [Karnataka] Societies Registration Act, 1960, shall stand dissolved and all property, movable and immovable, and all rights, powers and privileges of the said society which immediately before the appointed day belonged to or vested in the said society shall vest in the Mysore City Library Authority and shall be applied for purposes specified in this Act and such other purposes as may be prescribed.

1. Adapted by the Karnataka Adaptations of Laws Order 1973 w.e.f. 1.11.1973

(c) As from the appointed day, all debts and liabilities of the said society shall stand transferred to and vest in the Mysore City Library Authority.

(d) Every employee of the said society shall, as from the appointed day, become an employee of the State Government and shall hold his office under the State Government as a member of the [Karnataka State Library Service]1 on the same tenure, at the same remuneration and upon the same terms and conditions and with the same rights and privileges as to provident fund, gratuity and other matters, as he would have held the same as an employee of the said society, and shall continue to do so unless and until his remuneration, terms and conditions are duly altered by the State Government.

1. Adapted by the Karnataka Adaptations of Laws Order 1973 w.e.f. 1.11.1973

(2) (a) The State Government may by notification transfer the Mahatma Gandhi Public Library, Mercara, to the Coorg District Library Authority, with effect from such date as may be specified in such notification.

(b) With effect from the day on which such transfer takes place, all assets and liabilities appertaining to the said library shall stand transferred to and vest in the Coorg District Library Authority.

(c) With effect from the day on which such transfer takes place, every person employed by the Government in connection with the said public library shall hold his office under the State Government as a member of the [Karnataka State Library Service]1 on the same tenure, at the same remuneration and upon the same terms and conditions and with same rights and privileges as to provident fund, gratuity and other matters, as he would have held the same if the transfer had not taken place and shall continue to do so unless and until his remuneration, terms and conditions are duly altered by the State Government.

1. Adapted by the Karnataka Adaptations of Laws Order 1973 w.e.f. 1.11.1973

(3) (a) Notwithstanding anything contained in section 47, with effect from such date as the State Government may by notification appoint (hereinafter referred to in this sub-section as the specified day), the entire management and control of Karnad Sadashiva Rao District Central Library, Mangalore shall stand transferred to the Mangalore City Library Authority.

(b) As from the specified day, the assets and liabilities of the South Kanara District Library Authority appertaining to the said District Central Library shall vest in the Mangalore City Library Authority, and the South Kanara District Library Authority in such proportion and in such manner as the State Government may direct.

(c) Every employee of South Kanara District Library Authority who was employed by the said Authority wholly or mainly in connection with the said District Central Library shall, as from the specified day, become an employee of the State Government and shall hold his office under the State Government as a member of the [Karnataka State Library Service] on the same tenure, at the same remuneration, and upon the same terms and conditions and with the same rights and privileges as to provident fund, gratuity and other matters, as he would have held the same as an employee of the South Kanara District Library Authority, and shall continue to do so unless and until his remuneration, terms and conditions are duly altered by the State Government.

1. Adapted by the Karnataka Adaptations of Laws Order 1973 w.e.f. 1.11.1973

51. Amendment of the Press and Registration of Books Act, 1867 in its application to the [State of Karnataka] .- The Press and Registration of Books Act, 1867 (Central Act XXV of 1867) shall, in its application to the [State of Karnataka] , be amended as follows:-

1. Adapted by the Karnataka Adaptations of Laws Order 1973 w.e.f. 1.1.1973

(i) In the first paragraph of section 9, for clause (a), the following clause shall be substituted, namely:-

"(a) in any case, within one calendar month after the day on which any such book shall first be delivered out of the press, three such copies, and";

(ii) In the last paragraph of section 9, for clause (i), the following clause shall be substituted, namely:-

"(i) any second or subsequent edition of a book in which edition no additions or alterations either in the letter-press or in the maps, block prints or other engraving belonging to the book have been made, and three copies of the first or some preceding edition of which book have been delivered under this Act, or "

(iii) in section 11, for the first sentence, the following sentence shall be substituted, namely:-

"Out of the three copies delivered pursuant to clause (a) of the first paragraph of section 9 of this Act, one copy shall be sent to the State Central Library, Bangalore, referred to in the [Karnataka] Public Libraries Act, 1965, and the remaining two copies shall be disposed of in such manner as the State Government may, from time to time determine."

1. Adapted by the Karnataka Adaptations of Laws Order 1973 w.e.f. 1.1.1973

52. Repeal and savings:

(1) The Madras Public Libraries Act, 1948 (Madras Act XXIV of 1948) and the Hyderabad Public Libraries Act, 1955 (Hyderabad Act III of 1955) are hereby repealed.

(2) Notwithstanding such repeal,-

(a) The members of the Local Library Authorities constituted under the Madras Public Libraries Act, 1948, and holding office immediately before the commencement of this Act shall be deemed to be the members of the Local Library Authorities constituted under this Act and shall exercise all powers and perform all duties conferred on such Authorities in the respective areas in which they are functioning at such commencement until their present term expires or until new authorities are constituted under this Act, whichever is later;

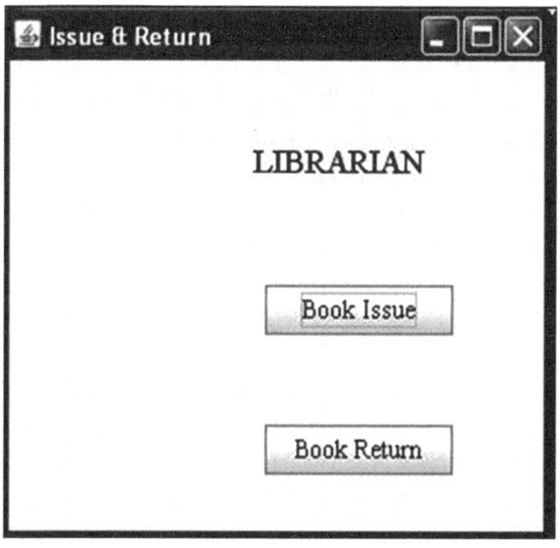

(b) Anything done or any action taken (including any appointment or delegation made, fee or cess imposed, notification, order, instrument or direction issued, rule, regulation, form, or scheme framed) under the said Acts and in force at the commencement of this Act, shall be deemed to have been done or taken under the provisions of this Act and shall continue to be in force accordingly until they are superseded or modified by anything done or any action taken under this Act.

Book Issue Details

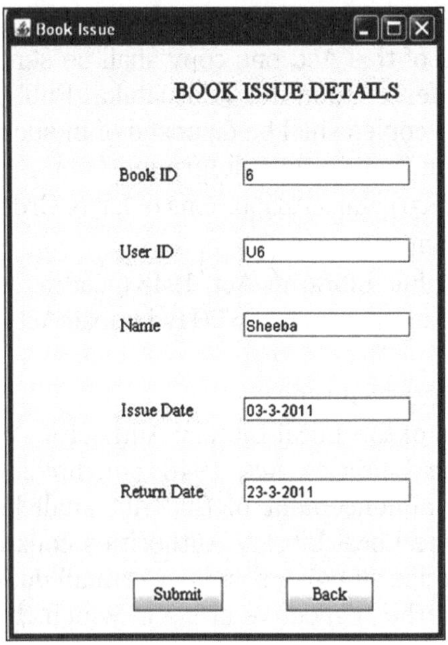

Book Return Details

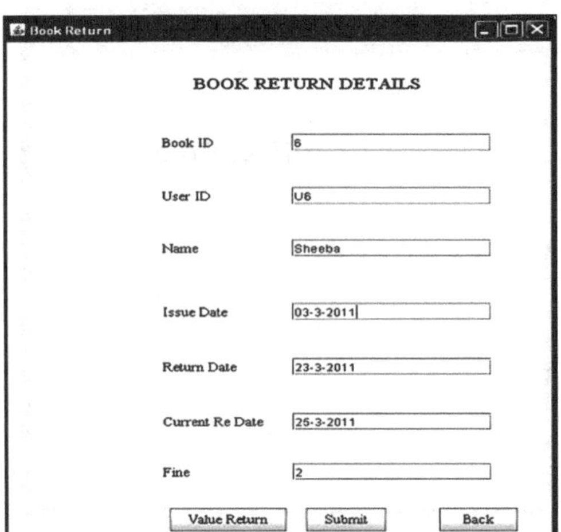

User Module

In the user module every authorized user has a unique login username and password. All these should be provided by the administrator. Through the login user, user can receive books from the library and return books to the library. All updation takes place in the library database.

Staff Module

All the staff have a unique login username and password. Staff have some additional feature compare to other user likewise they can take two more books and time extension compare to other user.

RESULT

Association rules can be implemented in a two-step process: find all frequent item sets: by definition, each of these item sets will represent the transaction, and then generate strong association rules from the frequent item sets: by definition, these rules must satisfy minimum support and minimum confidence.

Table. Association Rule Mining

Rule	Support	Confidence
In a semester if a book "Mobile Computing" was issued to a member then a book ".Net" also issued to the same member.	5%	75%
In a semester if Issue- Count of a book is between 20 to 30	2%	90%

CONCLUSION

This chapter describes the processes of selected techniques using association rule mining. It has been realised that all association mining techniques accomplish its goals perfectly, but this technique has its own characteristics and specifications that demonstrate its accuracy, proficiency and preference. It claims that new research solutions are needed for the problem of categorical data mining techniques, and presenting our ideas for future work. There is no effective technique in data mining. It is therefore recommended that these techniques should be used in cooperation with each other. For efficiently and effectively doing the library administration and extending library services, the need of library automation and digital library occur. But simply automating the library or developing digital library is not the only solution unless and until it is not able to explore the hidden information from the large amount of database. This can be done by applying the data mining in the library database.

Bibliography

A.A.N. Raju: *Facets of Library and Information Science*, Ess Ess Publications, Delhi, 2012.

Ajit Singh: *Siwatch Encyclopedic Dictionary of Library and Information Science, Vols. I to III*, Shree Publishers, Delhi, 2010.

Amjad Ali: *Ane's Encyclopedic Dictionary of Library and Information Science*, Ane Books India, Delhi, 2006.

Bharti Sharma and Jayanti Singh: *Serial Management in Academic Library*, Manglam Publications, 2011.

Brian Mathews: *Marketing Today's Academic Library: A Bold New Approach to Communicating with Students*, Ess Ess Publications, Delhi, 2010.

C Praveen Singh: *Library Automation in Modern Age*, Alfa Publications, Delhi, 2008.

G.K. Sampath Kumar: *Digital Library Automation Planning Designing and Development*, Akhand Publications, Delhi, 2012.

J. Sridevi and Vijay Laxshmi: *Model of Digital Library*, Shree Publications, Delhi, 2004.

Jagadeesha S. and Mahesh V. Mudhol: *Library Automation Using Foxpro 2.0*, Ess Ess Publications, Delhi, 1998

K. Nazeer Badhusha: *Digital Library Architecture*, Ane Books Pvt. Ltd., Delhi, 2008.

Kusum Verma: *Digital Library Preservation Strategies*, Akansha Publications, Delhi, 2005.

Manohar Nanda: *Library Automation*, Anmol Publications, Delhi, 2006.

Omesh Aadhavan: *Development of Digital Library*, Oxford Book Company, Jaipur, 2010.

Omesh Aadhavan: *Management of Digital Library*, Oxford Book Company, Jaipur, 2010.

P. Balasubramanian: *Library Automation and Networking*, Deep and Deep publications, Delhi, 2011.

Prabhat Pandey: *Recent Advances in Library Automation*, Mahamaya Publications, Delhi, 2010.

Publications, Delhi, 2011.

Purushotham Tiwari: *Digital Library*, APH Publications, Delhi, 2014.

R.K. Singh: *Basic Facts of Digital Library*, Shree Publications, Delhi, 2004.

R.S. Aswal: *Library Automation for 21 Century*, Ess Ess Publications, Delhi, 2006.

Raghunath Pandey and M.N. Velayudhan Pillai: *Digital Library: Trends and Prospects*, Jnanada Prakashan, Delhi, 2011.

Rajan Nagia: *Making of Software Packages for Library Automation*, Cyber Tech Publications, Delhi, 2012.

Rajneesh Agarwal: *Data Communication And Computer Networks*, Vikas Publications, Delhi, 2008.

Rashmi Upadhyay: *Digital Library Management*, Alfa Publications, Delhi, 2011.

Ritu Choudhary: *Computer Networks and Communications*, Centrum Press, Delhi, 2011.

S. K. Sangma: *Manual of Library Automation and Networking*, Centrum Press, Delhi, 2013.

S. Yadagiri and R.K. Pavan Kumar: *Library Automation: Perspectives and Challenges*, Swastik Publications, Delhi, 2013.

S.C. Dwivedi: *Digital Library (2 Vols-Set)*, Shree Publications, Delhi, 2005.

S.P. Singh: *Library Automation and Acquisition System*, Omega Publications, Delhi, 2009.

Savita Mittal: *Digital Library Resources*, Ess Ess Publications, Delhi, 2005.

Shiv Ram Verma: *Academic Library System*, Shree Publications, Delhi, 2005.

T. Bala Theresa, C. Ratna Kumari and B.A. Rani: *Information Technology and Library Automation*, Commonwealth

V.K. Iyenger: *Digital Library Use: Librarian's Guide to Internet*, Arise Publications, Delhi, 2011

V.K. Jain: *Information Technology for Digital Library Management and Automation*, Atlantic Publications, Delhi, 2009.

V.V.V. Satyanarayana: *Modern Librarianship Ushering in Digital Library*, Authorspress Publications, Delhi, 2006.

Vasantha N. and Mahesh V. Mudhol: *Software Packages for Library Automation*, Ess Ess Publications, Delhi, 2000.

Index